The Complete Guide to

SEWING

Made Easy

Copyright (c)2007
Creative Publishing international, Inc.
18705 Lake Drive East
Chanhassen, MN 55317
1-800-328-3895
www.creativepub.com
All rights reserved.

President/CEO: Ken Fund
Publisher: Bryan Trandem

Printed in China
10 9 8 7 6 5 4 3 2 1

CONTENTS

How to USE THIS BOOK

Welcome to the creative, sometimes challenging, but always rewarding world of sewing. *The Complete Guide to Sewing* is designed to make your learning experience as painless as possible and to instill confidence as you take on new projects and learn new techniques. Easy-to-follow instructions with colorful photographs help you build your sewing skills while making clothes, gifts, and home decorating items that really appeal to you.

QUICK REFERENCE

QUICK REFERENCE TEXT

GLOSSARY TEXT

Sewing enthusiasts enjoy this time-honored art for a multitude of reasons. Those of us who came into this world as Baby Boomers may have begun sewing as adolescents wanting to ride the wave of trendy fashion while saving money over store-bought clothes. While this is not always the case today, sewing our own clothes still gives us the advantage of personalized fit and individual expression. Home decorating items are popular projects for beginners and advanced sewers alike, partly because of the cost savings over purchased items. By sewing these items for the home, we also get to enjoy the creative fun of choosing styles, colors, and fabrics that fit our own personalities and tastes rather than those of the mass-produced market. But perhaps the greatest reason that sewing is so enjoyable is the mere satisfaction felt in creating something from scratch with your own two hands. Whether you are making something for yourself, your home, or to give to someone else, the ultimate reward is the intangible delight and personal fulfillment gained in the process.

The projects in this book are designed to guide you from your first nervous stitch at your sewing machine to comfortable familiarity. Each project will teach you new skills, listed under **What You'll Learn.** Throughout the book you will find tips and explanations to help you understand the "why" behind what you are doing. We also have included lots of variations for the projects, encouraging you to explore the unlimited design and fabric possibilities.

Use the first section of the book to acquaint yourself with your sewing machine and the techniques and supplies that encompass the art of sewing. Your sewing machine owner's manual is a necessity; refer to it first if you have questions or problems specific to your machine.

The first step in any sewing project is to read through the directions from beginning to end. Refer to the **Quick References** at the right side of the pages for definitions or elaborations on any words or phrases printed *like this* on the page. If the word or phrase is followed by a page number, its reference can be found on the page indicated. Words printed **LIKE THIS** can be found in the **Glossary** on pages 493 to 496. At the beginning of every project you will find a list telling you **What You'll Need.** Read through the information on fabric before you go shopping, so the fabric store will seem a little more user-friendly when you get there.

Above all, enjoy the process. Give yourself the opportunity to be creative and express yourself through the things you sew.

Sewing BASICS

The Sewing MACHINE

The principle parts common to all modern sewing machines are shown in the diagrams at right. The parts may look different on your model, and they may have slightly different locations, so open your owner's manual, also. If you do not have an owner's manual for your machine, you should be able to get one from a sewing machine dealer who sells your brand. Become familiar with the names of the parts and their functions. As you spend more time sewing, these items will become second nature to you.

   If you are buying a new machine, consider how much and what kind of sewing you expect to do. Talk to friends who sew and to sales personnel. Ask for demonstrations, and sew on the machine yourself. Experiment with the various features while sewing on a variety of fabrics, including knits, wovens, lightweights, and denim. Think about the optional features of the machine and which ones you want on yours. Many dealers offer free sewing lessons with the purchase of a machine. Take advantage! These lessons will be geared to your particular brand and model of sewing machine.

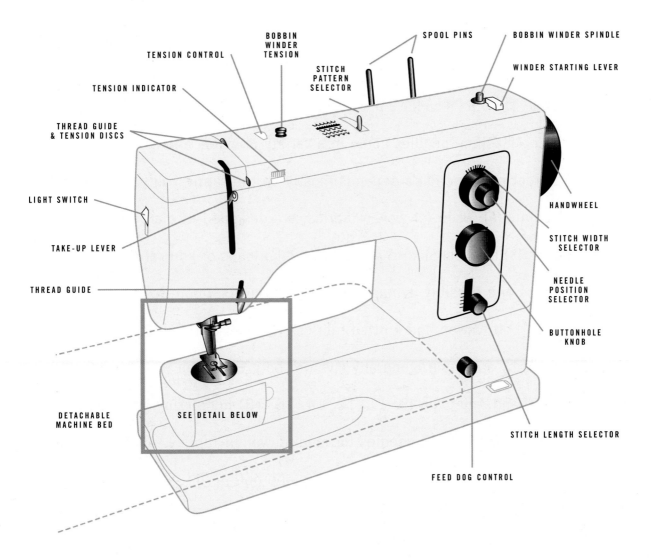

TENSION CONTROL

BOBBIN WINDER TENSION

SPOOL PINS

BOBBIN WINDER SPINDLE

STITCH PATTERN SELECTOR

WINDER STARTING LEVER

TENSION INDICATOR

THREAD GUIDE & TENSION DISCS

LIGHT SWITCH

TAKE-UP LEVER

THREAD GUIDE

HANDWHEEL

STITCH WIDTH SELECTOR

NEEDLE POSITION SELECTOR

BUTTONHOLE KNOB

DETACHABLE MACHINE BED

SEE DETAIL BELOW

STITCH LENGTH SELECTOR

FEED DOG CONTROL

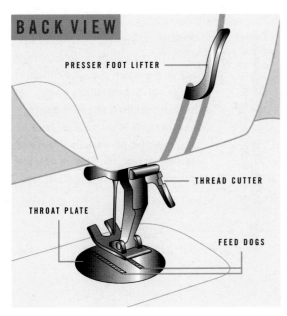

BACK VIEW

PRESSER FOOT LIFTER

THREAD CUTTER

THROAT PLATE

FEED DOGS

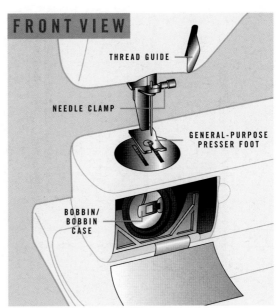

FRONT VIEW

THREAD GUIDE

NEEDLE CLAMP

GENERAL-PURPOSE PRESSER FOOT

BOBBIN/ BOBBIN CASE

Machine ACCESSORIES

SEWING MACHINE NEEDLES

Sewing machine needles come in a variety of styles and sizes. The correct needle choice depends mostly on the fabric you have selected. Sharp points **(A)**, used for woven fabrics, are designed to pierce the fabric. Ballpoints **(B)** are designed to slip between the loops of knit fabric rather than pierce and possibly damage the fabric. Universal points **(C)** are designed to work on both woven and knitted fabrics. The size of the needle is designated by a number, generally given in both European (60, 70, 80, 90, 100, 110) and American (9, 11, 12, 14, 16, 18) numbering systems. Use size 11/70 or 12/80 needles for mediumweight fabrics. A larger number means the needle is thicker and that it is appropriate for use with heavier fabrics and heavier threads.

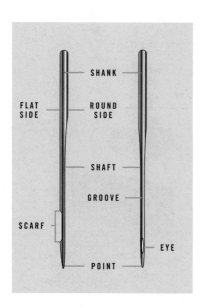

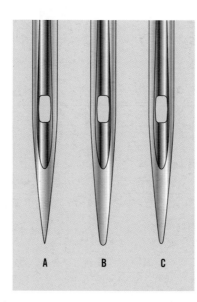

TIP Though needle style and size are usually indicated in some way on the needle, it is often difficult to see without a magnifying glass, and you most likely will not remember what needle is in the machine. As an easy reminder, when you finish a sewing session, leave a fabric swatch from your current project under the presser foot.

BOBBINS

Stitches are made by locking the upper thread with a lower thread, carried on a bobbin. Always use bobbins in the correct style and size for your machine. Bobbin thread tension is controlled by a spring on the bobbin case, which may be built in (A) or removable (B).

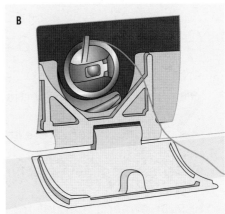

PRESSER FEET

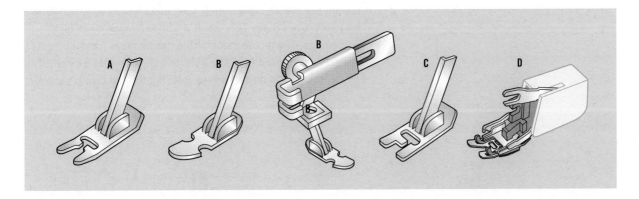

Every sewing machine comes with accessories for specialized tasks. More can be purchased as you develop your interest and skills. Your machine manual or dealer can show you what accessories are available and will explain how to use them to get the best results.

A general-purpose foot (A), probably the one you will use most often, has a wide opening to accommodate the side-to-side movement of the needle in all types of utility (nondecorative) stitches. It is also suitable for most straight stitching. A zipper foot (B) is used to insert zippers or to stitch any seam that has

more bulk on one side than the other. For some sewing machines, the zipper foot is stationary, requiring you to move the needle position to the right or left. For other styles, the position of the zipper foot itself is adjustable. A special-purpose or embroidery foot (C) has a grooved bottom that allows the foot to ride smoothly over decorative stitches or raised cords. Some styles are clear plastic, allowing you to see your work more clearly. A walking foot (D) feeds top and bottom layers at equal rates, allowing you to more easily match patterns or stitch bulky layers, as in quilted projects.

Getting Ready to SEW

Simple tasks of inserting the needle, winding the bobbin, and threading the machine have tremendous influence on the stitch quality and performance of your machine. Use this guide as a general reference, but refer to your owner's manual for instructions specific to your machine.

INSERTING THE NEEDLE

Loosen the needle clamp. After selecting the appropriate needle for your project (page 10), insert it into the machine as high as it will go. The grooved side of the needle faces forward, if your bobbin gets inserted from the front or top; it faces to the left, if your bobbin gets inserted on the left. Tighten the clamp securely.

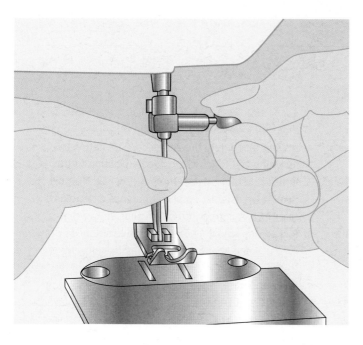

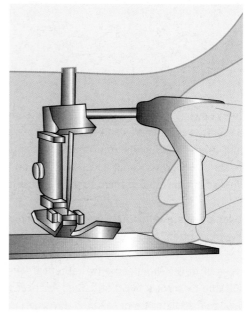

WINDING THE BOBBIN

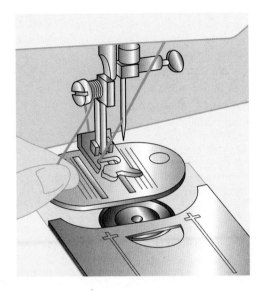

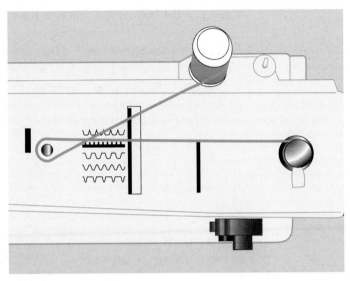

If the bobbin case is built in, the bobbin is wound in place with the machine fully threaded as if to sew (page 14).

Removable bobbins are wound on the top or side of the machine, with the machine threaded for bobbin winding, as described in your owner's manual.

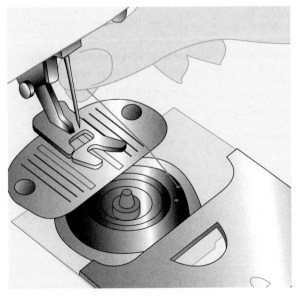

Bobbin thread must be drawn through the bobbin case tension spring. For wind-in-place bobbins, this happens automatically when you wind the bobbin, but you must do it manually when you insert a bobbin that already has thread on it.

THREADING THE MACHINE

Because every sewing machine is different, the threading procedure for your machine may differ slightly from the one shown here. Once again, it is important to refer to your owner's manual. Every upper thread guide adds a little tension to the thread as it winds its way to the needle. Missing one of them can make a big difference in the quality of your stitches.

1 Set the thread spool on the spindle.

A. Vertical spindle. Position the spool so that it will turn clockwise as you sew.

B. Horizontal spindle. The spool is held in place with an end cap. If your spool has a small cut in one end for minding the thread, position the spool with that end to the right.

TIP If the spool is new and has paper labels covering the holes, poke them in, completely uncovering the holes, to allow the spool to turn freely.

Unless your machine has a self-winding bobbin, you will want to wind the bobbin (page 13) before threading the machine.

2 Pull thread to the left and through the first thread guide.

3 Draw thread through the tension guide.

TIP It is very important to have the presser foot lever up when threading the machine, because the tension discs are then open. If the presser foot is down and the discs are closed, the thread will not slide between the discs, and your stitches will not make you happy.

4 Draw thread through the next thread guide.

5 Insert thread through the take-up lever.

6 Draw the thread through the remaining thread guides.

7 Thread the needle. Most needles are threaded from front to back; some, from left to right.

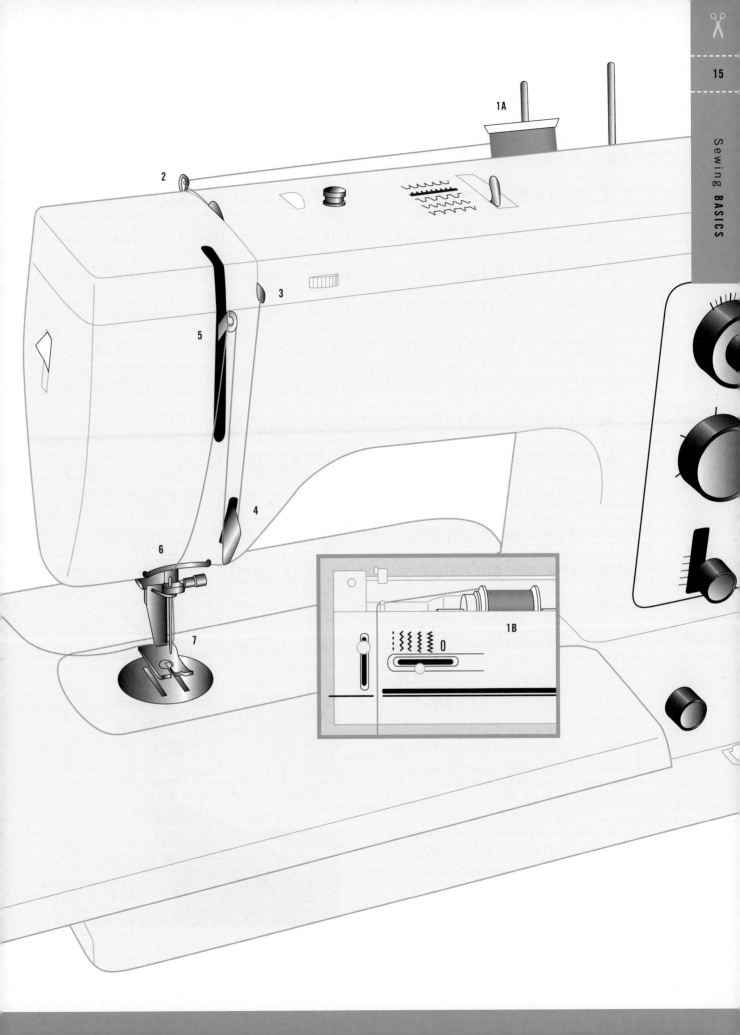

How to BALANCE TENSION

Your machine forms stitches by interlocking the bobbin thread with the needle thread. Every time the needle goes down into the fabric, a sharp hook catches the needle thread and wraps the bobbin thread around it. Imagine this little tug-of-war. If the needle thread tension is "stronger" than the bobbin thread tension, the needle thread pulls the bobbin thread through to the top. If the bobbin thread tension is "stronger," it pulls the needle thread through to the bottom. When the tensions are evenly balanced, the stitch will lock exactly halfway between the top and bottom of the layers being sewn, which is right where you want it.

Some machines have "self-adjusting tension," meaning the machine automatically adjusts its tension with every fabric you sew. For machines that do not have this feature, you may have to adjust the needle thread tension slightly as you sew different fabrics.

TESTING THE TENSION

1 Thread your machine and insert the bobbin, using two very different colors of thread, neither of which matches the fabric. Cut an 8" (20.5 cm) square of a smooth, mediumweight fabric. Fold the fabric in half diagonally, and place it under the presser foot so the fold aligns to your ½" (1.3 cm) seam guide. Lower the presser foot and set your stitch length at 10 stitches per inch or 2.5 mm long.

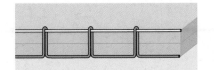

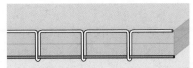

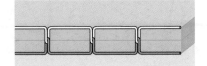

Top tension too tight   **Top tension too loose**   **Tensions even**

2 Stitch a line across the fabric, stitching ½" (1.3 cm) from the diagonal fold. Remove the fabric from the machine. Inspect your stitching line from both sides. If your tension is evenly balanced, you will see only one color on each side. If you see both thread colors on the top side of your sample, the needle tension is tighter than the bobbin tension. If you see both thread colors on the back side of your sample, the bobbin tension is tighter than the needle tension.

3 Pull on your stitching line until you hear threads break. (Because you stitched on the **BIAS**, the fabric will stretch slightly.) If the thread breaks on only one side, your machine's tension is tighter on that side.

ADJUSTING THE TENSION

Before adjusting the tension on your machine, first check:
• that your machine is properly threaded (page 14)
• that your bobbin is properly installed
• that your needle is not damaged and is inserted correctly

After checking these three things, you may need to adjust the tension on your machine. (Check your owner's manual.) Tighten or loosen the needle thread tension slightly to bring the needle thread and bobbin thread tensions into balance. Test the stitches after each adjustment, until you achieve balanced tension. If slight adjustments of the needle tension dial do not solve the problem, the bobbin tension may need adjusting. However, most manufacturers do not recommend that you adjust bobbin tension yourself, so unless you have received instructions for your machine, take your machine in for repair.

Sewing a SEAM

You may or may not be familiar with the very basic technique of running your machine and sewing a seam. Use this exercise as a refresher course whenever you feel you have lost touch with the basics or if your personal technique has become sloppy. Little frustrations, such as thread jams, erratic stitching lines, or having the thread pull out of the needle at the start of a seam, can often be prevented or corrected by following these basic guidelines. If you are really not sure where to begin, then you should probably begin right here!

1 Thread your machine (page 14) and insert the bobbin (page 13). Holding the needle thread with your left hand, turn the handwheel toward you until the needle has gone down and come back up to its highest point. A stitch will form, and you will feel a tug on the needle thread. Pull on the needle thread to bring the bobbin thread up through the hole in the throat plate. Pull both threads together under the presser foot and off to one side.

2 Cut two pieces of fabric and place them right sides together, aligning the outer edges. Pin the pieces together along one long edge, *inserting the pins* about every 2" (5 cm), *perpendicular to the edge.* Place the fabric under the presser foot so the pinned side edges align to the ½" (1.3 cm) *seam allowance guide* and the upper edges are just behind the opening of the presser foot. Lower the presser foot, and set your stitch length at 2.5 mm, which equals 10 stitches per inch.

3 Begin by *backstitching* several stitches to the upper edge of the fabric. Hold the thread tails under a finger for the first few stitches. This prevents the needle thread from being pulled out of the needle and also prevents the thread tails from being drawn down into the bobbin case, where they could potentially cause the dreaded **THREAD JAM**.

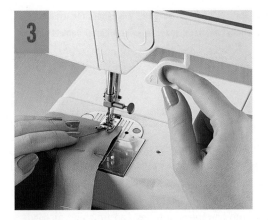

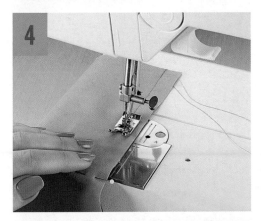

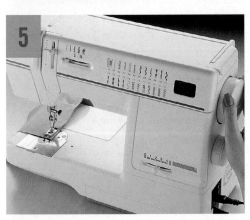

QUICK REFERENCE

Inserting the pins perpendicular to the edge. This makes it much easier to remove them as you sew. The pin heads are near the raw edge where you can easily grasp them with your right hand. In this position, you are much less likely to stick yourself with a pin as you sew.

Seam allowance guide. Most machines have a series of lines on the throat plate. These lines mark the distance from the needle (where a standard straight stitch seam would be) to the cut edges. Measure these lines on your machine to determine where the edge of your fabric should be for the width seam you are stitching.

Backstitching secures the beginning and end of your stitching line so that the stitches will not pull out. The method for backstitching varies with each sewing machine. You may need to lift and hold your stitch length lever, push in and hold a button, or simply touch an icon. Check your owner's manual.

Remove pins as you come to them. As tempting as it may be, don't sew over pins! You may be lucky and save a few seconds, or you could hit a pin and break your needle, costing you much more time in the long run.

4 Stitch forward over the backstitched line, and continue sewing the ½" (1.3 cm) seam. Gently guide the fabric while you sew by walking your fingers ahead of and slightly to the sides of the presser foot. Remember, you are only guiding; let the machine pull the fabric.

5 Stop stitching and *remove pins as you come to them.* When you reach the end of the fabric, stop stitching; backstitch several stitches, and stop again. Turn the handwheel toward you until the needle is in its highest position.

6 Raise the presser foot. Pull the fabric smoothly away from the presser foot, either to the left side or straight back. If you have to tug the threads, turn your handwheel slightly toward you until they pull easily. Cut the threads, leaving tails 2½" to 3" (6.5 to 7.5 cm) long.

TIP Straight stitching lines are easier to achieve if you watch the edge of the fabric along the seam guide and ignore the needle. Sew smoothly at a relaxing pace, with minimal starting and stopping, and without bursts of speed. You have better control of the speed if you operate your foot control with your heel resting on the floor.

More About SEAMS

Aside from the standard straight-stitch **SEAM**, your machine is probably capable of sewing several other stitches that are appropriate for various fabrics and situations. Whenever you sew with knits, for example, you want a seam that will stretch with the fabric. To prevent raveling of woven fabrics, **SEAM ALLOWANCE** edges must be finished. There are several finishing methods to choose from, depending on the fabric and the capabilities of your machine. These general guidelines will help you decide when to use these stitches and finishing methods. Your owner's manual is the best source of specific information for your machine.

STRETCH SEAMS

TIP The cut edges of knit fabrics do not ravel, but they often curl. To minimize this problem, the seam allowances are usually finished together and pressed to one side.

Double-stitched seam. Stitch on the seamline, using a straight stitch set at a length of 12 stitches per inch, which equals 2 mm long. Stretch the fabric slightly as you sew, to allow the finished seam to stretch that much. Stitch again 1/8" (3 mm) into the seam allowance. Trim the seam allowance close to the second stitching line. This seam is appropriate for fabrics with minimal stretch or for seams sewn in the vertical direction on moderate stretch knits.

Narrow zigzag seam. Stitch on the seamline, using a very narrow zigzag stitch set at 12 stitches per inch, which equals 2 mm long. If the fabric is very stretchy in the direction you are sewing, you may also stretch the fabric slightly as you sew. Trim the seam allowance to 1/4" (6 mm), if necessary. Set the zigzag wider, and stitch the seam allowance edges together. This seam is appropriate for very stretchy knits.

Built-in stretch stitch. Differing from brand to brand, these stitches are designed to incorporate stretch, so that you do not need to stretch the fabric as you sew. Some stitch styles, like the bottom two samples, are a pattern of zigzag and straight stitches that stitch and finish the seam in one pass. Check your manual for stitch settings.

SEAM FINISHES

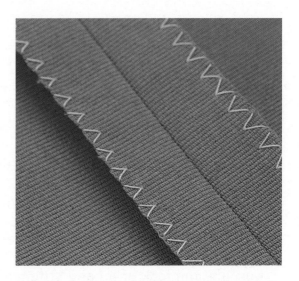

Stitched and pinked finish. Stitch ¼" (6 mm) from each seam allowance edge, using a straight stitch set at 12 stitches per inch, which equals 2 mm. Trim close to the stitching, using pinking shears (page 29). This finish is suitable for finely woven fabrics that do not ravel easily.

Zigzag finish. Set the zigzag stitch on or near maximum width and a length of 10 stitches per inch, which equals 2.5 mm. Stitch close to the edge of each seam allowance so that the right-hand stitches go just over the edge. If the fabric puckers, try a narrower zigzag width.

Multistitch-zigzag finish. If your machine has this stitch, check your owner's manual for directions on selecting the settings. Stitch near, but not over the edge of, each seam allowance.

Turn and zigzag finish. Set the zigzag stitch near maximum width at a length of 10 stitches per inch, which equals 2.5 mm. Turn under the seam allowance edge ⅛" to ¼" (3 to 6 mm). Stitch close to the folded edge so that the right-hand stitches go just on or over the fold. Use this finish on loosely woven fabrics, especially on garments, such as jackets, where the inside may be visible occasionally.

Hand STITCHES

While modern sewers rely on sewing machines for speedy garment construction, there are situations when hand stitching is necessary or preferable. You may need to slipstitch an opening closed in the lining of a vest, or perhaps you like the look of a hand-stitched blind hem (page 24). Of course, you'll also need to sew on buttons.

THREADING THE NEEDLE

Insert the thread end through the needle's eye, for sewing with a single strand. Or fold the thread in half, and insert the fold through the eye, for sewing with a double strand. Pull through about 8" (20.5 cm). Wrap the other end(s) around your index finger. Then, using your thumb, roll the thread off your finger, twisting it into a knot.

TIP Use a single strand when slipstitching or hemming. Use a double strand when sewing on buttons. To avoid tangles, begin with thread no longer than 18" (46 cm) from the needle to the knot. Run the thread through beeswax (page 27), if desired.

SLIPSTITCHING

1 Insert the threaded needle between the seam allowance and the outer fabric, just behind the opening. Bring it to the outside in the seamline. If you are right-handed, work from right to left; lefties work from left to right.

2 Insert the needle into the fold just behind where the thread came up, and run it inside the fold for about ¼" (6 mm). Bring the needle out, and draw the thread snug. Take your next stitch in the opposite fold, inserting the needle directly across from the previous stitch.

3 Continue, crossing from one fold to the other, until you have sewn past the opening. Secure the thread with several tiny stitches in the seamline. Then take a long stitch, and pull it tight. Clip the thread at the surface, and let the tail disappear inside.

SEWING ON A SHANK BUTTON

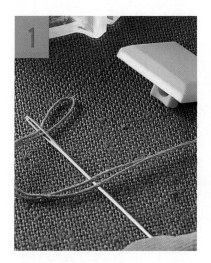

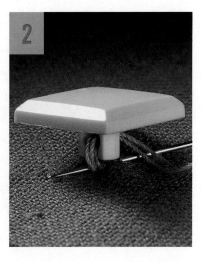

1 Place the button on the mark, with the shank hole parallel to the buttonhole. Secure the thread on the right side of the garment with a small stitch under the button.

2 Bring the needle through the shank hole. Insert the needle down through the fabric and pull the thread through. Take four to six stitches in this manner.

3 Secure the thread in the fabric under the button by making a knot or by taking several small stitches. Clip the thread ends.

SEWING ON A SEW-THROUGH BUTTON

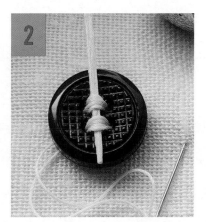

1 Place the button on the mark, with the holes lining up parallel to the buttonhole. Bring the needle through the fabric from the underside and up through one hole in the button. Insert the needle into another hole and through the fabric layers.

2 Slip a toothpick, match, or sewing machine needle between the thread and the button to form a shank. Take three or four stitches through each pair of holes. Bring the needle and thread to the right side under the button. Remove the toothpick.

3 Wind the thread two or three times around the button stitches to form the shank. Secure the thread on the right side under the button, by making a knot or taking several small stitches. Clip the threads close to the knot.

HEMS

There are a number of ways to hem the lower edges of skirts, pants, jackets, and shirts. Some hems are sewn by machine; others by hand. The method you choose will depend on the fabric, the garment style, and your own preference. For methods that do not involve turning under the raw edge, finish the edge (page 21) in an appropriate manner, before hemming.

HAND HEMS

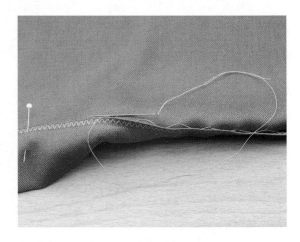

Blindstitch. Fold back the finished edge of the hem ¼" (6 mm). Take a small stitch to anchor the thread in a seam allowance. Work with the needle pointing in the direction you are going. Take a small horizontal stitch in the garment, catching only one or two threads. Take the next stitch in the hem, ¼" to ½" (6 mm to 1.3 cm) away from the first stitch. Continue alternating stitches; do not pull too tightly.

Blind catchstitch. Fold back the finished edge of the hem ¼" (6 mm). Take a small stitch to anchor the thread in a seam allowance. Work with the needle pointing in the direction opposite from the way you are going. Take a very small horizontal stitch in the garment, catching only one or two threads. Take the next stitch in the hem, ¼" to ½" (6 mm to 1.3 cm) away from the first stitch, crossing the stitches. Continue alternating the stitches in a zigzag pattern.

Slipstitch. Fold under the raw edge ¼" (6 mm), and press. Take a small stitch to anchor the thread in a seam allowance. Work with the needle pointing in the direction you are going. Follow the directions for slipstitching on page 22, catching only one or two threads with each stitch that goes into the garment.

MACHINE HEMS

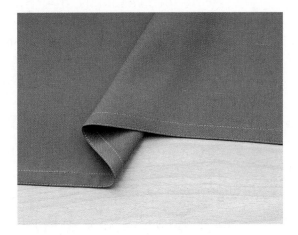

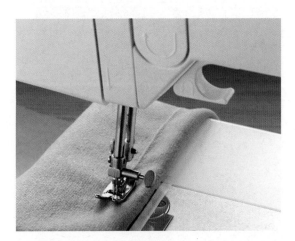

Machine blindstitch. Follow your manual for adjusting the stitch settings, and use the appropriate presser foot. Test the stitch on a scrap of the garment fabric until you are happy with the results. **(A)** Place the hem allowance facedown on the machine bed, with the bulk of the garment folded back. Allow about ¼" (6 mm) of the hem edge to extend under the presser foot, aligning the soft fold to rest against the guide in the foot. Stitch along the hem, close to the fold, catching only one or two threads of the garment with each left-hand stitch of the needle. **(B)** When complete, open out the hem, and press it flat.

Double-fold hem. This method results in one or two rows of straight stitches showing on the right side of the garment, which is generally a more casual appearance. Follow pages 101 and 102, steps 2 and 3. This method is most successful on straight edges where there is no excess fullness to ease in. It may be helpful to hand-baste the folds in place before machine-stitching.

Double-needle hem. Stitched from the right side of the fabric, this hem is suitable for knit garments, because it will stretch slightly. The farther apart the needles are spaced, the more stretch the hem will have. However, widely spaced needles will usually produce a ridge between the stitching lines. Using two thread spools on top, thread both needles. Place tape on the bed of the machine as a stitching guide.

Sewing SUPPLIES

Sewing involves many steps: measuring, laying out the pattern, cutting, marking, stitching, and pressing. For each of these steps there are special tools and supplies to make your sewing easier and help you complete your projects successfully. Don't feel you need to buy all the items before you start. For instance, a pair of sharp shears and a seam ripper will see you through most of the cutting tasks for the projects in this book. You will undoubtedly acquire additional tools as your skills and interests grow.

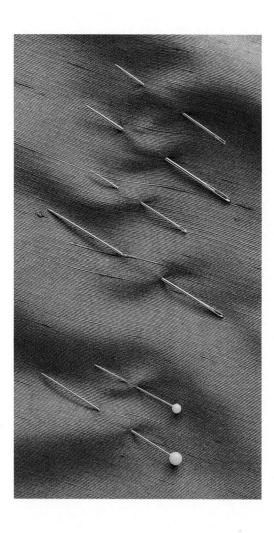

HAND-SEWING SUPPLIES

Needles and pins are available in a variety of sizes and styles. Look for rustproof needles and pins made of brass, nickel-plated steel, or stainless steel. Pictured from top to bottom:

Sharps are all-purpose, medium-length needles designed for general sewing.

Crewels are sharp, large-eyed medium-length needles, designed for embroidery.

Betweens are very short and round-eyed. They are useful for hand quilting and making fine stitches.

Milliner's needles are long with round eyes and are used for making long basting or gathering stitches.

Straight pins are used for general sewing. They should be slim and are usually 1¹⁄₁₆" (2.7 cm) long. Pins with colored ball heads are easier to see and are less likely to get lost than those with flat heads.

Quilting pins are 1¾" (4.5 cm) long. Their extra length makes them ideal for use on bulky fabrics or fabrics with extra loft.

A Thimble protects your finger while hand sewing. Available in a variety of styles and sizes, it is worn on whichever finger you use to push the needle through the fabric. Most people prefer either the middle or ring finger. Using a thimble is an acquired habit. Some people can't get along without one, while others feel they are a nuisance.

B Pincushion provides a safe and handy place to store pins. One style is worn on the wrist for convenience. Another style, a magnetic tray, attracts and holds steel pins. Be careful not to place any magnetic tools near a computerized machine, because the magnet may interfere with the machine's memory.

C Needle threader eases threading of hand and machine needles. This is especially useful if you have difficulty seeing something that small.

D Beeswax with holder strengthens thread and prevents tangling while hand sewing.

MEASURING & MARKING TOOLS

A Transparent ruler allows you to see what you are measuring and marking. It also is used to check fabric grainline.

B Yardstick (meterstick) should be made of smooth hardwood or metal.

C Tape measure has the flexibility helpful for measuring items with shape and dimension. Select one made of a material that will not stretch.

D Seam gauge is a 6" (15 cm) metal or plastic ruler with a sliding marker. It helps make quick, accurate measurements and can be used to measure seam allowance widths.

E Transparent T-square is used to locate grainlines and to measure 90° angles.

F Marking chalk is available in several forms; as powder in a rolling wheel dispenser, as a pencil, or as a flat slice. Chalk lines are easily removable from most fabrics.

G Fabric marking pens are available in both air-erasable and water-erasable forms. Air-erasable marks disappear in 48 hours; water-erasable marks wash off with a sprinkling of water.

H Narrow masking tape is an alternative method for marking fabrics when other methods are less suitable.

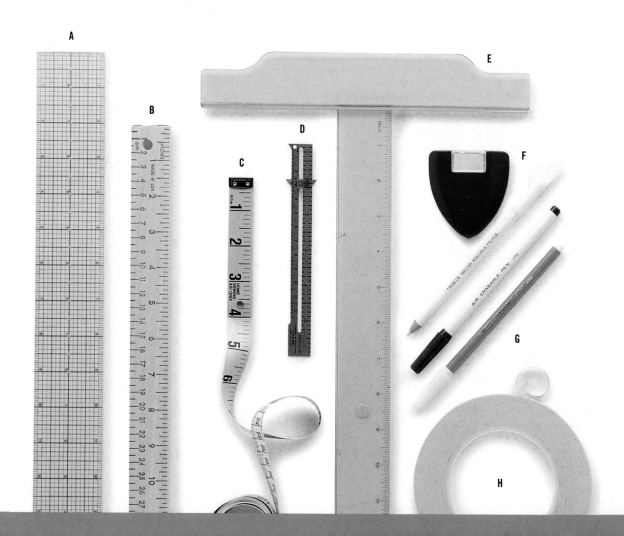

CUTTING TOOLS

Buy quality cutting tools and use them only for your sewing! Cutting paper or other household materials will dull your cutting tools quickly. Dull tools are not only tiresome to work with, they can also damage fabric. Scissors have both handles the same size; shears have one handle larger than the other. The best-quality scissors and shears are hot-forged, high-grade steel, honed to a fine cutting edge. Blades should be joined with an adjustable screw to ensure even pressure along the length of the blade. Have your cutting tools sharpened periodically by a qualified professional.

I Bent-handled dressmaker's shears are best for cutting fabric shapes because the angle of the lower blade lets fabric lie flat on the cutting surface. Blade lengths of 7" or 8" (18 or 20.5 cm) are most popular, but lengths of up to 12" (30.5 cm) are available. Select a blade length appropriate for the size of your hand; shorter lengths for smaller hands. Left-handed models are also available. If you intend to sew a great deal, invest in a pair of all-steel, chrome-plated

shears for heavy-duty cutting. Lighter models with stainless steel blades and plastic handles are fine for less-frequent sewing or lightweight fabrics.

J Sewing scissors have one pointed and one rounded tip for clipping threads and trimming and clipping seam allowances. A 6" (15 cm) blade is suitable for most tasks.

K Seam ripper quickly removes stitches and opens buttonholes. Use it carefully to avoid cutting the fabric.

L Rotary cutter works like a pizza cutter and can be used by left-handed or right-handed sewers. A locking mechanism retracts the blade for safety. Use the rotary cutter with a special plastic mat available in different sizes, with or without grid lines. The self-healing mat protects both the work surface and the blade.

M Pinking shears and pinking rotary cutters are used to finish seams. They cut fabric in a zigzag or scalloped pattern instead of a straight line.

Sewing **BASICS**

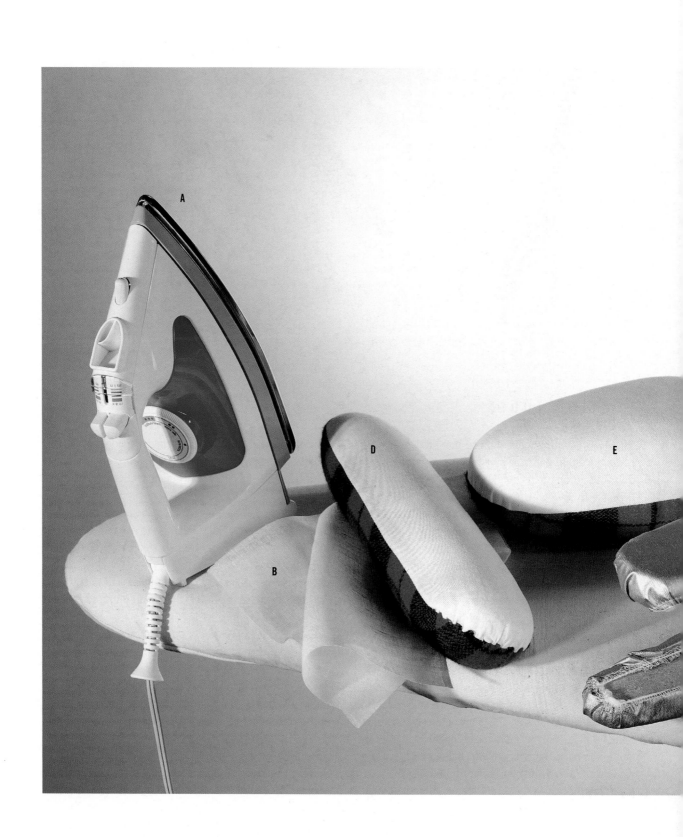

PRESSING TOOLS

Pressing at each stage of construction is the secret to a perfectly finished project. The general rule is to press each stitched seam before crossing it with another.

A Steam/spray iron should have a wide temperature range to accommodate all fabrics. Buy a dependable, name-brand iron. An iron that steams and sprays at any setting, not just the higher heat settings, is helpful for fabrics with synthetic fibers.

B Press cloth helps prevent iron shine and is always used when applying fusibles. The transparent cloth allows you to see if the fabric is smooth and the layers are properly aligned.

C Teflon™-coated sole plate guard, available to fit most irons, eliminates the need for a press cloth.

D Seam roll is a firmly packed cylindrical cushion for pressing seams. The bulk of the fabric falls to the sides away from the iron, preventing the seam from making an imprint on the right side of the fabric.

E Pressing ham is a firmly packed cushion for pressing curved areas of a garment.

F Sleeve board looks like two small ironing boards attached one on top of the other. It is useful for pressing sleeves or other tubular shapes one layer at a time to avoid unwanted creases.

Special PRODUCTS

Many special products and gadgets are designed to assist you in various steps of the sewing process. Before using a new product, read the manufacturer's instructions carefully. Learn what special handling or care is required, and for what fabrics or sewing techniques it is especially suited. Here are some specialized products, available in fabric stores, that you may find helpful in sewing your clothes, accessories, or home décor items.

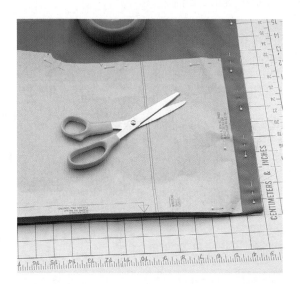

Cutting boards protect table finishes from scratches. Available in cardboard, plastic, or padded styles, these boards also hold fabric more securely while cutting. Square off fabric using the marked lines, and use the 1" (2.5 cm) squares as an instant measure.

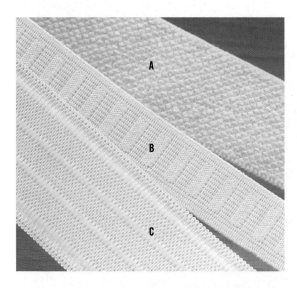

Elastics can be purchased in a variety of widths and styles, either in precut packages or by the yard (meter). Softer elastics **(A)** are suitable for pajamas or boxer shorts; nonroll elastic **(B)** stays flat in the casing; some wide elastic has channels for topstitching **(C)**.

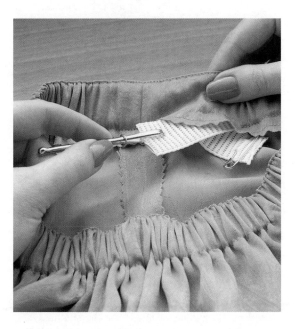

Bodkin is used to thread elastic or cording through a **CASING**. One end holds the elastic or cord tightly while you feed the tool through the narrow casing.

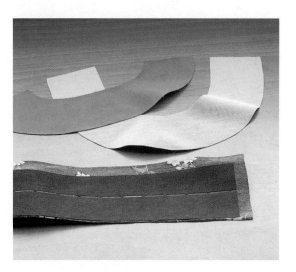

Interfacing plays a supporting role in almost every garment. It is an inner layer of fabric, used to stabilize the fabric in areas like necklines and waistbands, or give support behind buttons and buttonholes. Interfacings may be woven, nonwoven, or knit; the easiest forms to use are heat fusible.

Point turner is helpful for perfecting corners, such as at the top of a pocket, at the ends of a waistband, or inside a pillow cover. Slip the tool inside the item, and gently poke the fabric out into a point.

Liquid fray preventer is a colorless plastic liquid that prevents fraying by stiffening the fabric slightly. It is helpful when you have clipped too far into a seam allowance or want to reinforce a buttonhole. It may discolor some fabrics, so test before using, and apply carefully. The liquid may be removed with rubbing alcohol. It dries to a permanent finish that will withstand laundering and dry cleaning.

CONTINUED

Glue stick is a convenient substitute for pinning or basting when you need to hold an item in place temporarily before stitching. The temporary adhesive in a retractable tube can be applied in small dots. It won't discolor the fabric and washes out completely, if necessary. It will not harm your machine or gum up your needle as you stitch through it.

Buttonhole cutter is a handy tool for making precision cuts down the center of buttonholes. It comes with a wooden block to place under the fabric, to protect your work surface and accept the sharp thin blade of the cutter. While buttonholes can be cut open with small scissors or a seam ripper, a buttonhole cutter is more accurate and less likely to cut the stitches.

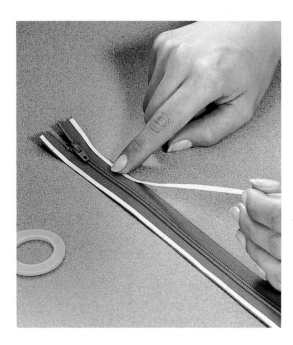

Basting tape is double-faced adhesive tape used instead of pinning or basting. It is especially helpful for matching prints, applying zippers, and positioning trims. Some manufacturers advise that you avoid stitching through the tape because the adhesive may collect on your needle.

Paper-backed fusible web is sold on rolls, in various narrow widths. It is also available as a wide sheet rolled on a bolt for purchase by the yard (meter). It is a timesaving product used for adhering two pieces of fabric together. For instance, you may use narrow strips of it to secure the side hems of a Roman shade instead of stitching them. A protective paper backing is removed from one side after the other side has been fused to the fabric.

Welting is a fabric-covered cording, sewn into a seam or around an outer edge to provide extra strength and a decorative finishing touch. It is available in many colors and various diameters to purchase by the yard (meter) or in precut packaged lengths.

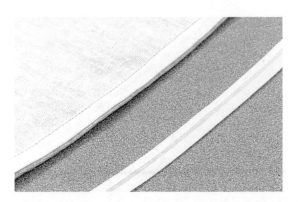

Single-fold bias tape is useful for hemming curved edges, such as a round tablecloth. The manufacturer has already cut the bias strips, sewn them together, and pressed in precise folds to make your sewing easier. The tape is available in packaged lengths in a wide range of colors.

Batting. Low-loft cotton, polyester, or poly/cotton blend batting, sold in packages, is used for quilted projects, such as channel-quilted placemats. It is soft and drapable.

Blanket binding resembles a wide satin ribbon that has been pressed in half for encasing the raw edge around a blanket. Packaged in a convenient length for sewing baby blankets, the binding is available in assorted soft colors and white. Because of its stability and permanent crease, it is easy to work with, yet feels silky smooth against your baby's skin.

Twill tape is a sturdy nondecorative fabric strip that has many sewing uses. For instance, lengths of twill tape are sewn at the corners inside the duvet cover for tying the duvet in place, a convenient feature rarely found in ready-made bedding. Packaged white twill tape is available in a choice of narrow widths.

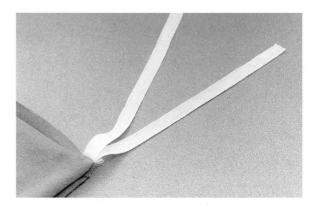

Buttons for covering are available in kits, complete with a button front and back and the tools for covering the button. Dampen the fabric to make it easier to handle. The fabric may shrink slightly as it dries to fit more smoothly around the button. Use the eraser end of a pencil to secure the fabric to the prongs of the button front, working back and forth across the button to tuck all the fabric into the button front.

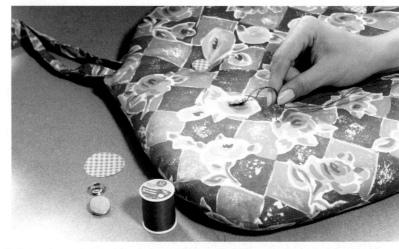

Button and carpet thread is a strong, heavy thread recommended for hand sewing when long-term durability is necessary, such as button-tufting a cushion. The thread has a polyester core wrapped with cotton. A polished glacé finish prevents thread abrasion and tangling.

Zippers come in a wide range of styles for many different uses. For the zipper closure on a pillow, choose a conventional polyester coil zipper (not a separating style) in a color to match your fabric.

Flat decorator trims and grosgrain ribbons can be machine-sewn to some items, such as decorator pillows, for a designer touch. Bulkier trims can be stitched on by hand.

Polyurethane foam can be purchased at most fabric stores that have home decorating areas or from specialty foam stores. It is available in various thicknesses, densities, and widths. The store will usually cut foam to the size you need, or you can cut thinner foam yourself using sewing shears, a serrated knife, or an electric knife.

Pillow forms offer you the convenience of being able to "stuff" and "unstuff" your pillow quickly and neatly. Inexpensive forms, stuffed with generous amounts of polyester fiberfill, are available in a range of rectangular and round sizes. For extra softness and luxury, you may want to pay the higher price for down-filled pillow forms.

Fabric INFORMATION

Selecting the right fabrics for your projects may seem like an overwhelming task, but there are a few simple guidelines to help narrow the field. One good way to learn about fabrics is to browse through a fabric store, handling the fabrics and reading the fiber content information and care instructions printed on the ends of the bolts. You may already know whether you want a solid color, a printed pattern, or perhaps a multicolored fabric. Do you need a fabric that can be laundered frequently? Do you want smooth or textured, stiff or drapable, lightweight or heavy? Some basic fabric knowledge and a thought-out plan will help you make wise choices and avoid costly errors.

FIBER CONTENT

Natural fabrics are made from plant or animal fibers, spun into yarns: cotton, wool, silk, and linen are the most common. Naturals are often considered the easiest fabrics to sew. Synthetic fabrics, made from chemically produced fibers, include nylon, acrylic, acetate, and polyester. Rayon is a man-made fiber made from a plant source. Each fiber has unique characteristics, desirable for different reasons. Many fabrics are a blend of natural and synthetic fibers, offering you the best qualities of each, such as the breathable comfort of cotton blended with the wrinkle resistance of polyester.

LINEN

COTTON PRINT

WOOL MELTON

WOVEN ACRYLIC

ACETATE

DUPIONI SILK

POLYESTER

RAYON VELVET

CRINKLED NYLON

Synthetic fabrics are made to resemble the look and feel of natural fabrics. Polyester may look like cotton or silk, acetate and nylon shimmer like silk, and acrylic mimics the texture and appearance of wool.

More About FABRIC

WOVEN FABRICS

Woven fabrics have straight lengthwise and crosswise yarns. The pattern in which the yarns are woven gives the fabric its characteristic surface texture and appearance. The outer edges of woven fabrics are called **SELVAGES**. As a general rule, they should be trimmed away because they are often heavier than the rest of the fabric, and they may shrink when laundered or pressed. Grainlines are the directions in which the fabric yarns run. Strong, stable lengthwise yarns, running parallel to the selvages, form the **LENGTHWISE GRAIN**. The **CROSSWISE GRAIN** is perpendicular to the lengthwise grain and has a small amount of give. Any diagonal direction, called the **BIAS,** has a fair amount of stretch.

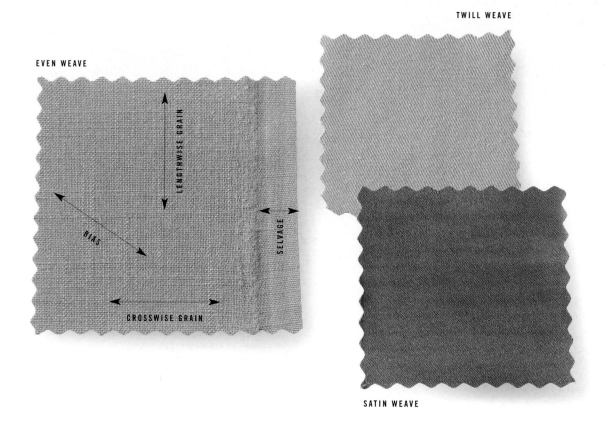

TWILL WEAVE

EVEN WEAVE

LENGTHWISE GRAIN

BIAS

SELVAGE

CROSSWISE GRAIN

SATIN WEAVE

KNIT FABRICS

Knit fabrics consist of rows of interlocking loops of yarn, as in a hand-knit sweater, but usually on a finer scale. Knit fabrics are more flexible than other fabrics, and they all stretch. These features mean that garments made of knits require less fitting and offer more freedom of movement. When sewing with knits, select patterns that are specifically designed for knit fabrics.

Knit fabric is made from interlocking looped stitches. The lengthwise rows of stitches are called **RIBS**; the crosswise rows are called **COURSES**. These ribs and courses correspond to the lengthwise and crosswise grains of woven fabrics.

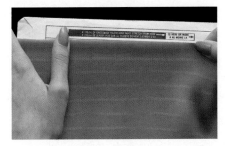

Patterns designed for knit fabrics have a stretch gauge. Fold over the fabric along a crosswise course several inches (centimeters) from a cut end, and test its degree of stretch against the gauge. If the fabric stretches the necessary amount without distortion, it is suitable for the pattern.

STRETCH TERRY

SYNTHETIC FLEECE

DOUBLE KNIT

SWEATSHIRT FLEECE

NOVELTY KNIT

MOIRÉ

COTTON
SATEEN
PRINT

JACQUARD

TWILL WEAVE
(TOP, RIGHT)

NOVELTY WEAVE

COTTON SATEEN

Even More About FABRIC

SHOPPING

Fabrics in a store are divided into fashion fabrics and decorator fabrics. Decorator fabrics are generally more durable than fashion fabrics; most have stain-resistant finishes. They are designed for pillows, slipcovers, window treatments, and other home decorating projects. They are manufactured in widths (crosswise grain) of 48" or 54" (122 or 137 cm), though occasionally you may find some wider. To prevent creases, decorator fabrics are rolled on tubes.

Fashion fabrics are usually folded double and rolled on cardboard bolts. They vary in width; the most common are 36", 45", and 60" (91.5, 115, and 152.5 cm). Though fashion fabrics are intended for apparel, many of them are also suitable for home decorating. Most stores arrange their fashion fabrics according to the fiber content or fabric style. For instance, all the wools and wool blends, suitable for skirts, slacks, and jackets, may be found together in one area of the store; all the bridal and special-occasion fabrics located in another area; quilting fabrics (lightweight cottons) in another. This is not a hard-and-fast rule, however, so you will want to spend time getting acquainted with the fabric stores you shop.

FABRIC PREPARATION

PRESHRINK washable fabric before cutting out the project, by washing and drying it in the same way you will care for the finished item. Because most decorator fabrics are not washable and require dry cleaning when necessary, preshrink them by pressing with steam, moving the iron evenly along the grainlines. Allow the fabric to dry before moving it.

The "right" side of the fabric will usually be obvious, and you will usually want to use it, but sometimes the "wrong" side of the fabric will actually be the side you prefer. Go ahead! Part of the fun of sewing is doing what looks right to you!

COTTON
CORDUROY

SILK

POLYESTER FLEECE

COTTON DENIM

LINEN

Cutting DECORATOR FABRICS

C utting into a new piece of fabric may seem a little scary, considering the investment you have just made. Here are a few guidelines for accurate cutting that should boost your confidence.

After preshrinking, straighten the cut ends of the fabric, using one of the three methods opposite. Then mark the other cutting lines, using the straightened edge as a guide. Before cutting full-width pieces of fabric for large home décor projects, such as tablecloths, window swags, or Roman shades, pin-mark the placement of each cut along the **SELVAGE**. Mark out pieces for smaller projects, like decorator pillows or napkins, with chalk. Double-check your measurements and inspect the fabric for flaws. Once you have cut into the fabric, you cannot return it. To ensure that large décor items will hang or lay straight, the fabric lengths must be cut on-grain. This means that the cuts are made along the exact **CROSSWISE GRAIN** of the fabric. Patterned decorator fabrics are cut following the **PATTERN REPEAT** rather than the grainline so they must be *printed on-grain*.

Printed on-grain. This means the pattern repeat coincides exactly with the crosswise grain of the fabric. To test fabric before you buy, place it on a flat surface and fold the cut edge back, aligning the selvages on the sides. Crease the fold with your fingers, then unfold the fabric and check to see if the crease runs into the selvage at exactly the same point in the pattern on both sides. Slight differences of less than 2" (5 cm) can usually be corrected by stretching the fabric diagonally. Avoid buying fabric that is printed more that 2" (5 cm) off-grain, as you will not be able to correct it, and the finished project will not hang straight.

For tightly woven fabrics without a matchable pattern, mark straight cuts on the crosswise grain, using a carpenter's square. Align one edge to a selvage and mark along the perpendicular side.

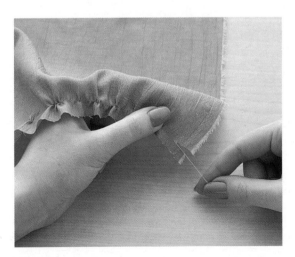

For loosely woven fabrics, such as linen tablecloth fabric, pull out a yarn along the crosswise grain, from selvage to selvage. Cut along the line left by the missing yarn.

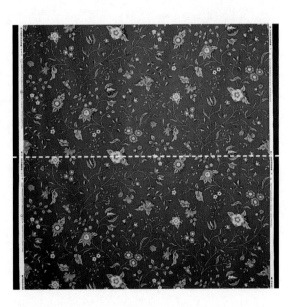

For tightly woven patterned decorator fabric, mark both selvages at the exact same point in the pattern repeat. Using a long straightedge, draw a line connecting the two points. If you will be stitching two or more full widths of fabric together, make all the cuts at the same location in the repeat. This usually means that you cut the pieces longer than necessary, stitch them together, and then trim them to the necessary length.

Matching DESIGNS

Stitching **SEAMS** in printed fabrics and fabrics with woven-in patterns requires a few extra steps to make sure the pattern will flow uninterrupted from one fabric width to the next.

1 Place two fabric widths right sides together, aligning the **SELVAGES**. Fold back the upper selvage until the pattern matches. Adjust the top layer slightly up or down so that the pattern lines up exactly. **PRESS** the foldline.

2 Unfold the pressed selvage, and pin the fabric widths together, inserting the pins in and parallel to the foldline.

3 Turn the fabric over, and check the match from the right side. Make any necessary adjustments.

4 Repin the fabric so the pins are perpendicular to the foldline. Stitch the seam following the foldline; remove the pins as you come to them.

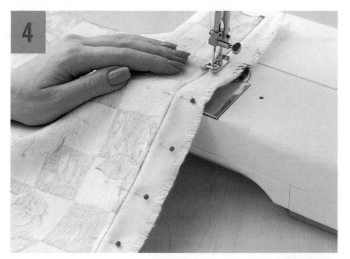

5 Check the match from the right side again. Make any necessary adjustments. Trim away the selvages, cutting the **SEAM ALLOWANCES** to ½" (1.3 cm).

6 Trim the entire fabric panel to the necessary **CUT LENGTH** as determined in the project instructions. (Remember your initial cut length for the patterned fabric included extra length to accommodate the **PATTERN REPEAT**.)

Selecting a PATTERN

Major pattern companies follow a uniform sizing based on standard body measurements. This is not exactly the same as ready-to-wear sizing.

DETERMINING SIZE

To select the right pattern size, first take your standard body measurements. Wear your usual undergarments and use a tape measure that doesn't stretch. It may be easier to have another person measure you. Record your measurements and compare them with the size chart on the back of the pattern or in the back of the pattern book.

TAKING STANDARD BODY MEASUREMENTS

 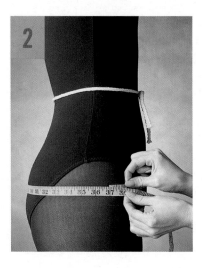

1 **Waistline.** Tie a string or piece of elastic around your middle, and allow it to roll to your natural waistline. Measure at this exact location with a tape measure. Leave the string in place as a reference for measuring your hips and back waist length.

2 **Hips.** Measure around the fullest part of your hips. This is usually 7" to 9" (18 to 23 cm) below the waistline, depending on your height.

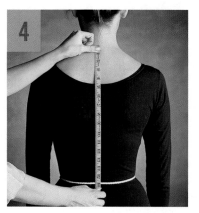

3 **Bust.** Place the tape measure under your arms, across the widest part of the back and the fullest part of the bustline.

4 **Back waist length.** Measure from the middle of the most prominent bone at the base of the neck down to the waistline string.

PATTERN SELECTION

Selecting a pattern for a garment allows for more creativity than shopping from a ready-to-wear catalog. Pattern catalogs don't limit you to certain fabric, colors, skirt lengths, or types of trims shown on the pages. You are free to choose a combination of features that best reflect your style and are most flattering to you.

Major pattern companies publish new catalogs with each season, which means that designer trends seen in clothing stores are reflected in the newest pattern catalogs along with more classic styles. You'll find simple patterns for sewers who prefer the quick and easy styles, and more detailed patterns for experienced sewers. The number of pattern pieces listed on

the back of the pattern will provide a clue to the complexity of the pattern. The fewer pieces, the easier the project. Also, the pattern may indicate whether it is intended for knits only.

Pattern catalogs are usually divided into categories by garment types and marked by index tabs. The newest fashions often appear in the first few pages of each category. Pattern illustrations are accompanied by information on recommended fabrics and yardage requirements. An index at the back of the catalog lists patterns in numerical order along with their page numbers. The back of the catalog also includes a complete size chart for every figure type.

All About **PATTERNS**

The pattern envelope is a selling tool and an educational device. The front generally has a photograph of the finished garment and several drawings of the variations that can be sewn using the pattern. On the pattern back, you'll find detailed information to help you select fabric and all the notions necessary to complete your project.

THE ENVELOPE FRONT

Pattern company name, and style number that corresponds to the number in the catalog, are displayed prominently.

Photograph or fashion illustration shows the main pattern design made up in suitable fabrics. It also indicates how closely or loosely the pattern is intended to fit.

Size or sizes included in the pattern are indicated near the number. Most patterns include several sizes.

Labels may indicate special considerations: that a pattern is suitable for knits only, is easy to sew, has special fitting or size-related information.

Views, labeled with letters, are alternate designs that can be sewn using the pattern. They may include variations in length, fullness, or other design details.

THE ENVELOPE BACK

Fabric amounts required for each view in all the available sizes are listed in a chart. Locate the style view and the fabric width at the left; match it with your size at the top. The number where the two columns meet is the amount of fabric you need to buy. Interfacing (page 33) and elastic (page 32) requirements are also listed. Metric equivalents are given in a separate chart.

Fabrics recommended for sewing the garments are listed to help you make your selections. This paragraph will also tell you if certain fabrics are unsuitable, such as stripes or one-way designs.

Style number is repeated on the pattern back.

Number of pattern pieces gives you an idea of how easy or complicated the pattern is to sew.

Descriptions of the garment include its style, how it is intended to fit, and construction information for each of the views.

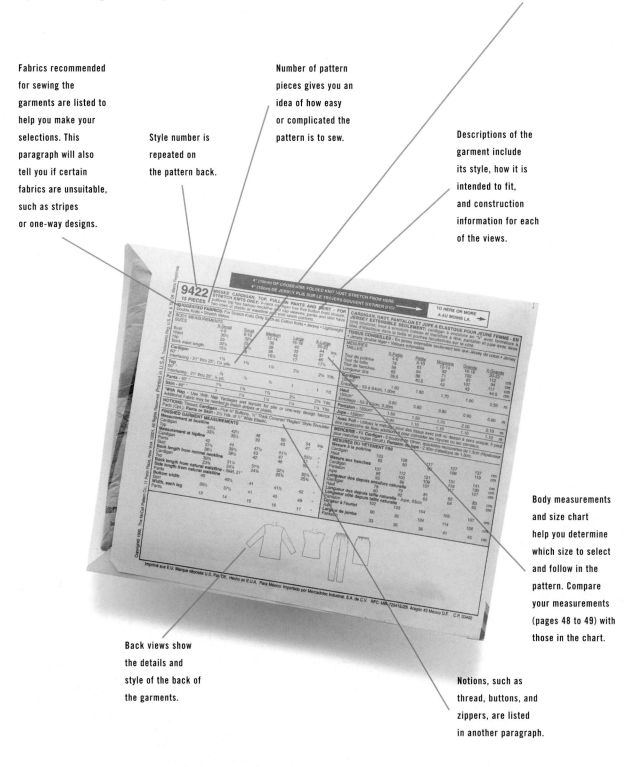

Body measurements and size chart help you determine which size to select and follow in the pattern. Compare your measurements (pages 48 to 49) with those in the chart.

Back views show the details and style of the back of the garments.

Notions, such as thread, buttons, and zippers, are listed in another paragraph.

Inside the PATTERN

Even if you love a good puzzle, your first peek at the pattern innards can be scary. Here's what to expect.

YOU'LL FIND...

Detailed sketches show you both front and back of each view.

General sewing directions, given as a short refresher course, include a key to the symbols used on the pattern pieces, and some basic construction techniques.

Cutting layouts for different fabric widths are shown for each view, in every size. Alternative layouts are shown for fabric with or without NAP.

Pattern key, identifying every pattern piece by name and number.

Sewing directions are a step-by-step guide through the construction of the garment. Each step is accompanied by a sketch. The right side of the fabric usually appears shaded; the wrong side is plain. Interfacing is often indicated with dots.

PATTERN MARKINGS

GRAINLINE: Place on straight grain of fabric, an even distance from selvage or fold.

FOLD LINE: Place on fold of fabric.

CUTTING LINE: For cutting.

SEAM LINE: For stitching.

SEAM ALLOWANCE: Distance between cutting and seam lines, usually 5/8" (1.5cm). On multi-sized patterns seam allowance is included, but not printed on tissue.

NOTCHES AND CIRCLES: For matching pattern pieces.

FINISHED GARMENT MEASUREMENT SYMBOL: The finished garment measurements at bust and/or hip are printed on your **Front** pattern pieces. The measurement includes **Body Measurement + Wearing Ease + Design Ease.** The measurement excludes pleats, tucks, darts and seam allowances. Measurements are also printed on the back of the pattern envelope, when space is available.

ADJUST IF NECESSARY

A pattern is made to fit body measurements, with extra ease for comfort and style. Adjust pieces before placing on fabric. Adjust back waist, sleeve and finished garment lengths, using McCALL's Easy-Rule Guide.

TO SHORTEN: Crease on Easy-Rule Guide. Fold necessary amount. Tape in place.

TO LENGTHEN: Cut on dotted lines of Easy-Rule Guide. Spread necessary amount. Tape over paper.

When Easy-Rule Guide is not on tissue, lengthen or shorten at lower edge.

CUTTING AND MARKING

SHRINK FABRIC not labeled pre-shrunk. Press.

CIRCLE LAYOUT for View, Size, Fabric Width. Fit garment

Use WITH NAP layout for fabrics with one-way designs, nap, pile or surface shading. Because most knits have surface shading, a with nap layout is used. For **DOUBLE THICKNESS (WITH FOLD)** - fold fabric with Right Sides Together.

DOUBLE THICKNESS (WITHOUT FOLD) - For fabrics with nap, fold fabric crosswise, RIGHT SIDES TOGETHER. Mark as shown. Cut along crosswise fold of fabric (A). Turn upper layer 180° so arrows go in same direction and place over lower layer, RIGHT SIDES TOGETHER (B)

For **SINGLE THICKNESS** - place fabric Right Side Up. Before **CUTTING** place all pieces on fabric according to layout. Overlap margins. Pin. Cut **ACCURATELY** through fabric and pattern on cutting line. Cut notches outward.

BEFORE REMOVING PATTERN, transfer markings to Wrong Side of fabric. Two ways which may be used quickly are the Pin and Chalk Pencil method or Tracing Paper and Dressmaker Wheel.

PIN AND
Pin or ba
Fit garme

WITH A
STITCH
allowance
guide lin
for accur
PRESS
stated. C

WITH AI
SERGE
allowan
specified
OVERE
cutting a

For **FUS**

CUTTING LAYOUTS

■ Black area denotes interlock.

NOTE: Pattern pieces may interlock more closely for smaller sizes.

✱ The finished garment measurements at breast and/or hip printed on your pattern tissue = Body Measurement + Wearing Ease + Design Ease.

NOTE: This SELECT-A-SIZE pattern has cutting lines for several sizes. Choose the proper cutting line for your size.

IMPORTANT: Layouts illustrated are suitable for corresponding Miss or Miss Petite sizes.

IMPORTANT: For layouts marked "✱", cut two pieces of fabric; place one layer over the other, RIGHT SIDES TOGETHER, so nap runs in one direction.

☐ Pattern pieces to be placed with printed side up
▨ Pattern pieces to be placed with printed side down

VIEW A OR B

TOP
View A - use pieces 7 thru 10, 12
View B - use pieces 7, 8, 11, 12

44" 45" (115cm) fabric
with nap or without nap
all sizes

OPEN FABRIC TO CUT RIGHT SIDE UP

sizes 10-12-14-16-18-20-

PANTS
use pieces 13, 14, 15

44" 45" (115cm) fabric
with nap or without nap
sizes 6-8

sizes 10-12-14-16-18-20-

CARDIGAN
use pieces 1 thru 6

44" 45" (115cm) fabric
with nap or without nap
sizes 6-8-10

OPEN FABRIC TO CUT RIGHT SIDE UP

sizes 12-14-16-18-20-22-24

58" 60" (150cm) fabric
with nap or without nap
all sizes

58" 60" (150cm) fabric
with nap or without nap
sizes 6-8-10-12-14-16

OPEN FABRIC TO CUT

PATTERN PIECES — TOP A-B

CARDIGAN

5, 6, 3, 2, 4, 1 — 11 B, 10 A, 9 A, 12, 8, 7

14, 15, 13 — **LEGGINGS** — 17, 16

PANTS

CARDIGAN
1. POCKET
2. CARDIGAN FRONT
3. CARDIGAN BACK

TOP A-B
7. TOP FRONT
8. TOP BACK
9. FRONT NECK FACING A

PANTS
13. PANTS FRONT
14. PANTS BACK
15. POCKET

FABRIC KEY
RIGHT SIDE   WRONG SIDE   INTERFACING   LINING

9039 - PAGE 2 of 4

SEWING DIRECTIONS

CARDIGAN

1. FRONTS AND BACK

NOTE: Pockets are optional.

Finish upper edge of POCKET (1) with a zigzag stitch or turn under 1/4" (6mm) and edge-stitch with a conventional machine or overedge using an overlock machine (serger).

Turn upper edge of pocket to OUTSIDE on hemline. Stitch hem to pocket at sides. Cut upper corners diagonally.

Turn hem to INSIDE. Press under 5/8" (1.5cm) on sides and lower edge below hem, folding in corners.

Stitch hem in place 1" (2.5cm) from upper edge.

Pin pockets to position on each CARDIGAN FRONT (2). Stitch close to sides and lower edge of pocket.

Pin each cardigan front to CARDIGAN BACK (3) at shoulders, RIGHT SIDES TOGETHER, matching notches. Stitch.

2. FACING

Baste interfacing to WRONG SIDE of each FRO and BACK FACING (5).

Stitch each front facing to back facing at shoulders. Cut interfacing close to stitching.

Finish UN-NOTCHED edge of front facing and lower edge of back facing with a zigzag stitch or turn under 1/4" (6mm) and edge-stitch with a conventional machine or overedge using an overlock machine (serger).

Press seam allowances toward facing. UNDERSTITCH by stitching through facing and seam allowances close to seam. (This prevents facing from rolling to outside.)

Turn facing to INSIDE. Press.

Baste raw edges of facing and jacket together at armholes, matching seams.

3. SLEEVES AND UNDERARM SEAMS

With RIGHT SIDES TOGETHER, pin SLEEVE (6) to armhole

CLIP

and sleeve, matching armhole
g free below circle if using slits.

titch again just inside previous

if necessary to press open.

ORCEMENT STITCHING

Turn up a 1¼" (3.2cm) hem on lower edge of sleeve. Press.

Open out hem and finish raw edge same as facing.

Replace hem and hand-sew in place. Press.

4. FINISHING

HEM - WITHOUT SLITS

Turn lower edge of facing to OUTSIDE on seam. Pin lower edges together. Stitch across lower edge of facing and turn up a 1¼" (3.2cm) seam allowance.

Cut corners diagonally. Cut facing seam allowance to only 1/4" (6mm).

HEM - WITH

Press under
pressed edge

Press under
gan, opening

Turn facings
on crease. S
seam allow

Turn facing to INSIDE. again

Turn hem an
on lower edg

Stitch hem a
and above c

BUTTONING

Pattern LAYOUT

All pattern companies use a universal system of symbols on their pattern pieces. These symbols help you lay out the pattern, show you where to cut, help you match up seamlines, show you where to sew, and give placement guides for things like buttons, buttonholes, and hems. Along with the symbols, you will also find essential instructions printed on the pattern pieces.

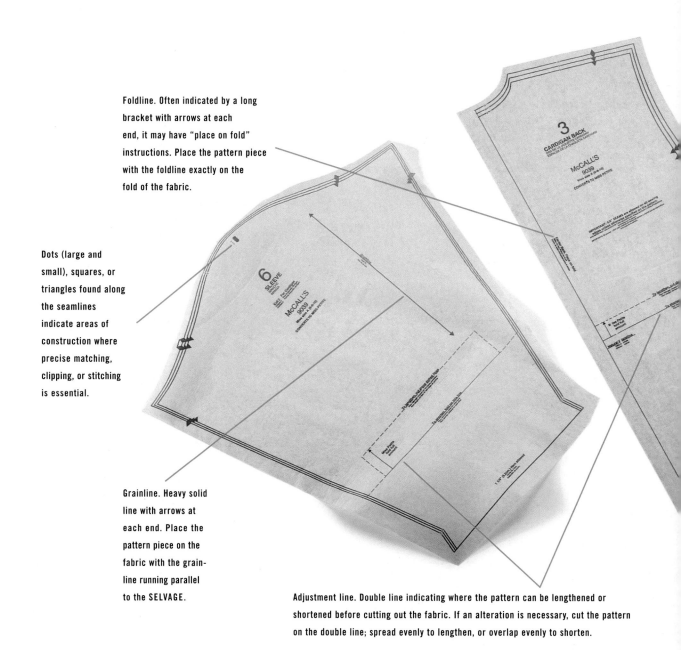

Foldline. Often indicated by a long bracket with arrows at each end, it may have "place on fold" instructions. Place the pattern piece with the foldline exactly on the fold of the fabric.

Dots (large and small), squares, or triangles found along the seamlines indicate areas of construction where precise matching, clipping, or stitching is essential.

Grainline. Heavy solid line with arrows at each end. Place the pattern piece on the fabric with the grainline running parallel to the SELVAGE.

Adjustment line. Double line indicating where the pattern can be lengthened or shortened before cutting out the fabric. If an alteration is necessary, cut the pattern on the double line; spread evenly to lengthen, or overlap evenly to shorten.

Seamlines. Long, broken line, usually 5/8" (1.5 cm) inside the cutting line. Multisize patterns often do not have seamlines printed on them.

Cutting line. Heavy solid line along the outer edge of the pattern, often shown with a scissors symbol. Cut on this line. When more than one size is printed on one pattern, the cutting lines may be various styles of solid, dotted, or dashed lines, to help you distinguish one size from the next.

Notches. Diamond shapes along the cutting line, used for matching seams. They may be numbered in the order in which the seams are joined.

Button and buttonhole placement marks. Solid lines indicate the length of the buttonhole, if you are using the button size suggested on the pattern back. "X" or a button symbol shows the button size and placement.

Detail positions. Broken or solid lines indicating the placement for pockets or other details. Mark the position for accurate placement.

Hemline. Hem allowance is printed on the cutting line. Turn the hem up the specified amount, adjusting as necessary.

CONTINUED

Pattern LAYOUT

CONTINUED

Prepare a large work area, such as a dining room table covered with a cutting board (page 32). Assemble all the pattern pieces you will be needing, and press out any wrinkles with a warm, dry iron.

Locate and circle the correct pattern layout diagram (page 51) on your pattern guide sheet. These diagrams usually show you the easiest, most efficient way to lay out your pattern. Some fabrics have a **NAP**, meaning they have definite up and down directions. For these fabrics, pattern pieces must all be laid out in the same direction.

Fold the fabric in half, lengthwise. Smooth it out on the work surface, so that the **SELVAGES** align and the **CROSSWISE GRAIN** is perpendicular to them. Arrange the pattern pieces as indicated in the layout diagram. White pattern shapes indicate the piece is to be placed with the printed side up. Shaded pieces are

to be placed with the printed side down. Be sure to follow any other incidental directions that pertain to your layout. After all the pieces are in place, pin them to the fabric. Do not begin cutting until all the pattern pieces are in place.

PINNING

A First, position the pattern pieces that are to be cut on the fold. Place each one directly on the folded edge of the fabric. Pin the corners diagonally. Then continue pinning near the outer edge, placing the pins parallel to the cutting line. Space the pins about 3" (7.5 cm) apart; closer together on curves.

B Place the straight-grain pattern pieces on the fabric, with the grainline arrow parallel to the selvages on woven fabrics or parallel to the **RIBS** on knits. Measure from each end of the arrow to the selvage, shifting the pattern until the distances are equal. Pin both ends of the grainline so the pattern will not shift. Then pin the outer edges.

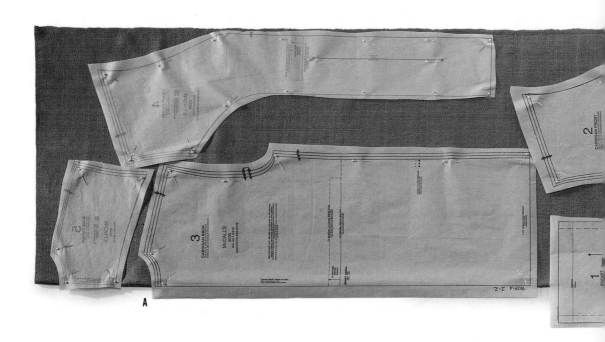

A

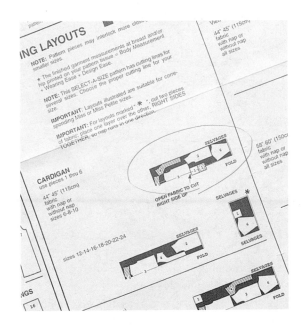

QUICK REFERENCE

Fold the fabric in half, lengthwise. When your fabric is folded like this, you will end up with mirror-image pieces for the left and right sides of the garment. Pattern directions usually suggest folding right sides together. Sometimes there are advantages to folding wrong sides together, such as having a better view of the fabric design or ease in marking. Either way will work.

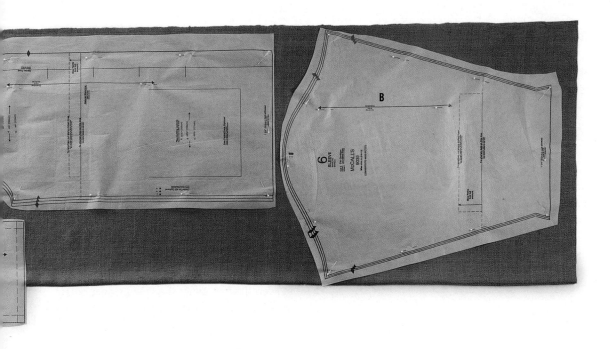

Cutting & MARKING

Don't be intimidated! Locate the correct cutting lines, and cut with confidence. Transfer the necessary marks, and you'll be ready to sew!

CUTTING

Accuracy is important, since mistakes made in cutting cannot always be corrected. Before cutting, double-check the placement of the pattern pieces.

Using bent-handled shears, cut with long, firm strokes, cutting directly on the cutting line. Take shorter strokes around curves. If you are using a multisize pattern, be sure that you follow the correct cutting line all the time.

Notches can be cut outward, especially if the fabric is loosely woven or if the pattern calls for ¼" (6 mm) **SEAM ALLOWANCES**. Cut multiple notches as one unit, not separately. Or, you can cut directly through the notches, and then mark them with short snips into the seam allowances.

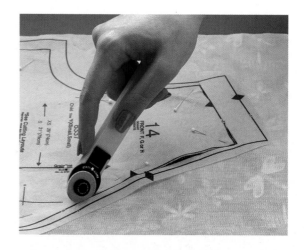

If you prefer to use a **ROTARY CUTTER AND MAT**, be sure to keep the mat under the area being cut. Use steady, even pressure, and, above all, keep fingers and small children away from the rotary cutter.

MARKING

Keep the pattern pieces pinned in place after cutting.
Transfer pattern symbols to the appropriate side
of the fabric, using one of the following methods.

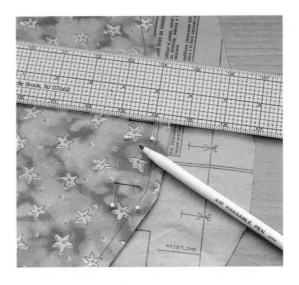

Erasable fabric markers are felt-tip pens designed
specifically for sewing needs. Air-erasable marks
disappear within 48 hours. Water-erasable marks
disappear with a spritz of water.

Pins are a quick way to transfer marks. Since they
may fall out easily, use pin marks only when you
intend to sew immediately. Or pin-mark first,
remove the pattern, and mark again, using chalk or
erasable fabric marker.

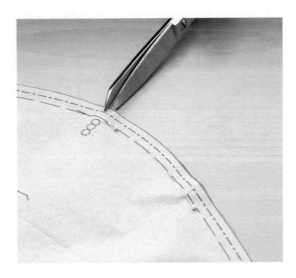

Snips are handy for marking things like dots at
shoulder seams. Make shallow snips into the seam
allowances at the dot locations.

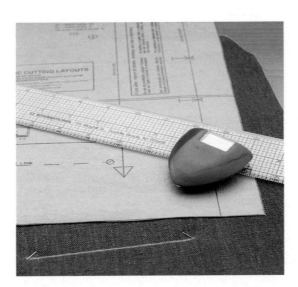

Chalk is available in pencil form or as a powder in a
rolling-wheel dispenser.

Sewing GARMENTS

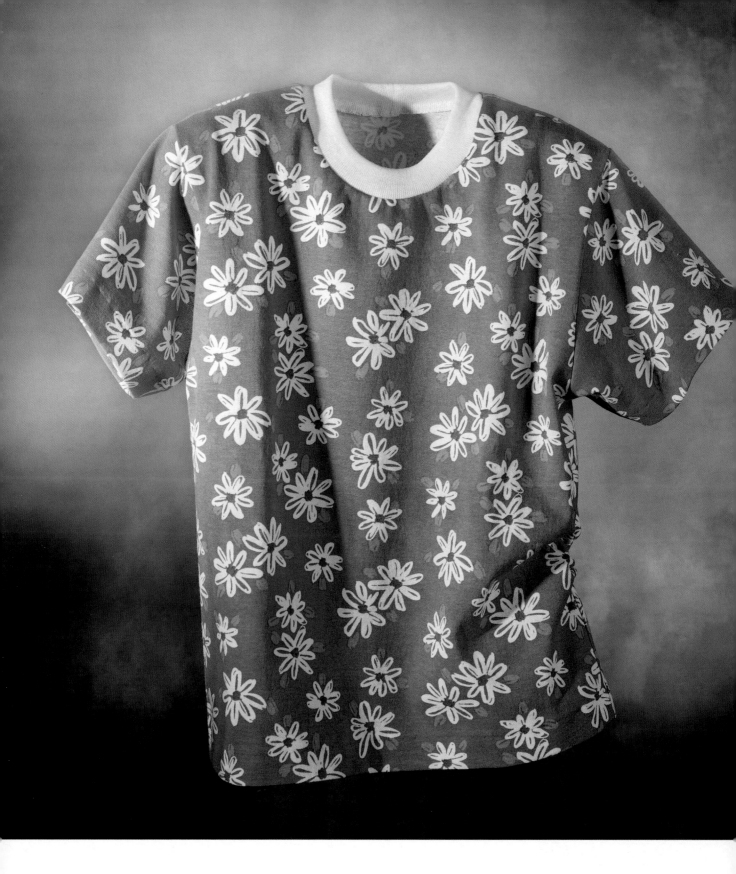

T-SHIRTS

T-shirts are classic and versatile; it seems you can never have too many. As you become more experienced, you'll be surprised how quickly you are able to make them. The fun begins in selecting your knit fabric (page 41) from the array of stripes, prints, and colorful solids available. To help you decide which pattern to buy, note the way the T-shirts fit the models or sketches on the package front. Some patterns are designed for an "oversized" look, others are meant to fit the form of your body more closely. Your pattern should have four pieces: front, back, sleeve, and neck **RIBBING**. Some may also have a piece for sleeve ribbing.

The fit of the T-shirt will vary with the fabric's degree of stretch. T-shirt patterns, designed for knits only, indicate the amount of stretch required of the fabric. For instance, "25% stretch crosswise" would indicate that 4" (10 cm) of fabric will stretch on the **CROSSWISE GRAIN** an additional 1" (2.5 cm). Always test the degree of stretch in the fabric, especially if you are making a close-fitting T-shirt.

WHAT YOU'LL LEARN

Techniques for sewing with knits

How to sew in sleeves

How to apply ribbing to a neckline

WHAT YOU'LL NEED

T-shirt pattern (designed for stretch knits)

Knit fabric (check pattern for amount)

Scraps of fusible knit interfacing (page 33)

Ribbing (check pattern for amount)

Matching all-purpose thread

How to Sew a T-SHIRT

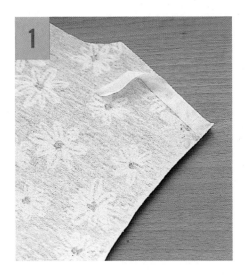

LET'S BEGIN

1 Prepare the fabric (page 31); however, don't wash the ribbing, as the raw edges are likely to stretch out of shape. T-shirts are easiest to sew using ¼" *(6 mm) seam allowances*. If your pattern pieces have ⅝" (1.5 cm) **SEAM ALLOWANCES**, trim them down to ¼" (6 mm) before laying out the pattern. Lay out the pattern (page 54), and cut the fabric (page 58). Transfer any necessary marks (page 59). Insert a ballpoint sewing machine needle; size 11/70 or 12/80 is suitable for most knits. Cut two ½" (1.3 cm) strips of fusible interfacing the length of the shoulder **SEAM**. Place a strip even with the cut edge of each back shoulder, on the wrong side of the fabric. Fuse the strips in place, *following the manufacturer's directions*. This is done to *stabilize the shoulder seams*.

2 Place the T-shirt front over the back, right sides together, aligning the shoulder seam allowance edges. Pin, inserting the pins perpendicular to the edges. Stitch the front and back T-shirt sections together at the shoulder seams, using a ¼" (6 mm) seam allowance; *backstitch (p. 19)* a few stitches at each edge. Since the shoulder seams are stabilized, a straight stitch is appropriate here.

3 Add a second row of machine stitching (either a straight stitch or a narrow zigzag) next to the first row, within the seam allowance. **PRESS** the shoulder seam allowances toward the shirt back.

4 Mark the center front and center back of the neckline with pins. Then bring the two centers together and mark the points halfway between with pins. (These marks should be slightly ahead of the shoulder seams.) The neckline is divided into fourths.

5 Sew the short ends of the *ribbing, right sides together,* forming a circle. Use ¼" (6 mm) seam allowance, and sew with a short straight stitch. *Press the seam open with your fingers.*

6 Fold the ribbing in half, lengthwise, with the raw edges even and the seam allowances on the inside. Divide the ribbing into fourths, as you did the neckline. Mark these sections with pins.

CONTINUED

QUICK REFERENCE

¼" (6 mm) seam allowances. Some patterns made especially for knits are designed with ¼" (6 mm) seam allowances, rather than ⅝" (1.5 cm). In many cases, running the outside edge of the presser foot along the cut edge of the fabric results in a ¼" (6 mm) seam. Run a test to be sure.

Follow the manufacturer's directions. The interfacing bolt is wrapped with a long sheet of plastic on which the directions are printed. Have the store clerk cut off a section of the directions for you to take home.

Stabilize the shoulder seams. Shoulder seams follow the crosswise grain, the direction in which knit fabrics stretch the most. However, it is not desirable or necessary to have shoulder seams that stretch. Narrow strips of fusible interfacing help the seams keep their intended length. You'll also find that this makes sewing in the stretchy direction much easier.

Ribbing, right sides together. Sometimes knit fabrics and ribbings do not have a right or wrong side. To test, gently stretch the raw edge on the crosswise grain of the ribbing. If the edge curls to one side, that side is the right side of the fabric. If it doesn't curl to either side, either side can be used on the outside.

Press the seam open with your fingers. Avoid pressing ribbing with an iron, as this may destroy its elasticity.

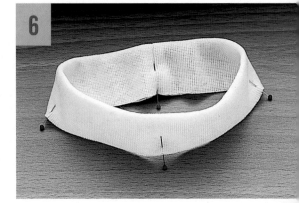

How to Sew a T-SHIRT

7 Pin the ribbing to the right side of the neckline, aligning the ribbing seam to the center back pin mark; match up the remaining pin marks.

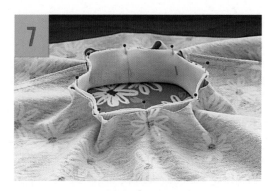

8 Place the fabric under the presser foot, with the ribbing facing up. Stitch with a narrow zigzag or stretch stitch (page 20), keeping the raw edges even and stretching the ribbing evenly to fit each section between pins. Remove the pins as you come to them.

9 Stitch again next to the first row, using a narrow, medium-length zigzag stitch. Gently press the ribbing toward the shirt, being careful not to stretch the ribbing.

10 Make sure you have marked the top of the sleeve and any other notches on the sleeve and shirt as indicated on the pattern pieces. With right sides together, pin the sleeve to the armhole of the shirt, matching the top dot or notch to the shoulder seam, and aligning any other notches. Pin frequently, easing in any extra sleeve fullness.

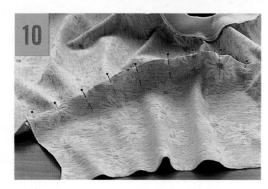

11 Stitch the armhole seam, using a narrow, medium-length zigzag stitch; remove the pins as you come to them. Stitch again next to the first row, within the seam allowance.

12 Repeat steps 10 and 11 for the other sleeve. Press the seams toward the sleeves. With the right sides together, pin the shirt front to the shirt back along the sides and sleeves, matching the underarm seams.

13 Stitch and finish the seams in the same manner as for the sleeve seams, beginning at the lower edge of the shirt and sewing continuously to the lower edge of the sleeve. Press the seams toward the back.

TIP You can press the side seams, simply by slipping the shirt over the end of the ironing board. Insert a seam roll or sleeve board (page 31) into the sleeve, so you can press the seam allowance to the side without pressing unwanted creases into the opposite side of the sleeve.

14 Turn under the lower *hem allowance,* as specified by your pattern. Stitch the hem by hand (page 24) or by machine (page 25); select a method that will allow the hem to stretch, if necessary. Hem the lower edges of the sleeves in the same manner.

QUICK REFERENCE

Hem allowance. The pattern has allowed a predetermined extra length for turning under and finishing the sleeves and lower edge. This amount is indicated on your pattern.

APPLAUSE

Who knew T-shirts could be so easy to make? Now there are no limits to what you can create.

Change the **LOOK**

If the neckline slips easily over the head, you can use the shirt fabric rather than ribbing at the neckline. TOPSTITCH close to the seam for added detail. Double-needle hems (page 25) provide the perfect finishing touch.

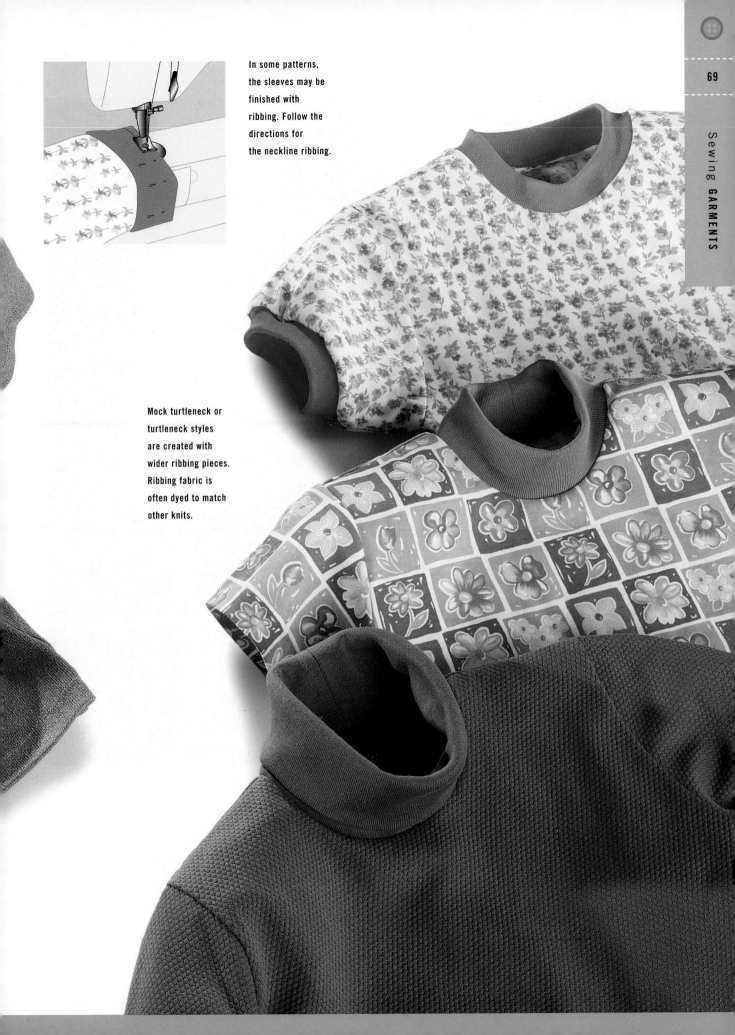

In some patterns, the sleeves may be finished with ribbing. Follow the directions for the neckline ribbing.

Mock turtleneck or turtleneck styles are created with wider ribbing pieces. Ribbing fabric is often dyed to match other knits.

Pull-on SKIRTS

Skirts with elastic waistbands are classic, comfortable, and easy-care. Straight or flared versions in varying lengths can be coordinated with a variety of sweaters or other tops for business, dress, or casual wear. Check the pattern envelope for recommended fabrics. Some patterns are designed only for knits and generally fit the body closer, counting on the stretchiness of the fabric to allow you to slide the skirt over your hips. Patterns suitable for woven fabrics will include extra fullness. The first set of directions works for woven or knit fabrics. Alternate steps for sewing with knits begin on page 77. These directions may differ from your pattern; be sure to use the **SEAM ALLOWANCE** given in your pattern. Select a pattern with two pieces: a front and a back. An elastic **CASING** at the waistline is formed from excess fabric length at the skirt top. The skirt itself may be constructed of two, three, or four sections, depending on whether or not there are center front or back **SEAMS**.

WHAT YOU'LL LEARN

Two methods for sewing elastic waistlines

Hem alternatives for skirts

How to sew and finish (page 21) side, front, and back seams

WHAT YOU'LL NEED

Skirt pattern with elastic waistline

Fabric (check pattern for amount)

Matching all-purpose thread

1" (2.5 cm) nonroll elastic, enough to go around your waist

How to Sew a PULL-ON SKIRT

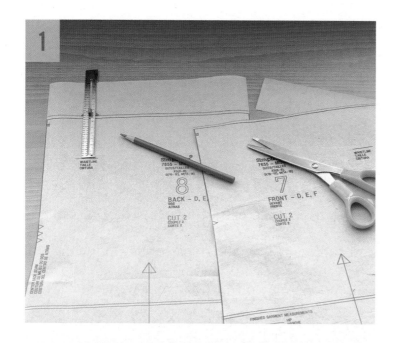

LET'S BEGIN

1 To construct the skirt following these directions, 2¾" (7 cm) of fabric must be allowed for the casing above the waistline. This may be different from the casing allowance already on your pattern. Measure this distance from the waistline, and mark a cutting line on your pattern. (Add extra paper, if necessary.) Be sure to mark both front and back pattern pieces.

2 Prepare the fabric (page 43), lay out the pattern (page 57), and cut the fabric (page 58). Transfer any necessary marks (page 59). Insert a size 11/70 or 12/80 sharp or universal sewing machine needle. If your pattern does not have center front or back seams, move on to step 4. If your pattern has a center front seam, place the skirt front pieces right sides together, aligning the center cut edges and matching the notches. Insert pins perpendicular to the center front seam.

TIP Be sure you are not pinning the pieces together along the side seams. Sometimes it is difficult to tell the difference. Check your pattern to be sure.

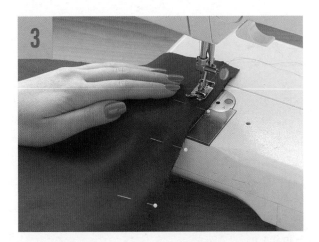

3 Place the fabric under the presser foot with the cut edges aligned to the ⅝" (1.5 cm) seam allowance guide. Stitch the center front seam, *backstitching (p. 19)* a few stitches at the upper and lower edges. If your pattern has a center back seam, stitch it in the same manner.

TIP **If your skirt has side seam pockets, follow the pattern directions carefully, as methods vary.**

4 If it is difficult to tell the skirt front from the skirt back, mark the wrong side of the skirt back, using chalk. Place the front and back skirt pieces right sides together, aligning the side edges and matching the notches. *Insert pins perpendicular to the sides (p. 19).* Stitch the side seams, backstitching at the upper and lower edges, and *removing pins as you come to them (p.19).* If you are sewing on a woven fabric, finish (page 21) the edges of all the seam allowances.

5 **PRESS** all the seams flat to set the stitching line in the fabric. This may seem unnecessary, but it really does give you a better-looking seam in the end. Then press the seam allowances open.

TIP **To prevent the cut edge of the seam allowance from imprinting the front of the fabric, press seams open over a seam roll or hard cardboard tube.**

CONTINUED

How to Sew a PULL-ON SKIRT

CONTINUED
---

6 **BASTE** the seam allowances open flat from the upper edge down about 4" (10 cm) (arrows). This will keep them from getting in the way when you insert the elastic in step 9. Finish the waistline edge, using a multistitch-zigzag (page 21). Fold the upper edge 1½" (3.8 cm) to the wrong side, and press. Insert pins along and perpendicular to the fold.

7 **EDGESTITCH** close to the fold around the upper edge of the waistline. Begin and end at a side seam, overlapping the stitches about ½" (1.3 cm).

TIP Sometimes it is difficult to tell the skirt front from the back when the garment is finished. We've sewn a short loop of twill tape under the casing seam to identify the back.

8 Insert pins along the lower edge of the casing. Place a piece of tape on the bed of your machine 1¼" (3.2 cm) from the tip of the needle. Stitch the lower edge of the casing, guiding the upper edge along the tape. Leave a 2" (5 cm) opening at one side seam.

9 Fasten a safety pin or bodkin (page 33) to one end of the elastic, and insert the elastic through the casing opening. Push and pull the safety pin all the way to the opposite side of the opening. Remove the basting threads from step 6.

TIP Insert a large safety pin across the free end of the elastic so that it will not get pulled into the opening.

10 Try on the skirt. Pull up the elastic to fit your waist snugly, yet comfortably; pin the ends together.

11 Take off the skirt. Pull the pinned ends of the elastic several inches (centimeters) out of the casing. Trim the overlapped ends to ½" (1.3 cm), if necessary. Place them under the presser foot, and stitch through both layers, using a multistitch-zigzag.

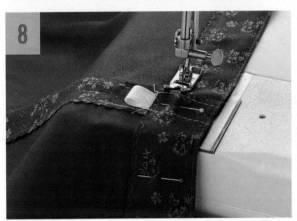

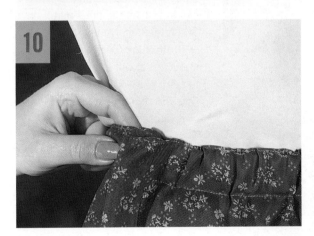

CONTINUED

How to Sew a PULL-ON SKIRT

CONTINUED

12 Machine-stitch the opening in the casing closed. Distribute the casing fullness evenly around the elastic. *Stitch in the ditch* at the seams to keep the elastic from shifting or rolling.

13 Try on the skirt, and have someone *mark the hem length* for you, using chalk or pins.

14 Take off the skirt, and trim the hem allowance to an even depth. (Check the pattern for hem allowance.) Turn under the hem along the markings, and pin. For double-fold hems on slightly flared skirts, it is helpful to hand-baste on the inner fold. Stitch the hem by hand (page 24) or by machine (page 25); select a method that will allow the hem to stretch, if you are using a knit. Give the skirt a final pressing, and give yourself a pat on the back.

ALTERNATE STEPS FOR A KNIT PULL-ON SKIRT

1 To construct a knit skirt following these directions, an amount of fabric equal to *twice the width of the elastic* must be allowed above the waistline. Measure this distance from the waistline, and mark a new cutting line on your pattern. (Add extra paper, if necessary.) Be sure to mark both front and back pattern pieces. Follow steps 2 to 5 on pages 72 and 73, sewing with the seam allowances designated by your pattern. It is not necessary to finish seams on knit skirts.

TIP **Read your pattern directions. Some patterns, especially those that have ¼" (6 mm) seam allowances, instruct you to sew your elastic waistline with this method. There is no need to alter those patterns, as they already allow this amount of fabric at the top.**

2 Cut a piece of elastic to fit your waist snugly, yet still stretch to fit over your hips. Overlap the ends ½" (1.3 cm), and stitch them together, using a wide zigzag stitch or multistitch-zigzag. Divide both the elastic and the upper edge of the skirt into fourths, and pin-mark. Pin the elastic to the wrong side of the skirt, aligning the edges and matching the pin marks; insert the pins perpendicular to the edges.

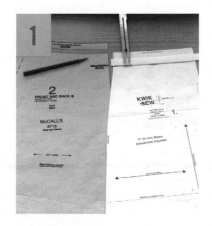

QUICK REFERENCE

Stitch in the ditch. Stitching from the right side and using short stitches, stitch directly into the well of the seam. Your stitches will practically disappear.

Mark the hem length. During the marking, stand straight, wearing the shoes you will be wearing with the skirt. The person marking should measure up from the floor to the desired length, moving around you as necessary. Otherwise, the hem will be uneven. If you don't have help, turn up the hem to the desired length and check in a mirror for even length.

Twice the width of the elastic. For this method, 1" (2.5 cm) elastic works well, though you may decide to use a different width. Some specialty elastics have channels for topstitching, giving the look of multiple rows.

CONTINUED

ALTERNATE STEPS FOR A KNIT PULL-ON SKIRT

CONTINUED

3 Insert four more pins, evenly spaced, between the quarter marks, distributing the fabric fullness evenly. Set your machine for a medium-width multistitch-zigzag. Place the skirt under the presser foot with the elastic on top. Align the edge of the foot to the elastic and fabric edges. Stitch, *stretching the elastic to fit between the pins* and keeping the edges aligned. Remove pins as you come to them, stopping with the needle down in the fabric.

4 Fold the elastic to the wrong side of the skirt, so the fabric encases the elastic. From the right side of the skirt, *stitch in the ditch (p. 77)* of the seam through all the waistband layers, at each seam. This step makes step 5 easier.

TIP Stretch the waistband slightly to give yourself a clear view of your target.

5 With the right side facing up, **TOPSTITCH** through all layers of the waistband, stretching the elastic as you sew. Use either a zigzag or multistitch-zigzag, with medium width and length, and stitch near the lower edge of the elastic. These stitches will allow the skirt to stretch as it goes over your hips. Finish the skirt, following steps 13 and 14 on page 76.

QUICK REFERENCE

Stretching the elastic to fit between the pins. Grasp the fabric and elastic behind the presser foot with one hand and ahead of the presser foot with the other hand, working in small sections at a time. Stretch the elastic only far enough to take up the slack in the fabric. Keep an even tension on the elastic, allowing the feed dogs to feed the fabric at a steady pace. Stop sewing to move your hands.

Simple Skirt VARIATIONS

For woven skirts, sew multiple-channel casings to handle two rows of ⅜" (1 cm) elastic or three rows of ¼" (6 mm) elastic. See the directions for pull-on-pants (page 79). To create this look with knit fabric, sew in one circle of wide elastic that has channels for topstitching (page 32).

Vary the hem treatment (pages 24 and 25) to suit the skirt style or to add design interest. A narrow, double-fold hem is suitable for a slightly flared skirt. Use a double-needle hem to give knits a little stretch. Stitch invisible hems in dressy skirts, either by hand or by machine.

Pull-on PANTS

Pull-on pants with elastic waists are easy to fit and easy to sew. When sewn in supple, lightweight wovens, such as rayon or microfiber, they are elegant enough for evening wear. For sportier looks, cotton, cotton blends, linen, or seersucker work well and can be paired with simple T-shirts or blouses. Consider purchasing enough fabric to make a matching jacket or vest to go with your pants and complete the outfit.

Select a pants pattern with two main pieces: the front and the back. The elastic **CASING** for the waist is formed from excess fabric at the top. These instructions are for pants without pockets. The method for sewing side-seam pockets varies greatly from pattern to pattern. Once you understand the basics of sewing pull-on pants, you can advance to a pattern with pockets, following the pattern instructions closely.

WHAT YOU'LL LEARN

How to alter the crotch length of a pattern

How to alter the leg length of a pattern

How to make a multi-row elastic waistband

WHAT YOU'LL NEED

Pants pattern; loose-fitting with elastic waistline

Fabric (check pattern for amount)

Matching all-purpose thread

⅜" (1 cm) elastic, enough to go twice around your waist

How to Sew PULL-ON PANTS

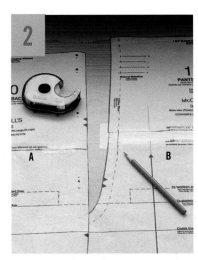

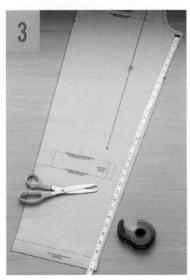

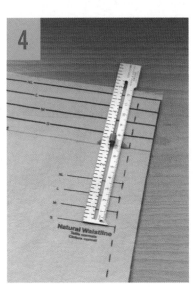

1 Measure the crotch seam length on a pair of pants that fits you comfortably. Start from the bottom of the waistband in the front and measure the distance to the bottom of the waistband in the back. On your pattern, measure the total crotch length, standing the tape measure on edge and measuring along the seamline of the center front and center back. Begin and end at the waistline mark; don't include the ⅝" (1.5 cm) **SEAM ALLOWANCES** at the inseam.

2 Compare the pants crotch length to the pattern crotch length. Alter your pattern, if necessary. Cut the pattern pieces apart on the horizontal adjustment line. Then lap the pieces *by half the total amount needed* to shorten (**A**), or separate the pieces by half the total amount needed to lengthen (**B**). Insert a paper strip to lengthen; tape the pieces in place.

3 Compare the inseam measurements on your pants and on your pattern, measuring from the crotch seamline to the hemline. Make any necessary alteration at the horizontal adjustment line.

4 To construct the pants following these directions, 2¾" (7 cm) of fabric must be allowed for the casing above the waistline. Measure distance from waistline, and mark a new cutting line on your pattern. (Add extra paper, if necessary.) Mark both front and back pattern pieces.

QUICK REFERENCE

By half the total amount needed.
For example, if you need to shorten the crotch 1" (2.5 cm), shorten the pants front ½" (1.3 cm), and shorten the pants back ½" (1.3 cm).

5 Prepare the fabric (page 43), lay out the pattern (page 54), and cut the fabric (page 58). Transfer any necessary marks (page 59). Set your sewing machine on a straight stitch of 10 to 12 stitches per inch, which is 2 to 2.5 mm. Insert a sewing machine needle suitable for your fabric (page 10). Place the right front over the right back, right sides together, along the inner leg. Pin them together, matching notches and ***inserting the pins perpendicular to the edges (p. 19).*** Stitch the **SEAM**, using ⅝" (1.5 cm) seam allowance unless your pattern indicates another seam allowance. Repeat for the left front and back legs.

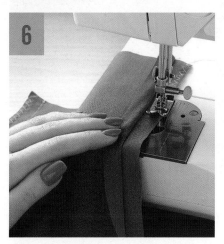

6 Finish (page 21) the edges of the seam allowances. **PRESS** the seams flat; then press them open.

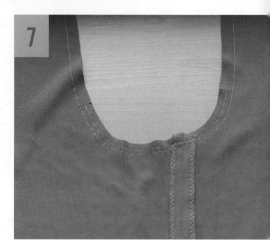

7 With right sides together, pin the sewn right and left pants sections together at the crotch seam. Line up the inner leg seams, and match any notches. Stitch the entire seam. Then stitch the curved area of the seam between the notches a second time, ¼" (6 mm) from the first stitching.

CONTINUED

How to Sew PULL-ON PANTS

CONTINUED
---

8 Trim the seam in the curved area of the crotch close to the second stitching line. Finish the trimmed seam allowances. Then also finish the remaining seam allowances separately. Press the seam allowances open in the front and back, above the trimmed portion of the seam.

9 Pin the front and back, right sides together, at the side seams, matching notches and any other marks. Stitch a ⅝" (1.5 cm) seam from the bottom of the leg to the upper edge. Repeat for the other side seam.

10 Finish the seam allowances separately. Press the seams flat; then press them open, using a seam roll. **BASTE** all the seam allowances open flat from the upper edge down about 4" (10 cm). This will keep them from getting in the way when you insert the elastic in step 15.

11 Finish the waistline (page 21). Fold the upper edge 1½" (3.8 cm) to the wrong side, and press. Insert pins along and perpendicular to the fold.

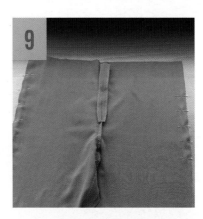

12 **EDGESTITCH** close to the fold around the upper edge of the waistline. Begin and end at a side seam, overlapping the stitches about ½" (1.3 cm).

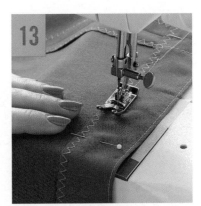

13 Place a piece of tape on the bed of your machine 1¼" (3.2 cm) from the tip of the needle. Stitch the lower edge of the casing, guiding the upper edge along the tape. Leave a 2" (5 cm) opening at one side seam.

14 Measure from the upper edge of the waist to a point halfway between the two stitching lines. Place tape on the machine bed as a sewing guide. Stitch, leaving a 2" (5 cm) opening just above the first opening.

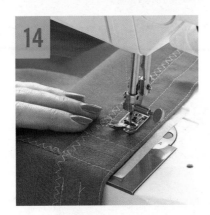

TIP To use three rows of ¼" (6 mm) elastic in your waistline casing, divide the space into even thirds.

15 Cut two pieces of ⅜" (1 cm) elastic a little larger than your waist measurement. Fasten a safety pin or bodkin (page 33) to one end of one elastic, and insert the elastic through the casing opening into the top channel. Push and pull the safety pin through all the way to the opposite side of the opening, taking care not to let the free end disappear into the opening. Then do the same with the second piece of elastic, inserting it into the lower channel. Secure the ends of both pieces with safety pins.

CONTINUED

How to Sew PULL-ON PANTS

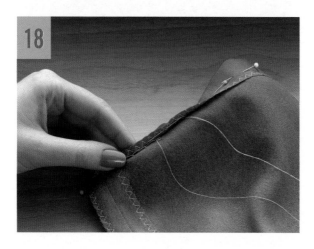

CONTINUED

16 Try on the pants. Pull up the elastic to fit your waist snugly, yet comfortably; pin the ends together. Take off the pants. Pull the pinned ends of the top elastic several inches (centimeters) out of the casing. Trim the overlapped ends to ½" (1.3 cm), if necessary. Place them under the presser foot, and stitch through both layers, using a multistitch-zigzag. Repeat for the lower elastic.

17 Machine-stitch the openings in the casing closed. Distribute the casing fullness evenly around the elastic. *Stitch in the ditch (p. 77)* at the seams to keep the elastic from shifting or rolling. Remove the basting stitches from step 10.

18 Turn under the hem allowance, and pin in place. Try on the pants, and adjust the length, if necessary. Take off the pants, and trim the hem allowance to an even depth. Press the fold. Finish the lower edge. Stitch the hem by hand (page 24) or by machine (page 25). Give the pants a final pressing, and they're ready to wear!

More Styles of PULL-ON PANTS

You'll find pants with
various leg widths. These
instructions work
for pull-on shorts and
culottes, too.

VESTS

Vests, in a variety of styles, enhance wardrobes by complementing skirts, slacks, or dresses. They can be worn over knit tops, turtlenecks, or blouses, to fit the occasion.

For easy sewing, we've selected a loose-fitting, lined vest. Look for a pattern with two main pattern pieces: a front and a back. Good choices of fabric for a loose-fitting vest include cotton, cotton blends, rayon, linen, denim, wool crepe, wool gabardine, and corduroy. Select lining fabric made specifically for that purpose, or use lightweight cotton or blends.

WHAT YOU'LL LEARN

How to sew lining in a vest

How to sew buttonholes

How to sew on buttons

WHAT YOU'LL NEED

Vest pattern; lined, loose-fitting, with button closure

Fabric for vest (check pattern for amount)

Lining fabric (check pattern for amount)

Matching all-purpose thread

Lightweight to medium-weight fusible interfacing (page 33), enough to cover the vest fronts

Buttons

How to Sew a VEST

1 Prepare the fabric (page 43).
Lay out the pattern and
cut the fabric (pages 54 to 58) for
the two back pieces, reserving
enough fabric for the fronts. Fuse
interfacing to the wrong side of
the reserved fabric, *following
the manufacturer's directions (p. 65)*.
This will give support to buttons
and buttonholes.

2 Lay out the vest front pieces
on the interfaced fabric; cut.
Lay out and cut the lining pieces.
Transfer any necessary marks
(page 59). Set your sewing
machine on a straight stitch of 10
to 12 stitches per inch, which
equals 2 to 2.5 mm. For most
fabrics, a universal machine needle
size 12/80 will work fine.

3 Place the vest fronts over the
vest back, right sides together,
aligning the shoulder **SEAM
ALLOWANCE** edges and matching
any notches. *Insert pins* along the
shoulders, *perpendicular to the
cut edges (p. 19)*. Stitch ⅝" (1.5 cm)
shoulder **SEAMS**, *backstitching
(p. 19)* at the beginning and end
and *removing the pins as you come
to them (p. 19)*.

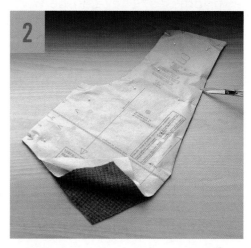

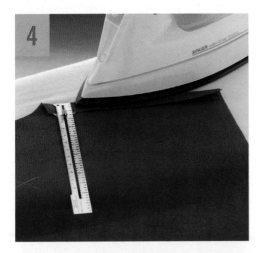

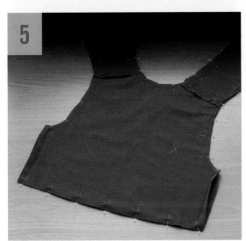

QUICK REFERENCE

Press the lining side seam allowances under ⅝" (1.5 cm).
You'll understand the importance of this when you get to steps
14 and 15. It is much easier to measure and press under
the side seam allowances of the lining now, but unfold them
to complete the next few steps.

4 Repeat step 3 for the lining
pieces. For both the vest and
the lining, **PRESS** the shoulder
seams flat; then press them open.
*Press the lining side seam allowances
under ⅝" (1.5 cm).*

TIP Because all the seam
allowances will be enclosed
between the vest and the lining, it is not
necessary to finish them.

5 Place the vest and the lining
right sides together, matching
the raw edges and any notches.
Insert pins perpendicular to the
edges along all but the side seams.

6 Stitch the ⅝" (1.5 cm) seam
across the bottom of the vest
back. Then stitch the armhole seams.

CONTINUED

How to Sew a VEST

CONTINUED
---

7 Beginning at the lower edge of one side, stitch one continuous seam along the bottom and center edges of one vest front, around the back neckline, and around the center and bottom edges of the other vest front, ending at the lower edge of the opposite side. Stop with the needle down in the fabric to **PIVOT** at each corner.

8 Trim the vest seam allowances to ¼" (6 mm); trim the lining seam allowances to ⅛" (3 mm). This step, called **GRADING**, reduces bulk. Do not trim the side seam allowances.

TIP Trimming to these widths works well for tightly woven fabrics like this wool. For looser weaves that tend to ravel easily, trim the seam allowances wider.

9 **CLIP** into the curved neckline and armhole seam allowances every ½" (1.3 cm), clipping up to, but not through, the stitches. Clipping allows the seam allowance to turn smoothly to the inside and lie flat.

10 Put your hand through one of the open side seams of the back and through the shoulder of that side; grab the front of the vest. Pull it through the lining and vest at the shoulder and out the side seam, turning it right side out. Turn the other front right side out through the same side opening. Turn the back right side out.

11 Insert a point turner (page 33) or similar tool into an opening, and gently push out any corners as necessary. Press all the seamed edges of the vest, centering the seam on the edge, with the lining to the inside.

12 Pin the vest front and back, right sides together, along the side seams, keeping the lining free. Match up the armhole seams, placing a pin directly in the seamline and turning the seam allowances toward the lining. Match up the lower seams in the same way. Then pin the lining front and back together 1" to 2" (2.5 to 5 cm) beyond the seams.

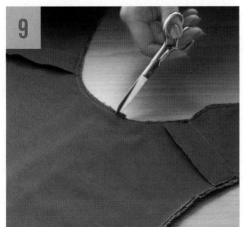

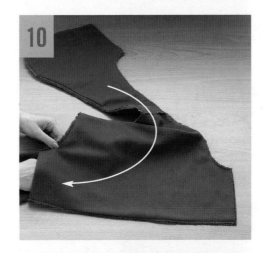

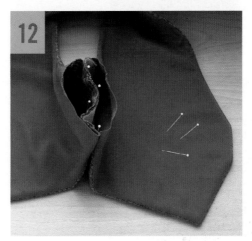

CONTINUED

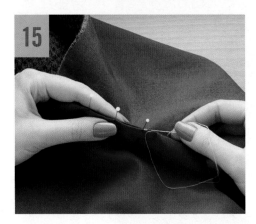

CONTINUED

13 Sew a ⅝" (1.5 cm) seam where you have pinned, backstitching at each end. As you cross the seam allowances at the armhole and lower edge, keep them turned toward the lining; remove pins as you come to them.

TIP This is an awkward seam to sew, especially at the beginning and end. Use the pressed foldlines of the lining (step 4) as seam guides. Take your time, and be careful to keep the rest of the vest out of the way so that you do not catch unwanted fabric in the stitches.

14 With your fingers, press the seam allowances open; turn in the lining seam allowances along the previously pressed lines. Press with your iron.

15 Pin the openings in the lining side seams closed. Slipstitch the edges together as on page 22.

16 TOPSTITCH ⅜" (1 cm) from the edge, around the armholes and around the lower, front, and neck edges.

17 Transfer the buttonhole markings from your pattern to the vest (page 59). Make sure they are all the same distance from the front edge and uniform in size. Usually a buttonhole is ⅛" (3 mm) longer than the button diameter. To sew the buttonholes, follow the instructions in your sewing machine manual.

TIP Remember, buttonholes go on the right front for females or on the left front for males. Don't cut them open until you have double-checked for accuracy in placement and size.

18 Overlap the vest fronts at the center front. Insert pins through the buttonholes at the outer ends; mark the locations for sewing the buttons on the other vest front.

19 Sew on the buttons as on page 23.

TIP Running thread through beeswax before sewing on the buttons will make the thread stronger and help prevent it from tangling. After running the thread through beeswax, run it through your fingers to melt the wax into the thread.

!

BRAVO

As you have discovered, sewing a lined vest is a piece of cake!

Vest VARIATIONS

Make a reversible vest by lining it with a fabric that can be worn on the outside rather than with lining fabric. Omit buttons and buttonholes, or sew sets of buttons to each side.

Vests have become the palette for a variety of artistic techniques. Add embroidery, beading, or painting to personalize your vest. Lining fabric is often used for both the inside and the outside of the vest back.

Before lining your vest, sew **PATCH POCKETS** to the fronts, following steps 2 to 6 on page 108; see page 117 for rounded-corner pockets.

Wrap SKIRTS

This wrap skirt is made from a rectangle of fabric; no pattern is needed. The rectangle size is determined from your own measurements, so the skirt is sure to fit. The upper edge is softly gathered onto a flat waistband, which is secured with a button closure.

A wrap skirt is the perfect candidate for a **BORDER-PRINT** fabric. The continuous design that runs along one **SELVAGE** becomes the lower edge of the skirt. Other suitable fabrics include solid colors and small, **NONDIRECTIONAL PRINTS**.

WHAT YOU'LL LEARN

How to **GATHER** fabric

How to sew a waistband

How to sew double-fold hems

WHAT YOU'LL NEED

Border-print (optional) lightweight woven fabric, length determined in step 1

Perforated waistband interfacing, for 1¼" (3.2 cm) waistband, enough to go around your waist plus 12" (30.5 cm)

Matching all-purpose thread

Two buttons

How to Sew a WRAP SKIRT

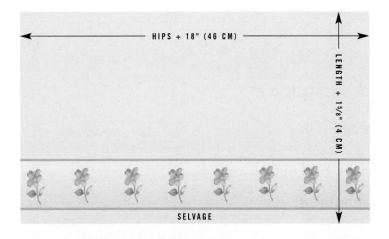

HIPS + 18" (46 CM)

LENGTH + 1⅝" (4 CM)

SELVAGE

LET'S BEGIN

1 Measure your hips at the widest location. Add 18" (46 cm) to this measurement to determine the width (side to side) of the rectangle. This is also the amount of fabric you need to buy. Decide how long you want the skirt, from your waist to the hem, and add 1⅝" (4 cm), to determine the length (top to bottom) of the rectangle. Cut a rectangle of fabric with these measurements. If you are using a border print, cut the rectangle with the width running on the **LENGTHWISE GRAIN**, and the lower edge just above the selvage on the border side.

2 Turn under the lower edge of the rectangle 1" (2.5 cm), and **PRESS**. Unfold the edge and turn the raw edge in to meet the pressed fold; press again. Then refold the edge, forming a *double-fold hem. Insert the pins perpendicular to the folds (p. 19).*

QUICK REFERENCE

Double-fold hem. Double-fold hems are made with two folds of equal depths, encasing the cut edge in the crease of the outer fold. Pressing the first fold to the total hem depth, in this case 1" (2.5 cm), allows you to be more accurate in turning and pressing.

3 Stitch along the inner fold, *removing the pins as you come to them (p. 19).* **EDGESTITCH** the outer fold. Hem each end of the rectangle in the same way, *backstitching (p. 19)* a few stitches at the bottoms and tops of the hems.

TIP At this point, check to be sure that both short ends of the skirt rectangle are exactly the same length. If one is slightly longer, trim them off evenly at the top edge.

4 Set your machine to sew long straight stitches. Beginning at one side hem, stitch a scant ⅝" (1.5 cm) from the edge along the top of the rectangle, stitching from the right side of the fabric. Stop stitching at the opposite side hem. Stitch a second row of long stitches ¼" (6 mm) closer to the edge. Leave thread tails at both ends.

TIP To stitch the second row, guide the fabric with the first stitching row along the left edge of the presser foot.

CONTINUED

How to Sew a WRAP SKIRT

CONTINUED

5 Cut *perforated waistband interfacing* 12" (30.5 cm) longer than your waist measurement. Fuse the interfacing to the fabric, with the *wider side of the interfacing along the selvage.* Cut out the waistband, allowing ½" (1.3 cm) excess fabric at the ends and ⅝" (1.5 cm) on the long edge for **SEAM ALLOWANCES**.

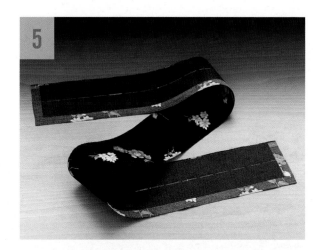

6 Mark the cut edge of the waistband ½" (1.3 cm) from each end. Then divide the remaining length into four equal parts, and mark, using chalk pencil or erasable marker. Divide the upper edge of the skirt into four equal parts, and mark.

7 With right sides together, pin the cut edge of the waistband to the upper edge of the skirt, matching quarter marks. Insert pins from the skirt side. At one end, grasp both bobbin threads, and pull on them with equal tension, sliding the fabric along the thread to gather it.

8 Keep pulling on the bobbin threads, gathering the fabric, and distributing the gathers evenly between the pins on half of the waistband. When the skirt fabric is gathered up to fit that half, secure the bobbin threads by winding them in a figure eight around the end pin.

QUICK REFERENCE

Perforated waistband interfacing. You can buy this convenient product at the fabric store, by the yard (meter) or in prepackaged lengths. Check the product label to be sure it works with the waistband measurements given in these instructions. Or cut the waistband width as specified by the manufacturer.

Wider side of the interfacing along the selvage. Normally, you avoid using the selvage edge because it is more tightly woven than the rest of the fabric, and it may tend to pucker if used in a seam. However, for waistbands, using the selvage eliminates the need to finish the edge or turn it under, thus eliminating extra steps and extra bulk.

9 Pull the bobbin threads from the other end to gather the remaining half; secure the threads. Distribute all the gathered fabric evenly along the waistband, inserting pins frequently to hold the fabric in place.

10 Reset the stitch length for 10 to 12 stitches per inch, which is 2 to 2.5 mm. Place the fabric under the presser foot, with the waistband on the bottom. Stitch ⅝" (1.5 cm) from the raw edges, keeping the gathers even and removing the pins as you come to them.

CONTINUED

How to Sew a WRAP SKIRT

CONTINUED

11 **GRADE** the seam allowances, by trimming the skirt seam allowance to ⅜" (1 cm), just above the gathering stitches.

12 Turn the seam allowance toward the waistband, and press lightly with tip of the iron. Avoid pressing creases into the gathers.

13 Fold the waistband on the interfacing center foldline, right sides together. The selvage edge extends down flat; the other edge is pressed up. Stitch ½" (1.3 cm) from the edge at each end. Trim the seam allowances to ¼" (6 mm). Then trim the upper corners diagonally.

14 Turn the waistband right side out, and press. The selvage edge extends down over the seam on the wrong side. From the right side, pin in the ditch of the waistband seam, catching the selvage edge on the back. At the ends, turn the corner of the selvage under at an angle.

TIP Be sure to keep the seam allowance turned up as it was pressed. Check to be sure the selvage edge is pinned at a consistent depth and lies flat.

15 *Stitch in the ditch (p. 77)* of the seam from the right side of the skirt, backstitching at the ends and removing the pins as you come to them.

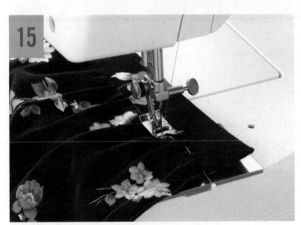

16 Try on the skirt, lapping the right side over the left side. Mark the waistband at each end, using a pin.

17 Stitch a buttonhole at each end of the waistband, following the directions in your owner's manual. Sew a button to the outside of the waistband on the left side; sew a button to the underside of the waistband on the right side.

Unlined JACKETS

Collarless jackets are versatile additions to any wardrobe. Those that are loose-fitting and unlined, with **DROP-SHOULDER** styling and **PATCH POCKETS**, are easy to make. Look for a pattern that includes pieces for front, back, sleeve, front **FACING**, back facing, and pocket. These directions are for square bottom front corners. If your pattern has round corners, pay close attention to the pattern directions when attaching the facing (step 11) and hemming the lower edge (steps 24 to 27).

As with any other project, the fabric of your jacket will determine whether it will be more suitable for casual, business, or dress. Cotton, cotton blends, and denim would be good choices to wear with jeans or casual slacks and skirts. Wool, wool blends, linen, and rayon work for business or dress. When you're feeling really confident, you might even consider making a jacket of suit-weight silk, like the one at left.

WHAT YOU'LL LEARN

How to sew a drop-shoulder sleeve

How to sew a patch pocket

How to apply fusible interfacing (page 33)

How to sew neck and front facings

WHAT YOU'LL NEED

Jacket pattern; unlined, loose-fitting

Fabric for jacket (check pattern for amount)

Matching all-purpose thread

Lightweight fusible interfacing (check pattern for amount)

Buttons

How to Sew an UNLINED JACKET

LET'S BEGIN
----

1 Prepare the fabric (page 43). Lay out the pattern pieces (page 54), and cut out (page 58) all but the facings. Fuse interfacing to the wrong side of the fabric for the facings, *following the manufacturer's directions (p. 65)*. Then cut out the facings. Transfer any necessary marks (page 59).

2 Turn under the top edge of the pocket ¼" (6 mm); **PRESS**. To finish the edge, set your machine for a zigzag stitch of medium length and width. Stitch close to the folded edge, so that the right-hand swing of the needle just clears the fold.

3 Turn the upper edge of the pocket (the facing) to the outside on the foldline; pin at the sides. Starting at the top of the pocket, stitch a ⅝" (1.5 cm) **SEAM** to the bottom of the facing on each side of the pocket, *backstitching (p. 19)* at the beginning and end. Trim the facing **SEAM ALLOWANCE** to ⅜" (1 cm). Trim the upper corners diagonally.

4 Turn the facing to the inside. Using a point turner or similar tool, gently push out the corners to square them off. Press the top fold. If the pocket has square bottom corners, turn under ⅝" (1.5 cm) on the bottom, and press. Then repeat for the side edges. For pockets with rounded corners, see the variation on page 117.

5 Set your sewing machine for a straight stitch of 10 to 12 stitches per inch, which is 2 to 2.5 mm. Measure the finished width of the facing; subtract ⅛" (3 mm). Mark this distance from the needle on the machine bed, using tape. **TOPSTITCH** the upper edge of the pocket, guiding the fold along the tape mark and catching the facing in the stitches.

6 Repeat steps 2 to 5 for the other pocket. Place the pockets on the jacket front, matching the upper corners to the markings transferred from the pattern. Pin them securely in place, *inserting the pins perpendicular to the edges (p. 19)*. **EDGESTITCH** around the sides and bottom of the pockets, backstitching at both upper corners. Stop with the needle down in the fabric to **PIVOT** at each corner. *Remove the pins as you come to them (p. 19)*.

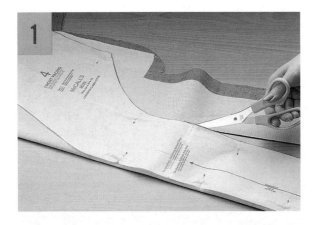

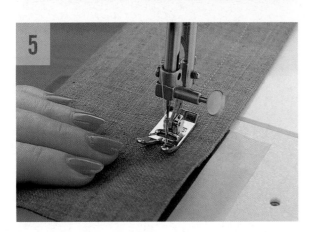

CONTINUED

How to Sew an UNLINED JACKET

CONTINUED
---

7 Pin the jacket fronts to the jacket back at the shoulders, with right sides together, aligning the cut edges and matching any notches. Insert the pins perpendicular to the edges.

8 Stitch the seams, guiding the cut edges along the ⅝" (1.5 cm) seam allowance guide. Press the seams flat; then press them open.

9 Sew the front facings to the back facing at the shoulders as in steps 7 and 8. Trim the seam allowances to ¼" (6 mm). Finish the inner, unnotched edges of the front facings and the lower edge of the back facing (arrows) as in step 2.

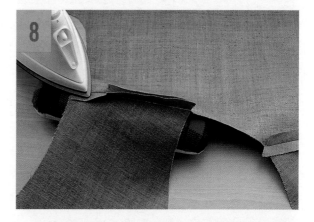

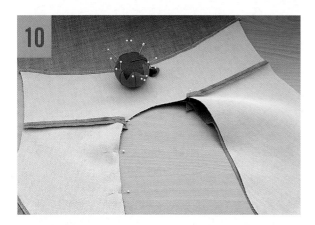

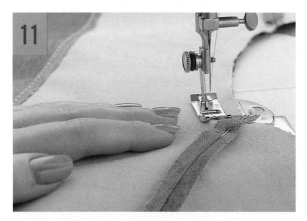

10 Pin the facing to the jacket, right sides together, aligning the cut edges. Match the shoulder seams and all notches. At the shoulders, insert a pin in the wells of the seams, to keep them aligned.

11 Stitch the facing to the jacket, guiding the cut edges along the ⅝" (1.5 cm) seam allowance guide. Stitch continuously from one lower edge, around the neckline, to the opposite lower edge; backstitch a few stitches at the beginning and end. Remove the pins as you come to them, and keep the shoulder seam allowances open flat.

12 **GRADE** the seam allowances by trimming the jacket neckline seam allowance to ⅜" (1 cm) and the facing seam allowance to ¼" (6 mm). **CLIP** into the neckline seam allowance every ½" (1.3 cm), clipping up to, but not through, the stitches. Clipping allows the facing to turn smoothly to the inside and lie flat.

CONTINUED

How to Sew an UNLINED JACKET

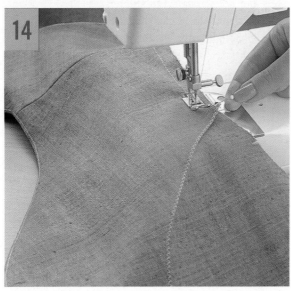

13 Press the seam allowances flat; then press them toward the facing. With the right side up, place the facing (**A**) under the presser foot, so the needle is aligned to enter the fabric just to the right of the seam at the lower left front; the jacket (**B**) extends off the left of the machine bed. Keeping the seam allowance turned toward the facing (arrows), stitch all around the fronts and neckline very close to the seam. You will be stitching through the facing and the seam allowance, but not through the jacket. This step, called **UNDERSTITCHING**, helps the facing lie flat.

> **TIP** Along the curve of the neckline, keep the facing lying flat, allowing the jacket to "bunch up" to the left of the curve. Stitch, following the curve of the facing. The clipped seam allowance will "fan out" underneath the facing.

14 Turn the facing to the inside; press. Align the shoulder seams, and smooth them out to the sleeve edge. Pin the facing to the sleeve edge, inserting the pins perpendicular to the edge. Set your machine for long straight stitches. **BASTE** the facings to the sleeve edges.

> **TIP** Some jacket patterns have facings that do not extend all the way to the sleeve edge. Align the shoulder seam allowances, and *stitch in the ditch (p. 79)* to secure the facing to the jacket.

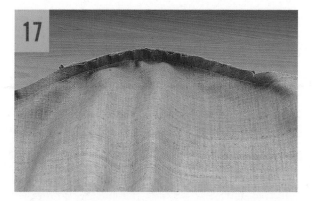

15 Pin the sleeve to the jacket, with right sides together. Align the cut edges, and match the notches. You probably also have a mark on the sleeve edge that aligns to the jacket shoulder seam. Count the notches to be sure you are pinning the correct sleeve. Pin frequently from the jacket side, easing the sleeve to fit smoothly.

16 Place the jacket under the presser foot, with the sleeve underneath. Stitch the seam, guiding the edges along the 5⁄8" (1.5 cm) seam allowance guide. Remove the pins as you come to them.

17 Check from the sleeve side, to be sure there are no puckers. If there are any, clip the stitches, using a seam ripper, and remove the stitches on either side of the pucker far enough to smooth it out; restitch.

18 Stitch a second line in the seam allowances, 1⁄4" (6 mm) from the first stitching line, from the notches to each end. Trim the seam allowances in this area close to the second stitching line.

CONTINUED

How to Sew an UNLINED JACKET

CONTINUED

19 Repeat steps 15 to 18 for the opposite sleeve. Set your machine for a medium-length, medium-width zigzag stitch. For each sleeve, finish the seam allowance edges together, stitching so that the right swing of the needle just clears the fabric edge. Press the seam allowances toward the sleeves.

20 Pin the jacket front to the jacket back, right sides together, along the side seams and extending on to the underarm sleeve seams. Match notches, and align the sleeve seams. Insert the pins perpendicular to the edges.

21 Stitch ⅝" (1.5 cm) seam from the bottom of one side continuously to the end of the sleeve. Keep the underarm seam allowances turned toward the sleeve. Repeat for the opposite side.

22 Finish the side and underarm seam allowances as in step 2. Press the seam allowances flat; then press them open.

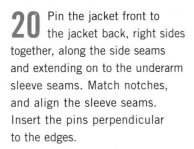

TIP **Press the seam allowances open over a seam roll** to prevent imprinting the seam allowance edges onto the right side of the jacket and to make it easier to press the sleeve seams open.

23 Finish the lower edge of the jacket as in step 2. Repeat for the lower edges of the sleeves. Turn under the remaining hem allowances on the sleeves, and press, using a seam roll or sleeve board (page 31). Slipstitch (page 22) the hems to the jacket.

24 Place the jacket on your ironing board, wrong side up; open the front facings. Turn under the remaining hem allowance on the lower edge, including the facings; press.

25 Unfold the lower edge. Turn the jacket over, and turn the facing to the outside, aligning the lower edges. Pin, keeping the facing seam allowances turned toward the facing. Stitch the facing to the jacket, stitching in the well of the pressed fold. Repeat for the opposite side.

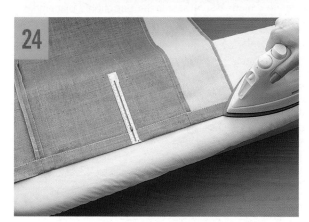

CONTINUED

How to Sew an UNLINED JACKET

CONTINUED

26 Trim the facing seam allowance to within ¼" (6 mm) of the stitches. Trim the corner diagonally, to within ⅛" (3 mm) of the corner stitch. Repeat for the opposite side. Turn the facings to the inside, and press.

27 Refold the remaining hem, and pin. Slipstitch the hem to the jacket. At the fronts, slipstitch the facings to the hem.

28 **TOPSTITCH** ⅜" (1 cm) from the edges along the fronts and neckline of the jacket, if desired. If your jacket has buttons, transfer the buttonhole placement marks from your pattern to the right jacket front. Make buttonholes, following the directions in your sewing machine owner's manual. Transfer the button placement marks to the left front. Sew buttons as on page 23.

!

YOU MUST BE PROUD

You will soon be getting rave reviews for your new jacket, and your sewing skills are growing by leaps and bounds.

Jacket VARIATIONS

Some jackets do not overlap at the front, but merely meet at the center. For these styles, you can add decorative closures, such as purchased frogs, toggles, or clips.

For pockets with round corners, machine-baste ¼" (6 mm) from the raw edge around the bottom corners. Make a cardboard template to help you get the sides of the pocket folded in and pressed evenly. Cut the template the size and shape of the finished pocket (the size of the pattern piece minus the seam allowances and facing). Before topstitching the facing, lay the template over the inside of the pocket, and push it up to the top under the facing. Press all the raw edges over the template, pulling up the basting threads around the corners to draw in the curves.

Sewing PILLOWS

Raw-edge Flange PILLOWS

A raw-edge flange pillow is a great first sewing project, requiring only very basic sewing skills and knowledge. This small 12" (30.5 cm) square pillow looks larger because of its flange, a border of flat fabric extending beyond the stitching line, around the outer edge of the pillow. We have selected synthetic fleece for this pillow project, because it is an easy fabric to work with; it does not ravel, and its natural loft will hide your stitches. In other words, don't be concerned if your stitching line wavers a bit; your pillow will still be gorgeous! You may recognize fleece as a popular fabric for ready-to-wear mittens, hats, and jackets. Imagine wonderful, cozy fleece pillows for a casual den or a child's bedroom. We have planned a 2½" (6.5 cm) flange around the pillow, so 5" (12.5 cm) must be added to the pillow dimensions.

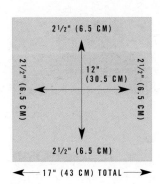

2½" (6.5 CM)

2½" (6.5 CM)

12" (30.5 CM)

2½" (6.5 CM)

2½" (6.5 CM)

17" (43 CM) TOTAL

WHAT YOU'LL LEARN

How to cut out fabric, following the fabric grainline

How to MARK fabric

How to match and pin edges together

How to sew a straight line and PIVOT at corners

That you can sew a great-looking pillow!

WHAT YOU'LL NEED

½ yd. (0.5 m) synthetic fleece fabric, 45" or 60" (115 or 152.5 cm) wide

Air-erasable marking pen or narrow masking tape

Thread in a color to match the fabric

12" (30.5 cm) square knife-edge pillow form

How to Sew a RAW-EDGE FLANGE PILLOW

LET'S BEGIN

1 Cut two 17" (43 cm) squares of fabric. Be sure to make your cuts on the fabric grainlines (page 40).

TIP Make yourself a paper pattern, and pin it to the fabric; then simply cut around it. This is easier than marking lines on the fleece.

2 Mark a square on the pillow front 2½" (6.5 cm) in from the four sides; this will be your stitching line. You can do this with an *air-erasable marking pen*, or place narrow strips of masking tape with one edge along the stitching line.

3 Pin the pillow front to the pillow back, with the right sides of the fabric facing out (wrong sides together). Insert the pins along the marked stitching line, inserting pins perpendicular to the line. This will make it easy to remove the pins as you sew. Leave a 7" (18 cm) section on one side unpinned. This is where you will leave an opening for inserting the pillow.

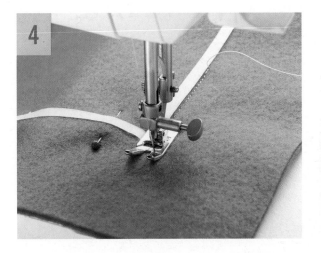

4 Place the pinned fabric under the presser foot, so that the opening will be just behind the presser foot. Begin sewing, stitching over the line if you marked it with a pen, or stitching right next to the tape, if you marked it with tape. Remove pins as you come to them; stitching over pins is hazardous to the health of your sewing machine. Stop sewing at the first corner, leaving the needle down in the fabric. (Turn the handwheel until the needle is down.)

5 Raise the presser foot and turn the fabric a quarter turn. Lower the presser foot and continue sewing to the next corner. Repeat this pivot procedure at each corner. Stop stitching when you reach the last pin, leaving the opening unstitched. *Remove the fabric from the machine.*

TIP Relax your shoulders and rest your elbows on the table next to your machine as you sew. Guide the fabric with your fingertips, moving your hands from the wrists. Let your machine work while you have fun!

QUICK REFERENCE

Air-erasable marking pen. This innovative tool marks the fabric with a fine colored line (usually purple or magenta). The "ink" evaporates and disappears within 48 hours, so you will want to mark your fabric just before you sew. Always test first on a scrap of fabric to make sure the marks will completely disappear.

Removing fabric from the machine. When you finish a stitching line, always stop with the needle out of the fabric and the take-up lever in the highest position. (Some newer machines automatically do this for you.) Raise the presser foot; pull the fabric to the side or toward the back. Clip the threads, leaving several inches of thread extending from the needle and bobbin.

CONTINUED

How to Sew a RAW-EDGE FLANGE PILLOW

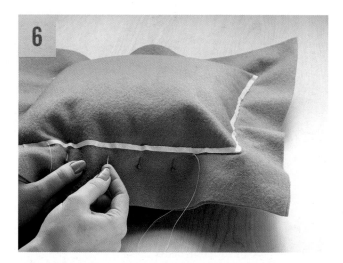

CONTINUED

6 Fold or bunch the pillow form and insert it through the opening. Allow the first and last stitches to loosen, if necessary, so the fleece is not damaged. Push the form away from the opening and pin the opening together, making sure the raw edges are aligned. Gently pull the thread tails to snug the loosened stitches.

7 Place the pillow back under the presser foot so that the opening is lined up in front of the presser foot and the end of the stitching line is visible just in front of the foot. Sew the opening closed, overlapping the ends of the previous stitching line by about 1" (2.5 cm). Remove the pillow from the machine and clip all the threads close to the fleece. If you marked your stitching line with tape, it is now safe to remove it!

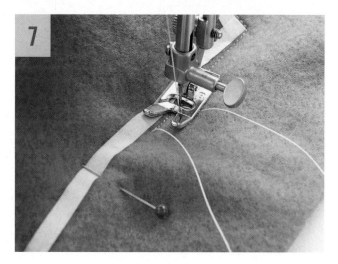

!

YOU DID IT

Sit back and admire your new pillow. You could make three more just like it in no time at all. Now that you are an expert on making raw-edge flange pillows, read the next page for some ideas to help you expand your repertoire!

Raw-edge Flange with a TWIST

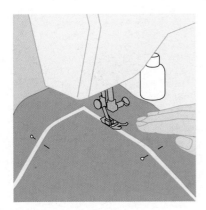

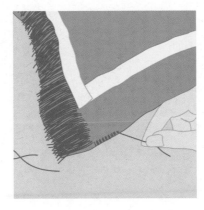

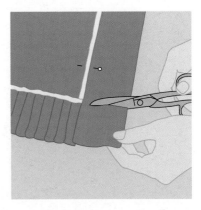

Use synthetic suede, such as Ultrasuede® for a luxurious formal look. To make stitching on synthetic suede easier, add one drop of silicone lubricant to the spool of thread before filling the bobbin and threading the machine. Also, apply a drop of lubricant to the needle, the bottom of the presser foot, and the throat plate.

Select a coarse, even-weave fabric such as this silk. Take special care to cut and sew the pillow following the grainlines. Stitch again ¾" (2 cm) beyond the first stitching line. Pull threads to fray the flange.

Cut fringe into the flange edges of a fleece or Ultrasuede pillow. Mark cutting guidelines ½" (1.3 cm) apart along each edge. Cut to within ⅛" (3 mm) of the stitches.

Knife-edge PILLOWS

The knife-edge pillow is probably the most versatile style for decorating your home. There are no limits to the variations you can create, not only in size, color, and texture, but also in added details that give your pillow a personal touch. The directions that follow are for a knife-edge pillow that is 14" (35.5 cm) square. For your first knife-edge pillow, we recommend a firmly woven mediumweight fabric.

Ready-made knife-edge pillow inserts come in a wide selection of sizes, including 12", 14", 16", 18", 20", 24", and 30" (30.5, 35.5, 40.5, 46, 51, 61, and 76 cm) squares and a 12" × 16" (30.5 × 40.5 cm) rectangle. By adapting these cutting instructions, you can sew a cover for any size pillow insert. You can also use these instructions to sew your own pillow inserts in any size you like, stuffing them to a plumpness that pleases you.

WHAT YOU'LL LEARN

How to *backstitch* (p. 19)

How to set and PRESS seams

Tricks for sewing perfect corners

How to slipstitch (page 22) an opening closed by hand

WHAT YOU'LL NEED

14" (35.5 cm) square pillow form

½ yd. (0.5 m) of fabric

Matching thread

Hand-sewing needle

Sewing PILLOWS

How to Sew a KNIFE-EDGE PILLOW

1 Cut two 15" (38 cm) squares of fabric, aligning the sides to the fabric grainlines (page 38). A ½" (1.3 cm) **SEAM ALLOWANCE** is needed on each side, so 1" (2.5 cm) is added to each dimension of the *desired finished size.*

2 Place the pillow front over the pillow back, right sides together, and align all four edges. Pin the layers together near the outer edges, *inserting the pins perpendicular to the edges (p. 19).* In the center of one side, leave a 7" (18 cm) opening unpinned.

3 Place the fabric under the presser foot, just ahead of the opening. Align the cut edges of the fabric to the ½" (1.3 cm) *seam allowance guide (p. 19)* on the bed of your machine. Remove the pin that marks the opening, before lowering the presser foot.

4 Backstitch three or four stitches; stop. Then, stitching forward, stitch the seam on all four sides, **PIVOTING** with the needle down at the corners. End the **SEAM** at the opposite side of the opening; backstitch three or four stitches.

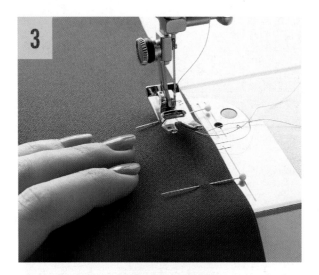

QUICK REFERENCE

Desired finished size. To make a knife-edge pillow of a different size, simply cut your fabric 1" (2.5 cm) larger in both directions than the desired finished size of your pillow. Cut 17" (43 cm) squares for a 16" (40.5 cm) pillow; cut 13" × 19" (33 × 48.5 cm) rectangles for a 12" × 18" (30.5 × 46 cm) pillow.

5 ***Remove the fabric from the machine (p. 123).*** Trim the threads close to the fabric. Press the seams flat to set the stitching line in the fabric. This may seem unnecessary, but it really does give you a better-looking seam in the end.

TIP Most machines have a handy thread cutter located within a few inches (centimeters) of the presser foot. By using this thread cutter, you are also pulling enough thread through the needle and up from the bobbin to help you prevent a THREAD JAM at the start of your next seam.

CONTINUED

How to Sew a KNIFE-EDGE PILLOW

CONTINUED

6 Turn back the top seam allowance, and press, applying light pressure with tip of the iron down the crease of the seam. In the area of the opening, turn back and press the top seam allowance ½" (1.3 cm).

7 Turn the cover over; turn back and press the remaining opening seam allowance.

8 At a *corner,* fold two seam allowances in, and then fold the other two seam allowances over them. Slip four fingers through the pillow opening and pinch the folded corner between your thumb and one finger. Turn that corner through the opening. Repeat with the other three corners. Your pillow cover has now been turned right side out.

9 Compress and insert the pillow form. Align the pressed edges of the opening, and pin the opening closed. Thread a hand needle and tie a knot in the end.

10 Slipstitch the opening closed, following the instructions on page 22.

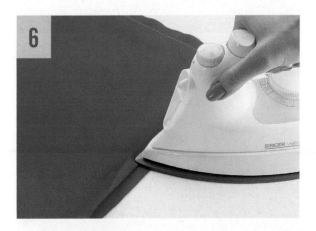

QUICK REFERENCE

Perfect corners. The corners of your pillow should be sharply squared, not rounded. To improve the appearance of a slightly rounded corner, you can push a pointed utensil into the corner from inside the pillow cover to force the stitches out to the corner. An inexpensive specialty tool, called a point turner (page 33), works well; or you can use a large knitting needle, a ballpoint pen with the inkball retracted, or something similar. Use light pressure, though, so that you don't punch a hole in the corner.

WAY TO GO

As you snip that last thread tail, you have finished sewing a knife-edge pillow. Plump it up, toss it in the air, and admire the daylights out of it! Just imagine all the ways you can get creative with a simple knife-edge pillow. Turn the page for a few examples to get you thinking.

Variations on a KNIFE-EDGE PILLOW THEME

Give a cozy chenille pillow a corded appearance. Then cinch in the center with two large buttons. Stitch ½" (1.3 cm) from the edge around the finished pillow. Attach shank buttons (page 23) with a single strand of heavy-duty thread; pull taut, compressing the pillow center before tying.

Use a tapestry pillow
panel for the pillow front.
Recut the edges if the
panel is not square.

Dress up a pillow
with decorative ribbon
tied in a bow.

Zipper CLOSURES

Pillows that get tossed around, leaned upon, and slid across the floor need occasional cleaning. A zipper closure sewn into a seam makes it much easier to remove and reinsert the pillow form. Any of the knife-edge-style pillows can be made with a zipper closure. Cut the fabric and prepare the pillow front and back according to the directions in the project. Then follow these directions to complete the pillow.

Purchase a conventional polyester coil zipper (not a separating style) to match your fabric, in the size indicated below.

ZIPPER	PILLOW
7" (18 cm)	12" to 14" (30.5 to 35.5 cm)
9" (23 cm)	16" to 18" (40.5 to 46 cm)
12" (30.5 cm)	20" (51 cm) or larger

How to Sew a ZIPPER CLOSURE

LET'S BEGIN

1 Place the pillow front over the pillow back, right sides together. Pin the side that will have the zipper. Center the zipper alongside the pinned edges, and **MARK** the **SEAM ALLOWANCES** just above and below the *zipper stops.*

TIP For best results, select a side that was cut on the **LENGTHWISE GRAIN** of the fabric. The lengthwise grain is more stable and will have less tendency to stretch as you sew.

2 Stitch a ½" (1.3 cm) **SEAM** from the upper edge to the mark, *backstitching (p. 19)* at the beginning and the end. Repeat at the lower edge. Leave the center section open.

3 *Machine-baste* on the seamline between the marks. Clip the basting stitches every 2" (5 cm) with a **SEAM RIPPER**. This will make the stitches easier to remove later.

QUICK REFERENCE

Zipper stops. Tiny metal bars are attached to the top and bottom of the zipper coil to prevent the zipper slide from sliding right off the end. On a conventional zipper, there is one wide stop at the bottom of the zipper and separate smaller stops at the top.

Machine-baste. Set the machine for the longest straight stitch possible. This stitching is temporary and will be easily removed later.

CONTINUED

How to Sew a ZIPPER CLOSURE

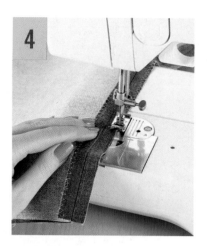

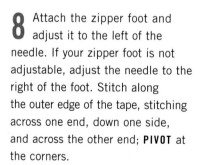

CONTINUED

4 **PRESS** the seam flat; then press the seam allowances open. Finish the seam allowances with a zigzag stitch (page 21).

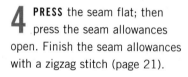 **TIP** If your fabric is loosely woven or tends to ravel easily, repeated washings could make the seam allowances ravel away and ruin your pillow. As a preventative measure, take the time to finish all of the seam allowances.

5 Apply *basting tape* to the right side of the zipper tape, running it along both outer edges.

6 Place the zipper facedown over the seam, with the zipper coil directly over the basted part of the seamline and the pull tab turned down. The zipper coil should be centered between the backstitched areas. Press with your fingers to secure the zipper to the seam allowances.

7 Spread the pillow pieces flat, right side up. Insert pins in the seamline, just above and below the zipper stops. Cut ½" (1.3 cm) transparent tape to fit between the pins; place it down the center of the seamline.

8 Attach the zipper foot and adjust it to the left of the needle. If your zipper foot is not adjustable, adjust the needle to the right of the foot. Stitch along the outer edge of the tape, stitching across one end, down one side, and across the other end; **PIVOT** at the corners.

9 Adjust the zipper foot to the right of the needle or adjust your needle to the left of the foot. Stitch over the previous stitches at one end, down the opposite side, and over the stitches at the other end. Clip the threads.

10 Remove the tape. Carefully remove the machine basting in the seamline, using a seam ripper.

11 Open the zipper. Pin the pillow front and back, right sides together, along the three remaining sides. Stitch ½" (1.3 cm) seam; press. Turn the pillow cover right side out and insert the pillow form through the zipper opening.

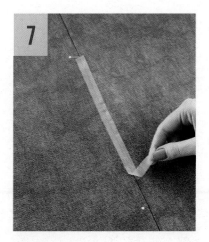

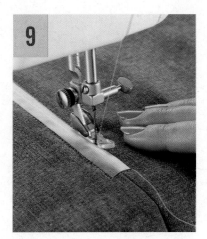

QUICK REFERENCE

Basting tape. This narrow tape is adhesive on both sides. As the tape comes off the roll, one side is sticky. After placing it on the zipper, remove the protective backing, exposing the other sticky side. Basting tape need not be removed after the zipper is stitched in place.

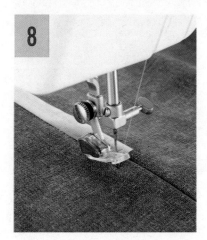

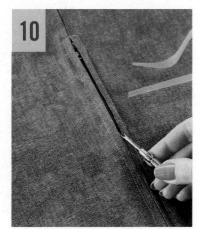

Tie-tab PILLOWCASES

This is a unique way to dress up a ho-hum knife-edge
pillow. Slip it inside a colorful pillowcase, tied with narrow

fabric ties. Create your own cheerful combo, beginning

with a basic knife-edge pillow (page 127). Then sew a pillowcase,

following these directions. Just think of all the interesting

variations and color combinations you can create.

WHAT YOU'LL LEARN

How to make fabric ties

How to sew a FACING

WHAT YOU'LL NEED

Knife-edge pillow in
desired size

Coordinating fabric for
the pillowcase, amount
determined by the
pillow size

Thread to match the fabric

How to Sew a TIE-TAB PILLOWCASE

LET'S BEGIN

1 Cut two rectangles of fabric for the front and back of the pillowcase, with the length equal to the length of the knife-edge pillow plus 1" (2.5 cm), and the width equal to the finished width of the knife-edge pillow. Cut a 2" (5 cm) strip of fabric for the facing with the length equal to two times the length of the pillow plus 1" (2.5 cm). Remember to follow the grainlines (page 40).

TIP The length here refers to the pillow from top to bottom, if you intend to place the ties at the pillow side. If you want the ties at the top, then length refers to the side-to-side measurement.

Cut twelve strips of fabric for the ties, 12" (30.5 cm) long and 1¼" (3.2 cm) wide. Cut them with the length running on the **LENGTHWISE GRAIN**.

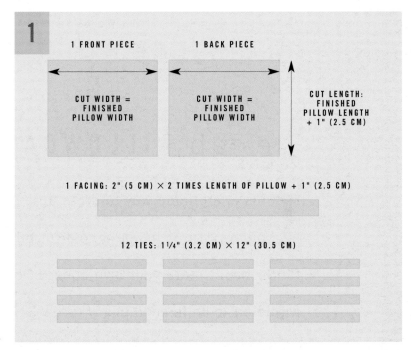

1 FRONT PIECE   1 BACK PIECE

CUT WIDTH = FINISHED PILLOW WIDTH   CUT WIDTH = FINISHED PILLOW WIDTH   CUT LENGTH: FINISHED PILLOW LENGTH + 1" (2.5 CM)

1 FACING: 2" (5 CM) × 2 TIMES LENGTH OF PILLOW + 1" (2.5 CM)

12 TIES: 1¼" (3.2 CM) × 12" (30.5 CM)

2 Place the pillowcase front over the back, right sides together, and align all four edges. Pin the layers together near three outer edges, leaving the fourth side (the side where the ties will go) open. Stitch ½" (1.3 cm) **SEAMS** along the three pinned sides, *backstitching (p. 19)* at the beginning and end.

3 **PRESS** the seams flat; then press them open. Turn the pillowcase right side out. Insert a point turner (page 33) or similar tool into the case to push the corners out gently, if necessary.

4 Pin two tie strips, right sides together, matching the raw edges. *Stitch ¼" (6 mm) seam* around the long edges and one short end. Repeat for the remaining five sets of ties.

CONTINUED

QUICK REFERENCE

Stitch ¼" (6 mm) seam. Sometimes the distance from the needle tip to the edge of the presser foot is ¼" (6 mm). If this isn't true for your machine, measure the distance and take note of the location on the presser foot or bed of the machine that measures an exact ¼" (6 mm).

Trim the corners diagonally. This minimizes the excess bulk to form a smoother corner when the piece is turned right side out.

Turn the ties right side out. There are special tools for turning narrow tubes inside out, including the FASTURN® shown in the photo. Because this is a frequently required task in sewing, it is worth it to buy one of these tools. In a pinch, you can probably get the job done by working the fabric over the eraser end of a pencil, but it's much harder to do.

5 ***Trim the corners diagonally. Turn the ties right side out.*** Use a point turner or similar tool to push the corners out gently, if necessary. Press the ties flat.

6 Pin the ties to the right side of the pillowcase along the unstitched edge, aligning the raw edges. Position one tie at the center of each side. Position the remaining four ties 2½" (6.5 cm) from the seams. Stitch ⅜" (1 cm) from the end of each tie, stitching only through one pillow layer.

7 Fold the facing strip, right sides together, matching the short ends. Stitch ½" (1.3 cm) seam across the short ends. Press the seam flat; then press it open.

How to Sew a TIE-TAB PILLOWCASE

CONTINUED

8 Press under ½" (1.3 cm) along one edge of the facing. Pin the unpressed edge of the facing to the open edge of the pillowcase, right sides together. Align the seam of the facing to one seam of the pillowcase.

9 Stitch ½" (1.3 cm) seam around the opening. Press the seam flat; then press it open.

10 Press the facing to the inside of the pillowcase, with the seam on the opening edge. The ties will now extend out from the opening. Pin the facing in place. Stitch along the inner fold of the facing, removing the pins as you come to them.

11 Tuck the knife-edge pillow into the pillowcase, and tie the ties. Now pat yourself on the back. You've just made a great-looking pillow!

Get CREATIVE!

Substitute narrow decorative cording for the fabric ties; use four or more sets, if desired. Tie knots about 2" (5 cm) from the ends of the cording and fray out the ends to look like tassels.

Make a collection of pillows with tie-tab cases. Select several coordinating fabrics, perhaps a floral print, a solid, and a stripe. Rearrange the fabrics for the pillows, ties, and cases of each set.

Nine-patch PILLOWS

Stitch nine squares of fabric together in a checkerboard pattern to create this interesting pillow top. Select two medium-weight fabrics that coordinate with each other; two prints, a print and a solid color, or two solids. Use one of the fabrics for the pillow back and five small squares; use the other fabric for the remaining four squares.

WHAT YOU'LL LEARN

The importance of accuracy in both cutting and stitching

Tricks for perfectly matched seams

Pressing is important

WHAT YOU'LL NEED

5/8 yd. (0.6 m) fabric A for pillow back and five pillow front squares

1/4 yd. (0.25 m) fabric B for remaining four pillow front squares

Thread to match or blend with the fabrics

12" (30.5 cm) zipper for closure, optional

18" (46 cm) square knife-edge pillow form

How to Sew a NINE-PATCH PILLOW

LET'S BEGIN

1 Cut a 19" (48.5 cm) square of fabric A for the pillow back. From the remaining fabric, cut five 7" (18 cm) squares. Cut four 7" (18 cm) squares from fabric B.

2 Pin one A square to one B square along one side, right sides together; align the cut ends and edges. Place the fabric under the presser foot, with the upper edges even with the needle hole in the throat plate. Align the cut edges of the fabric to the ¹⁄₂" (1.3 cm), *seam allowance guide (p. 19)* on the bed of your machine. Stitch ¹⁄₂" (1.3 cm) **SEAM**, *removing pins as you come to them (p. 19)*.

3 Pin another A square to the opposite side of the B square. Stitch ¹⁄₂" (1.3 cm) seam, forming a three-square strip. Repeat steps 2 and 3 to make another identical three-square strip. Then join the remaining three squares with an A square in the center. This will be the center strip.

4 **PRESS** all the seams flat to set the stitches. Then press the seams open. The strips should now measure 7" × 19" (18 × 48.5 cm).

5 Pin the top strip to the center strip, with right sides together and raw edges even. Align the seams, *inserting pins in the wells of the seams (p. 281).* Stitch 1/2" (1.3 cm) seam, removing pins as you come to them. Be sure that **SEAM ALLOWANCES** remain open as they were pressed.

TIP Slow your stitching as you approach each seam. Stopping with the needle down in the fabric, raise the presser foot. Lift the strips slightly from the machine bed, to be sure that the seam allowance on the underside is still open and lying flat. Then lower the presser foot and continue sewing across the seam.

6 Pin the remaining strip to the opposite side of the center strip, pinning as in step 5; stitch a 1/2" (1.3 cm) seam. Press the seam allowances flat; then press them open. Complete the pillow, following steps 2 through 8 on pages 128 to 130. Or, if you prefer, follow the directions for a zipper closure (page 135).

Harem PILLOWS

A harem pillow is really a basic knife-edge pillow with simple shaping at the corners to give it softness and depth. This floor pillow can be stuffed with a 24" (61 cm) pillow form. Or you can easily adapt the instructions to cover pillow forms in any size for your bed, sofa, and floor. Select an easy-care fabric that is also comfortable and durable. Because floor pillows get a lot of use and may require occasional cleaning, consider sewing the cover with a zipper closure, as on page 135.

WHAT YOU'LL LEARN

How to gather fabric

How to save many decorating dollars by making your own floor pillows

WHAT YOU'LL NEED

1½ yd. (1.4 m) fabric, 45" (115 cm) wide or ¾ yd. (0.7 m) fabric, 54" to 60" (137 to 152.5 cm) wide

Thread to match the fabric

24" (61 cm) square pillow form

Hand-sewing needle

How to Sew a HAREM PILLOW

1 Cut two 25" (63.5 cm) squares of fabric for the front and back of the pillow. Follow steps 2 through 7 on pages 128 to 130, for a pillow with a slip-stitched closure. Leave a 12" (30.5 cm) opening. Or follow steps 1 to 11 on pages 135 to 137 for a pillow with a zipper closure, leaving the pillow inside out.

2 Mark points 3" (7.5 cm) from a corner along each seam-line. Draw a diagonal line, connecting the points. Repeat this at each corner.

TIP Harem pillows can be made in any size. For pillows 16" (40.5 cm) or smaller, measure 2" (5 cm) from the corners.

3 Thread a needle with regular thread and knot the two ends together so you have a doubled thread. Insert the needle into the fabric near the cut edge and on the diagonal line. Pass the needle through the loop of the doubled thread just before the knot, and pull it taut. Hand-baste along the line with 1/4" (6 mm) running stitches for gathering.

4 Pull the doubled thread to gather the corner tight. Wrap the thread several times around the corner. Secure thread with a knot or several small stitches.

5 Repeat steps 3 and 4 at each corner. Turn the pillow right side out through the opening. Insert the pillow form.

6 Pin the opening closed. Slipstitch the opening as on page 22. Or, zip the pillow closed.

Mock Box **PILLOWS**

For a soft, chunky look, make mock box pillows. Simply modify the corners of a basic knife-edge pillow to give it a deeper, more squared appearance. Any size pillow will work. Keep in mind that when you square off the corners to increase the depth, the outer dimensions get slightly smaller. Use a pillow form the same size as the knife-edge pillow before squaring the corners.

As a bit of a challenge, we have designed this pillow from striped fabric. You will be able to match up the stripes, making them run continuously around the pillow, as long as the two pieces you cut are identical.

WHAT YOU'LL LEARN

How to match stripes

How to sew square corners

WHAT YOU'LL NEED

⅝ yd. (0.6 m) striped fabric

Thread to match the fabric

Square pillow form

Hand-sewing needle

How to Sew a MOCK BOX PILLOW

LET'S BEGIN
---

1 Cut two identical squares of fabric for the front and back of the pillow. The easiest way to do this is to cut the front first, and then use it as a pattern to cut the back, aligning the stripes.

2 Pin the pillow front to the pillow back, right sides together, *inserting pins perpendicular to the edges (p. 19).* Pin frequently along the edges where the stripes match up, inserting the pins through matching points in the stripes along the 1/2" (1.3 cm) seamline. Leave an opening for turning on a side where you do not have to match up stripes.

3 Follow steps 3 to 6 on pages 128 to 130 for a knife-edge pillow. Stitch slowly on the sides where stripes match up, stitching up close to each pin before removing it.

4 Separate the front and back at one corner. Center the **SEAMS** on each side of the corner, pinning through the seams to make sure they are aligned.

5 Measure along the seam and mark a point 2" (5 cm) from the corner. Draw a line, through the mark perpendicular to the seam, from fold to fold. This will give you a corner depth of 4" (10 cm).

TIP The distance you measure along the seam is equal to half the depth of the corner. So, if you want a depth of 3" (7.5 cm), measure 1½" (3.8 cm) from the corner; if you want a depth of 3½" (9 cm), measure 1¾" (4.5 cm) from the corner.

6 Stitch on the marked line, *backstitching (p. 19)* at the beginning and end. Do not trim the seam.

7 Repeat steps 4 to 6 at each corner. Turn the pillow cover right side out. Insert the pillow form, and slipstitch the opening closed (page 40).

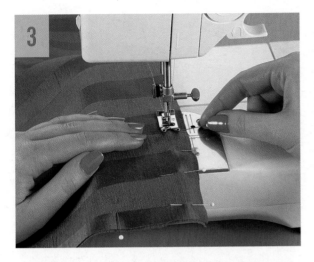

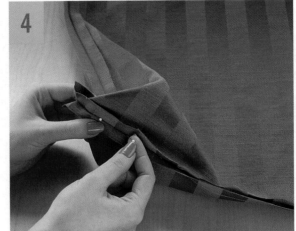

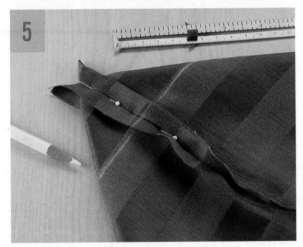

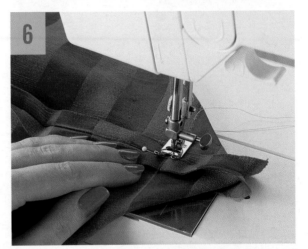

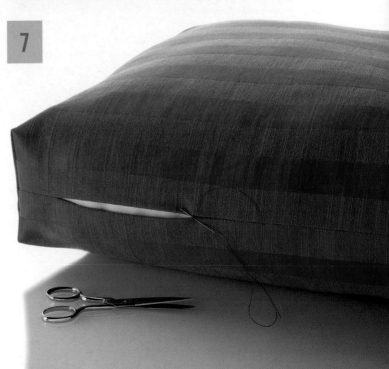

Decorator PILLOWS

Designer pillows are often expensive, but with a small amount of fabric and an interesting trim, you can create your own personally designed one-of-a-kind pillow. Choose complementary patterns and colors in mediumweight fabrics to make handsome decorator accents for your home. Because only a small amount of each fabric is required, check the remnant bins for some bargain-priced great finds.

These directions are for an 18" (46 cm) pillow, but you could easily adapt them for any size pillow. Simply graph out the pillow size you want, planning the center panel to measure about two-thirds of the total size. Add 1/2" (1.3 cm) **SEAM ALLOWANCE** to the outer edge of each piece.

WHAT YOU'LL LEARN

The importance of accurate measuring, cutting, and stitching

How to apply flat decorator trims easily

WHAT YOU'LL NEED

5/8 yd. (0.6 m) fabric for border and back of the pillow

3/8 yd. (0.35 m) fabric for pillow front center panel

1 3/4 yd. (1.6 m) flat decorator trim, braid, or grosgrain ribbon (page 29)

Threads to match trim and fabric

12" (30.5 cm) polyester coil zipper (page 28) (optional)

18" (46 cm) pillow form (page 29)

Fabric glue stick

Seam ripper (page 23)

Basting tape (page 26)

Transparent tape, 1/2" (1.3 cm) wide

How to Sew a DECORATOR PILLOW

LET'S BEGIN

1 Mark and cut one 13" (33 cm) square of fabric for the front center panel. Remember to trim away the **SELVAGE** and follow the **GRAINLINES**. Mark and cut a 19" (48.5 cm) square for the pillow back. Then mark and cut two rectangles each 4" × 13" (10 × 33 cm) and two rectangles each 4" × 19" (10 × 48.5 cm), for the front border strips.

2 Pin one 13" (33 cm) border strip to the upper edge of the center panel with the right sides together, aligning the cut edges. *Insert the pins perpendicular to the edges (p. 19).* Pin the other 13" (33 cm) strip to the lower edge of the center panel in the same way.

3 Set your machine for a straight stitch of 10 stitches per inch, which equals 2.5 mm. Place the upper pinned edges under the presser foot, aligning them to the 1/2" (1.3 cm) *seam allowance guide (p. 19)*. Stitch the 1/2" (1.3 cm) **SEAM**, *backstitching (p. 19)* at the beginning and end of the seam. *Remove the pins as you come to them (p. 19).* Stitch the lower seam in the same way.

4 **PRESS** over the stitching lines of the closed seams to set the stitches in the fabric. Then open the seam allowances and press them again.

5 Cut two 13" (33 cm) strips of decorator trim. Center a strip over each seamline. Hold the trim in place with the glue stick adhesive.

6 Stitch each trim in place, stitching along the outer edge of one side and then the other. Stitch in the same direction on both sides to keep the trim from puckering. Make sure the seam allowances on the underside remain open.

TIP Keep the trim strips "relaxed" as you position them in place. Stretching them will cause your fabric to pucker after stitching.

CONTINUED

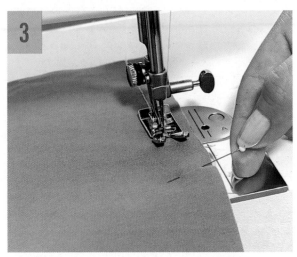

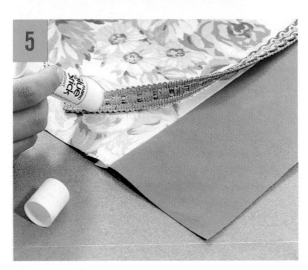

How to Sew a DECORATOR PILLOW

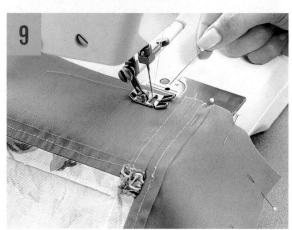

CONTINUED

7 Pin the two 19" (48.5 cm) border strips to the sides of the front pillow section, right sides together. Stitch ¹/₂" (1.3 cm) seams, sewing slowly through the areas where you cross the previous seams. Repeat steps 4 to 6 for the new seams to complete the pillow front. If you want to sew a zipper closure, complete your pillow following steps 1 to 11, pages 128 to 130.

8 Place the pillow front over the pillow back, right sides together, and align the four outer edges. Pin them together, inserting the pins perpendicular to the edges. In the center of the bottom, leave a 9" (23 cm) opening unpinned. Mark dots ¹/₂" (1.3 cm) from each corner.

9 Place the fabric under the presser foot, just ahead of the opening. Align the cut edges to the ¹/₂" (1.3 cm) seam allowance guide. Remove the pin that marks the opening, before lowering the presser foot.

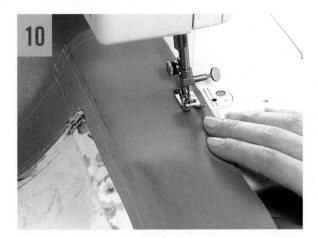

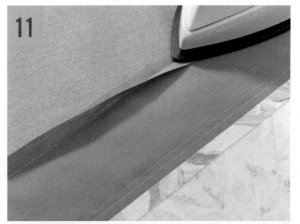

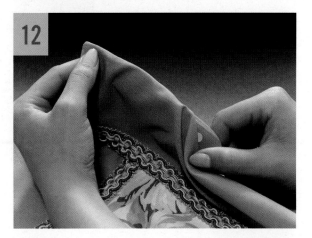

10 Backstitch three or four stitches; stop. Then, stitching forward, stitch the seam on all four sides, **PIVOTING** on the dots, with the needle down in the fabric at each corner. End the seam at the opposite side of the opening; backstitch three or four stitches.

11 Press the seam flat. *Turn back the top seam allowance (p. 101),* and press, using light pressure with the tip of your iron down the crease of the seam.

12 Reach in through the opening to grasp a corner and pull it out through the opening. Repeat with the other three corners to turn the pillow completely right side out. Use a point turner or similar tool to create *perfect corners (p. 53).*

13 Compress and insert the pillow form through the opening. Manipulate the form into the corners of the pillow. Slipstitch the opening closed, following the directions on page 40.

MORE IDEAS

Introduce a third fabric in
the border. Sew a set
of pillows, rearranging the
placement of the fabrics
in each one.

Sew a decorator pillow that
showcases a piece of needle-
work in the center square.
Accent the border seams with
flat lace trim or ribbon.

For an interesting tone-
on-tone effect, select a
reversible jacquard fabric.
Use one side up for
the center square and the
opposite side up for
the border.

Eliminate trims, and
hand-stitch large decorative
buttons to the corners of the
center square before
inserting the pillow form.
Sew tassels to the corners.

Envelope PILLOWS

This unique pillow cover is made from a single rectangle of fabric that wraps around the pillow form. One end, stitched to create a triangular flap, is secured with a button. The other end of the rectangle is folded inside the finished pillow and encloses the form to keep it neatly hidden. The pillow form is easily removed when you want to clean the pillow cover. For economical use of fabric yardage, cut the long rectangle on the **CROSSWISE GRAIN** of the fabric. Select fabric carefully. Suitable fabrics include stripes that run on the crosswise grain, solid colors, and small nondirectional prints. Avoid **DIRECTIONAL PRINTS** and stripes that run on the **LENGTHWISE GRAIN**.

The following directions are for a 16" (40.5 cm) pillow, though envelope pillows can be made in any size. For a different-size pillow, cut the fabric rectangle with the length equal to two-and-one-half times the size of the pillow form plus 6½" (16.3 cm) and the width equal to the size of the pillow form plus 1" (2.5 cm).

WHAT YOU'LL LEARN

How to finish a raw fabric edge with ZIGZAG STITCHES

Stitch settings are easily changed from straight stitch to zigzag stitch

How to sew, trim, and turn a point

How to sew a buttonhole

WHAT YOU'LL NEED

½ yd. (0.5 m) of 48" to 60" (122 to 152.5 cm) fabric

Matching thread

Decorative shank button, about 1" (2.5 cm) in diameter

Small sharp scissors or seam ripper

16" (40.5 cm) pillow form

Hand-sewn needle

How to Sew an ENVELOPE PILLOW

LET'S BEGIN

─────────────────────

1 Cut one rectangle of fabric, 46½" × 17" (118.3 × 43 cm). Draw light lines on the fabric with a fabric marker or light pencil. Or make a paper pattern first, if you prefer. Make sure the four corners of the rectangle are at right angles.

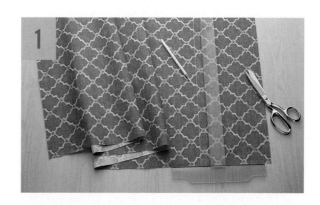

2 Fold one short end of the fabric rectangle in half, right sides together; pin. Stitch a ½" (1.3 cm) **SEAM**, *backstitching (p. 19)* at the beginning and end. This will form the triangular flap.

3 *Trim the seam allowance diagonally (p. 193)* at the folded end, trimming to within ⅛" (3 mm) of the stitches. **PRESS** the seam flat. Then press the seam allowances open.

> **TIP** Trim away slightly more than a 45-degree wedge. This will allow the point of the flap to lie flat and smooth when the fabric is turned right side out.

4 Turn the stitched flap right side out. Use a point turner or a similar tool to carefully push the point out, if necessary. Center the seam between the two long sides of the rectangle and press the diagonal folds. The seamed side of the flap is now the flap *facing*.

> **TIP** Remember that "press" means to lift the iron to move it to a new position. Avoid sliding the iron, which could cause this **BIAS** fold to stretch out of shape.

QUICK REFERENCE

Facing. This is a fabric extension or additional piece of fabric sewn as a backing to another piece to protect raw edges from raveling and give the item (in this case a pillow flap) a neat, finished appearance.

5 Set the pattern selector to **ZIGZAG** and your stitch width and length to medium. *Finish the raw edge (p. 201)* of the flap facing by zigzagging from one pressed fold, across the seam, to the opposite pressed fold. Also finish the opposite end of the rectangle with a zigzag stitch.

6 Mark a line ½" (1.3 cm) from the finished edge of the flap facing with an erasable fabric marker or chalk. Pin the flap facing to the flap as it was pressed, making sure both layers are smooth and the seam is still centered between the long sides. Insert the pins perpendicular to the marked line. Reset the pattern selector and stitch width to straight stitch settings. Stitch the facing to the flap along the marked line.

7 Fold the flap down along the stitching line; the facing will be against the wrong side of the fabric. Press along the stitching line. Pin-mark a point 6" (15 cm) from the lower edge on each long side of the rectangle. Fold the fabric, right sides together, aligning the pressed fold of the triangular flap with the pin marks.

CONTINUED

How to Sew an ENVELOPE PILLOW

CONTINUED

----

8 Fold the extra 6" (15 cm) of fabric, right side down, over the triangular flap. Pin the raw edges together along both sides. Stitch ½" (1.3 cm) seams. Press the seams flat, then open.

9 Turn the pillow cover right side out. The 6" (15 cm) extension becomes an inner flap that will wrap over the top of the pillow form. Press the pillow cover.

10 Push a pin through the seamline of the triangular flap facing 1¼" (3.2 cm) from the point. Insert a second pin 1⅛" (2.8 cm) above the first one. On the right side, mark a removable line between the two pins, for the buttonhole. Stitch the buttonhole and button as in steps 12 and 13 on page 211.

TIP This buttonhole size is appropriate for a relatively flat 1" (2.5 cm) button. If you select a different-size button, the correct buttonhole length is equal to the diameter of the button plus the thickness of the button plus ⅛" (3 mm). Always make a test buttonhole on a scrap of fabric.

MORE IDEAS

Hand-stitch fringe trim along the edge of the triangular flap, turning the ends under ³⁄₄" (2 cm). Apply liquid fray preventer on the ends of the trim to prevent raveling.

Block-print fabric paint designs on the finished pillow cover before inserting the pillow form. Allow the paint to dry completely; heat-set the designs with an iron. Attach beaded dangles to a stone ring for an eye-catching closure.

Sewing
WINDOW TREATMENTS

A

B

Roman SHADE

A Roman shade is a tailored, economical window treatment that controls light and provides privacy. This version is **LINED** to provide added body, prevent fabric fading, and create a uniform appearance from the outside. Mounted on a board, the shade can be installed as an **INSIDE MOUNT (A)**, securing it inside the upper window frame, flush with the front of the frame. For an **OUTSIDE MOUNT (B)**, the shade is installed on the wall at least 1" (2.5 cm) above the frame. Choose a sturdy, firm decorator fabric to give the shade a crisp look. These directions are suitable for a shade that is at least 2" (5 cm) narrower than the fabric width.

How to Sew a ROMAN SHADE

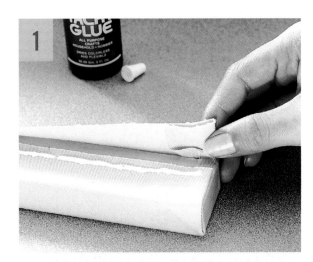

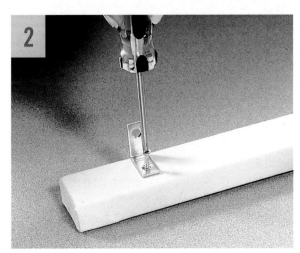

LET'S BEGIN

TIP Nominal lumber, angle irons, screw eyes, flat metal bars, awning cleats, and drapery pulls can all be purchased at a hardware store. If you do not have the proper tools, ask them to cut the lumber and metal bar to the size you need.

1 Measure the width of the window frame. Cut a 1 × 2 board 2" (5 cm) longer than the outside measurement, for an outside mount, or ½" (1.3 cm) shorter than the inside measurement, for an inside mount. Cut a strip of fabric for covering the board ½" (1.3 cm) wider than the board circumference and 2" (5 cm) longer than the board length. Center the board on the strip; wrap the fabric over the ends, and secure with glue. Then wrap the length of the board, overlapping the fabric down the center of one side and folding out excess fabric neatly at the ends; secure with glue. Allow to dry. Disregard steps 2 and 3 if you are installing an inside mount.

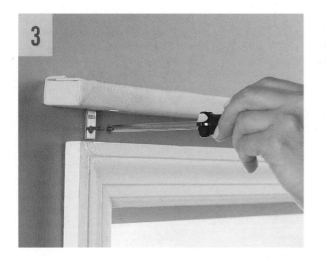

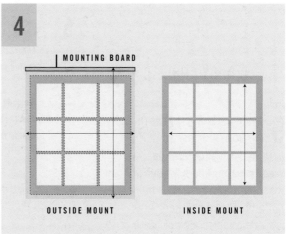

MOUNTING BOARD

OUTSIDE MOUNT   INSIDE MOUNT

2 Place the 1" (2.5 cm) angle irons on the side of the board opposite the overlap, about 2" (5 cm) from each end of the board. Mark the screw holes and, using a drill and appropriate drill bit, predrill holes into the board for the screws. Screw the angle irons to the board.

3 Hold the board above the window, making sure it is level and centered over the window frame; mark the screw holes on the wall. Secure the angle irons to the wall, using 1½" (3.8 cm) flat-head screws. If the angle irons are not at wall studs, use molly bolts or plastic anchors.

4 Determine the **FINISHED LENGTH** of the shade. For an outside mount, measure from the top of the mounting board to the sill or ½" (1.3 cm) below the apron; for an inside mount, measure the inside frame to the sill. The **FINISHED WIDTH** of the shade is equal to the length of the mounting board *plus ¼" (6 mm)*.

QUICK REFERENCE

Plus ¼" (6 mm). By sewing the shade slightly wider than the mounting board, you are sure to cover the entire board. There is always a little width and length lost in pressing and stitching the fabric.

CONTINUED

How to Sew a ROMAN SHADE

CONTINUED

5 Calculate the **CUT LENGTH** and **CUT WIDTH** of the fabric, working with this formula. (We used these numbers for our Roman shade on page 172; your numbers will probably be different.) Cut the shade fabric; do not use a **SELVAGE** as an edge. Cut the lining fabric with the width equal to the finished width and the length equal to the finished length plus 3½" (9 cm). Follow the guidelines for cutting decorator fabric on pages 44 and 45.

6 **PRESS** under 1" (2.5 cm) on the sides of the shade. Cut strips of ¾" (2 cm) paper-backed fusible web the length of each side. Turn back the hem and place the strips near the cut edge. Press over the strips to fuse them to the hem allowance, following the manufacturer's directions.

TIP Use a press cloth (page 31) to prevent any fusible adhesive from messing up the sole plate of your iron.

5			
Finished width:		45" (115 cm)	
Add 2" (5 cm) for side hems		+ 2" (5 cm)	
to find the cut width		= 47" (120 cm)	
Finished length:		50" (127 cm)	
Add 7" (18 cm) for hem and mounting		+ 7" (18 cm)	
to find the cut length		= 57" (144.5 cm)	

7 Place the lining over the shade fabric, wrong sides together, with the lower edge of the lining 3½" (9 cm) above the lower edge of the shade fabric; tuck the lining under the side hems. Remove the protective paper backing from the fusible web, and press to fuse the hems in place.

8 Press under ½" (1.3 cm) at the lower edge; then press under 3" (7.5 cm) to form the hem. (The second fold should be even with the lower edge of the lining.) Pin the hem, placing pins perpendicular to the hem.

9 *Edgestitch (p. 309)* along the inner fold-line of the hem, *backstitching (p. 19)* at the beginning and end, and *removing the pins as you come to them (p. 19)*. Press the entire shade lightly.

10 On the lining side, draw a line across the top of the shade at the finished length. Draw a second line 1½" (3.8 cm) above it for the *mounting board projection.* Cut off excess fabric along the top line. Pin the layers together, and finish the upper edges together using a wide zigzag stitch (page 21).

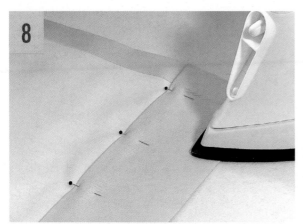

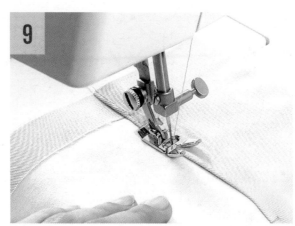

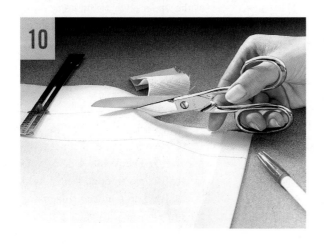

QUICK REFERENCE

Mounting board projection. The actual width of 1×2 nominal lumber is $1\frac{1}{2}$" (3.8 cm) which is how far the front of the mounting board (and the shade) will stand away from the wall on an outside mount.

CONTINUED

How to Sew a ROMAN SHADE

11 Diagram on graph paper the back side of the shade, indicating the finished length and width. Mark the hem 3" (7.5 cm) from the lower edge. Plan the *locations of rings* in columns spaced 8" to 12" apart (20.5 to 30.5 cm), with the outer columns ¾" (2 cm) from the outer edges of the shade. Space them in even horizontal rows 5" to 8" (12.5 to 20.5 cm) apart with the bottom row at the top of the hem and the top row on the line marked in step 10. Work through the following formula to determine ring locations. (We used these numbers for our shade on page 172; your numbers will probably be different.)

12 Mark the locations for the rings on the lining side of the shade, according to your diagram. The bottom row of rings is at the upper edge of the hem; the top row is the determined distance below the top marked line. (There are no rings on the top line.) Pin horizontally through both layers of fabric at each mark.

13 Thread a needle with a double strand of thread. Secure each ring with 4 or 5 small stitches, through both fabric layers. Reinforce all the rings in the bottom row with extra stitches because they carry the weight of the shade.

14 Insert the flat weight bar into the *hem pocket;* slipstitch (page 22) the end openings closed.

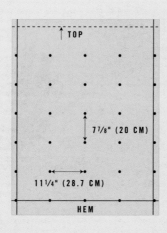

Finished width of shade:	45"	(115 cm)
Divide by 12" (30.5 cm)	÷ 12"	(30.5 cm)
and round up to the nearest whole number	= 3¾"	(9.5 cm)
to find the number of vertical spaces	4	
Divide the finished width	45"	(115 cm)
by the number of spaces	÷ 4	
to find distance between columns	= 11¼"	(28.7 cm)
Length of shade from top of hem:	47"	(120 cm)
Divide by 8" (20.5 cm)	÷ 8"	(20.5 cm)
and round up to the nearest whole number	= 5⅞"	(14.7 cm)
to find the number of horizontal spaces	6	
Divide the length	47"	(120 cm)
by the number of spaces	÷ 6	
to find distance between horizontal rows	= 7⅞"	(20 cm)

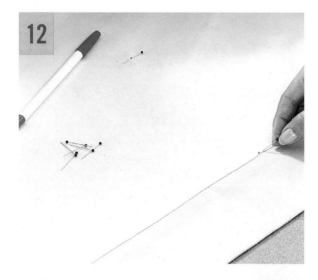

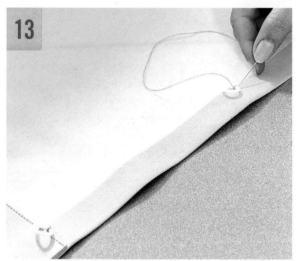

QUICK REFERENCE

Locations of rings. A system of evenly spaced rings through which cords are run on the back of the shade make it possible to raise and lower the shade. When the rings are spaced in even columns and rows, the shade will fold neatly at regular intervals when raised.

Hem pocket. In forming the hem at the lower edge, 3" (7.5 cm) openings were left on the sides so that the hem is really a tube or "pocket" into which you will slide the weight bar.

CONTINUED

How to Sew a ROMAN SHADE

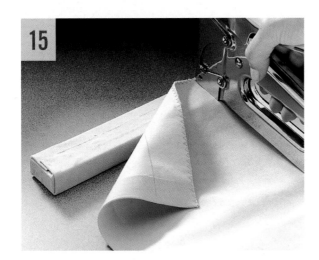

CONTINUED

15 Remove the mounting board from the angle irons, if you are installing an outside mount. Staple the shade to the top of the mounting board, aligning the marked line to the top front edge of the board.

16 Predrill the holes and insert screw eyes, centered, on the underside of the mounting board, aligning them to the columns of rings.

17 On the side where you want the cords to hang, run cord through the first column of rings, through the top screw eye, and *partway down the side.* Cut the cord and tie a nonslip knot at the bottom ring. Repeat for each column in order, running the cords also through the previous screw eyes. Apply glue to the knots for security.

18 Reattach the mounting board to the angle irons for an outside mount or install the mounting board directly to the underside of the window frame, inserting screws through predrilled holes, for an inside mount. Adjust the cords with the shade down so the tension on all cords is equal. Tie the cords in a knot just below the first screw eye. Braid the cords, insert them through a drapery pull, if desired, and knot and trim the ends.

19 Secure an awning cleat to the edge of the window frame or on the wall. Pull gently on the cords to raise the shade, *forming soft folds.* Wind the cord around the cleat to hold the shade in its raised position.

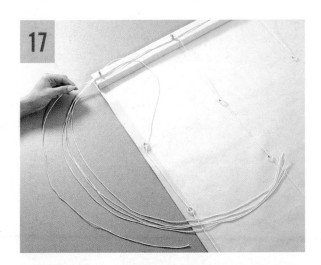

QUICK REFERENCE

Partway down the side. Work on one column at a time, cutting the cord only after you have run the cord through the appropriate rings and screw eyes and determined the extra length needed for raising and lowering the shade. The extra length needed may depend on the location of the window and whether or not you want it to be accessible to children.

Forming soft folds. The first time you raise the shade, you may have to "train" it where to fold. As you raise the shade, pull the excess fabric between horizontal rows forward, forming gentle rolls. To help it "remember," leave the shade in the raised position for a day or two.

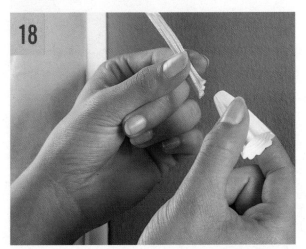

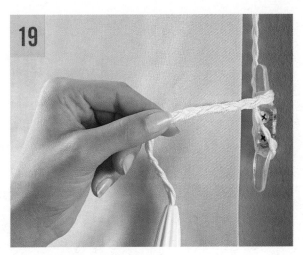

CONGRATULATIONS

With your own two hands, you have created a custom Roman shade that fits your window perfectly.

Draped Lace SWAGS

Very little sewing is required to achieve this elegant decorator look. The key is in the selection of the fabric. Many laces, ranging in width from 48" to 60" (122 to 152.5 cm), have decorative **SELVAGES**. From a short distance, most lace fabrics appear to be reversible, and, in some cases, you can use this fact to your advantage. In general, the right side of the lace has more texture, perhaps some raised, embroidered areas. The wrong side looks flat and less interesting. If you are unsure about which side is the right side, ask for clarification at the fabric store, and mark the right side.

You will use the entire width of the lace for the swag, running the **LENGTHWISE GRAIN** up one side, draping across the rod, and down the opposite side. Because the selvages are already finished, you merely sew narrow hems in the two cut ends of the lace. The effect is created in the way the lace is draped over the rod.

WHAT YOU'LL LEARN

How to measure the window for a swag

How to sew *double-fold hems (p. 101)*

Making decorator window treatments is easier than you thought!

WHAT YOU'LL NEED

Lace fabric in the amount determined in step 1

Thread to match the fabric

Decorative curtain rod of your choice, in a length suitable for the window width

Tools and hardware, for installing the rod

How to Sew a DRAPED LACE SWAG

LET'S BEGIN

1 Mount the rod above the window frame, with the outer brackets just clearing the frame sides. To determine the fabric length needed, drape a cord in the path you want the lower edge of the swag to follow. Cut the lace swag panel to this length, following the cutting directions on page 44.

2 *Press under* 1" (2.5 cm) on one end of the swag panel.

3 Unfold the pressed edge. Turn the cut edge back, aligning it to the first foldline; press the outer fold.

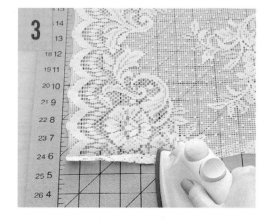

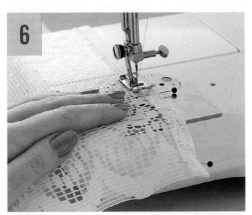

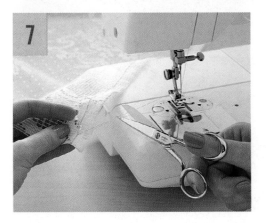

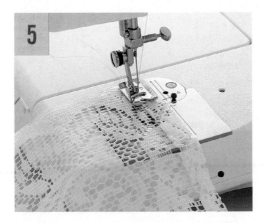

QUICK REFERENCE

Press under. Place the fabric facedown on your ironing board. Fold the cut edge back; measure, and press, keeping the width of the folded edge consistent across the entire edge.

4 Refold the edge along the pressed foldlines, encasing the raw edge to form a ½" (1.3 cm) double-fold hem. Pin the hem, *inserting the pins perpendicular to the folds (p. 19).*

5 Place the pinned hem under the presser foot of the machine, with the wrong side of the panel facing up. The bulk of the fabric is positioned to the left of the machine. The selvage of the panel should be even with the back of the presser foot, with the needle aligned to enter the fabric just inside the inner fold.

6 *Backstitch (p. 19)* along the inner fold to the selvage. Reverse the direction and stitch forward, stitching the entire length of the hem to the opposite selvage. *Remove pins as you come to them (p. 19).* Stop stitching at the opposite selvage. Backstitch for about ½" (1.3 cm).

7 Lift the presser foot, and *remove the fabric from the machine (p. 123).*

CONTINUED

How to Sew a DRAPED LACE SWAG

CONTINUED

8 Drape the swag panel over the rod, as shown in the photograph on page 182, placing the hemmed end in the desired location. Mark the unstitched end at the desired location for the opposite hem.

9 Remove the swag panel from the rod. Cut the panel 1" (2.5 cm) longer than the mark, allowing for the double hem. Stitch the remaining hem, following steps 2 to 7.

10 Fanfold the entire finished panel into gentle pleats of consistent depth. Tie the folded fabric at regular intervals, using ribbon or twill tape. Drape the folded panel over the rod, and arrange the folds as shown in the photograph on page 182.

More Draped Panel TREATMENTS

The basic construction steps for any of these treatments are the same as for the draped swag. Use lightweight to sheer reversible fabrics that have narrow, neat selvages. Drape the fabric panel over a decorative rod or through swag holders. Plan 15" to 20" (38 to 51 cm) of additional fabric length for each floor puddle.

Create multiple swags, wrapping the fanfolded fabric panel over the rod. Draw out folds gently to arrange swags. After arranging the folds, secure the swags to the rod, using double-stick tape.

Ornate shelf brackets are used as hardware for hanging this swag. Cording and tassels draped with the fabric give the swag a decorator look.

Self-lined Rectangle VALANCE

Top off a window with this simple, but stylish, self-lined valance. A long rectangle of fabric is folded in half lengthwise, with all the raw edges encased in **SEAMS**. Thus the same fabric forms the face of the valance as well as the **LINING**. The valance is stapled to a mounting board, forming gentle folds at the corners. Plan to mount the board just above the window, extending it 1" (2.5 cm) beyond the window frame on each side. This will allow room to install the board, using an angle iron at each end.

To avoid distracting seams in this valance, select a fabric that can be **RAILROADED**, such as a solid color or a print that can be turned sideways. After trimming the fabric to the necessary width, you can use the excess fabric to cover the mounting board.

WHAT YOU'LL LEARN

How to railroad fabric

How to PIVOT the stitching line at corners

How to encase SEAM ALLOWANCES

How to INTERLINE a treatment

How to install a board-mounted treatment

WHAT YOU'LL NEED

Decorator fabric; see step 1

Drapery lining, if the valance needs to be interlined; see step 1

Thread to match fabric

1 × 4 NOMINAL LUMBER

Heavy-duty stapler; staples

Angle irons and screws, for mounting board

How to Sew a SELF-LINED RECTANGLE VALANCE

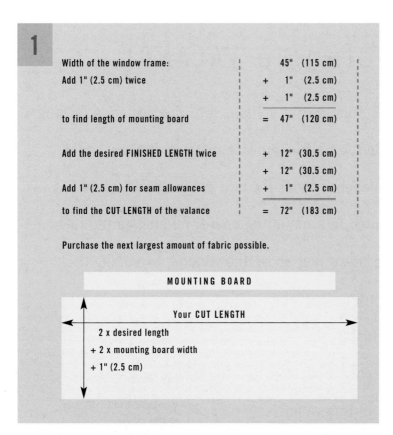

Width of the window frame:	45"	(115 cm)
Add 1" (2.5 cm) twice	+ 1"	(2.5 cm)
	+ 1"	(2.5 cm)
to find length of mounting board	= 47"	(120 cm)
Add the desired FINISHED LENGTH twice	+ 12"	(30.5 cm)
	+ 12"	(30.5 cm)
Add 1" (2.5 cm) for seam allowances	+ 1"	(2.5 cm)
to find the CUT LENGTH of the valance	= 72"	(183 cm)

Purchase the next largest amount of fabric possible.

MOUNTING BOARD

Your CUT LENGTH

2 x desired length
+ 2 x mounting board width
+ 1" (2.5 cm)

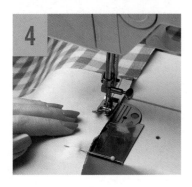

LET'S BEGIN

1 Measure the width of the window frame and determine how high above the frame you want to mount the valance. Then calculate the length of fabric needed for your valance, working with the formula at left. (We used these numbers for our valance on page 188; your numbers will probably be different.)

TIP If you select a print fabric for the valance, fold it in half and hold it up to the window to see if sunlight coming through the fabric will cause the print to show through to the front, muddying the design. If this happens, purchase the same amount of drapery lining, and follow the directions for interlining the valance.

2 Preshrink your fabric (page 43). Cut away the **SELVAGES**, cutting just beyond the tightly woven area. Cut a rectangle of fabric with the length equal to the cut length as determined in step 1. The width is equal to twice the desired valance length plus twice the width of the mounting board plus 1" (2.5 cm) for seam allowances. If you want to interline your valance, cut a rectangle of drapery lining with the same length as the valance fabric; the width is equal to exactly half the width of the valance fabric. Disregard steps 3 and 4 if your valance will not be interlined.

3 Place the interlining over the wrong side of the valance, aligning it to one long edge and the short ends. Pin the layers together near the outer edges, *inserting the pins perpendicular to the edges (p. 19).*

4 Set the stitch length on your machine to sew long stitches. Place the pinned fabric under the presser foot, aligning the cut edges to the 3/8" (1 cm) *seam allowance guide (p. 19)*. Stitch the interlining to the valance fabric along the three pinned sides. From this point on, *handle both layers together as one fabric.*

5 Fold the fabric in half lengthwise, with the right sides together. Align the cut edges at the short ends and along the long side. If your valance is interlined, the long free edge of the interlining should align to the folded edge of the valance. Pin the layers together near the outer raw edges, inserting the pins perpendicular to the edges. On the long side, leave a 10" (25.5 cm) opening.

6 Place the pinned fabric under the presser foot, so that the fold is aligned to the back of the presser foot. Align the cut edges of a short end to the 1/2" (1.3 cm) seam allowance guide. The bulk of fabric will extend to the left of the machine.

7 *Backstitch (p. 19)* to the fold; stop. Then, stitching forward, stitch the seam, guiding the cut edges along the 1/2" (1.3 cm) seam allowance guide. *Remove pins as you come to them (p. 19).*

8 Stop sewing at the first corner, leaving the needle down in the fabric. (Turn the handwheel until the needle is down.) Raise the presser foot and turn the fabric a quarter turn. Lower the presser foot and continue sewing. Stop stitching when you reach the last pin before the opening. Backstitch three or four stitches. *Remove the fabric from the machine (p. 19).*

CONTINUED

QUICK REFERENCE

Handle both layers together as one fabric.
Fold, stitch, and press both the decorator fabric and the lining fabric together as if they are one fabric, even though the directions may not specifically refer to the interlining.

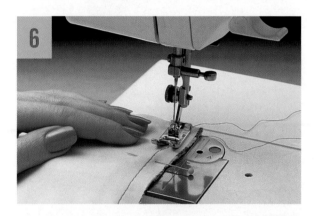

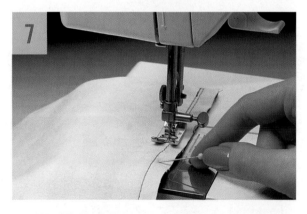

How to Sew a SELF-LINED RECTANGLE VALANCE

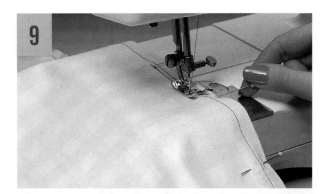

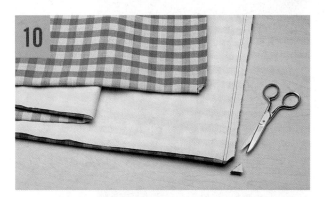

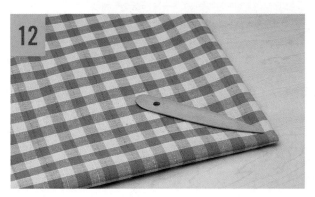

9 Reposition the fabric under the presser foot, just beyond the pin that marks the opposite side of the opening. Backstitch three or four stitches. Then stitch forward, completing the seam on the long edge. Pivot at the opposite corner, and continue stitching to the opposite fold; backstitch three or four stitches. Remove the fabric from the machine. Trim the threads close to the fabric.

10 *Trim the seam allowances diagonally* at the four corners. **PRESS** the seams flat to set the stitches in the fabric. This may seem unnecessary, but it really does give you a better-looking seam in the end.

11 Insert a heavy cardboard tube or a seam roll (page 31) into the opening. Press the seam allowance open, applying light pressure with the tip of the iron down the crease of the seam. Turn back the seam allowances 1/2" (1.3 cm) along the opening, and press.

12 Slip your hand into the opening; grasp one of the far corners of the valance. Pull it through the opening. Repeat this for all of the corners until the entire valance is turned right side out. Insert a point turner or similar tool into the valance through the opening, gently pushing the points out to form *perfect corners*.

13 Press the entire valance, including the fold at the lower edge. Pin the opening closed. Place the valance under the presser foot just behind the opening; the needle should be aligned to sew just inside the folded edges. Stitch the opening closed, backstitching a few stitches at the beginning and end of the stitching line. Remember to remove pins as you come to them.

14 Cut the mounting board 2" (5 cm) longer than the measured width of the window frame; cover it with fabric, if desired. Attach angle irons to the underside near the ends, with the corners aligned to the board back. Mount the board to the wall just above and outside the frame. Remove the board, leaving the angle irons on the wall. Center the valance over the top of the mounting board with the long stitched edge along the back of the board. The valance should extend the same distance off both ends and off the front of the board.

QUICK REFERENCE

Trim the seam allowances diagonally. This step eliminates the excess bulk at the corners, allowing them to lie flat and square after turning the valance right side out.

Perfect corners. The corners of your valance should be sharply squared, not rounded. To improve the appearance of a slightly rounded corner, you can push a pointed utensil into the corner from inside the valance to force the stitches out to the corner. An inexpensive specialty tool, called a point turner, works well; or you can use a large knitting needle, a ballpoint pen with the inkball retracted, or something similar. Use light pressure, though, so that you don't punch a hole in the corner.

15 Staple the valance to the mounting board, inserting the staples near the back of the board. Begin in the center and work toward the ends, spacing the staples 4" to 6" (10 to 15 cm) apart. Mount the valance on the angle irons, replacing the screws in their original holes. Adjust the front corners of the valance to fall in gently rounded folds as shown on page 188.

Strap-tied VALANCE

The versatile style of this **LINED-TO-THE-EDGE** board-mounted valance makes it suitable for many decorating schemes. Fabric choice determines whether it has a sleek, contemporary look; cozy, country appeal; or classic, traditional elegance. Excess length, fanfolded at the lower edge, is held in place with straps, forming pleated wings at the corners and a gentle swag in the middle.

Using one 54" (137 cm) width of decorator fabric, this valance is suitable for windows with inside frame measurements of 53" (134.5 cm) or less, with a frame depth deep enough to accommodate the mounting board.

WHAT YOU'LL LEARN

How to line a window treatment

How to reduce bulk at square corners

How to stitch and turn long straps

WHAT YOU'LL NEED

Two decorator fabrics; one for the valance and one for the **LINING** and straps

Thread to match

3/4" (2 cm) wooden dowel

Mounting board; 1 x 2 **NOMINAL LUMBER**

Heavy-duty stapler; staples

How to Sew a STRAP-TIED VALANCE

1

Desired **FINISHED LENGTH** at the strap:		12"	(30.5 cm)
Add 24" (61 cm) for fanfolds	+	24"	(61 cm)
Add ½" (1.3 cm) for seam allowance	+	½"	(1.3 cm)
Add the mounting board width	+	1½"	(3.8 cm)
to find the **CUT LENGTH** of the valance	=	38"	(96.5 cm)

Add ½ yd. (0.5 m) of fabric to allow for covering the mounting board and making the straps. Purchase the next largest amount possible for each of the two fabrics.

LET'S BEGIN

1 Determine how long you want your valance, measured at the strap. The center will swag down a distance equal to about one-sixth the width of the valance. Then calculate the length of fabric needed for your valance, working with the formula at left. (We used these numbers for our valance on page 194; your numbers will probably be different.)

TIP If you select two print fabrics for the valance, layer them and hold them up to the window to see if sunlight coming through the fabric will cause the lining print to show through to the front, muddying the design. If this happens, purchase the same amount of drapery lining, and follow the directions for **INTERLINING** the valance.

2 Preshrink your fabric (page 43). Cut away the **SELVAGES**, cutting just beyond the tightly woven area. Cut a rectangle of fabric with the length equal to the cut length as determined in step 1. The **CUT WIDTH** is equal to the inside frame measurement of the window plus 1" (2.5 cm) for **SEAM ALLOWANCES**. Cut the lining fabric to the same size. If you want to interline your valance, cut drapery lining to the same size as the valance and lining pieces. Disregard steps 3 and 4 if your valance will not be interlined.

3 Place the interlining over the wrong side of the valance, aligning all the cut edges. Pin the layers together near the outer edges, *inserting the pins perpendicular to the edge (p. 19).*

4 Place the pinned fabric under the presser foot, aligning the cut edges to the 3/8" (1 cm) *seam allowance guide (p. 19). Machine-baste* the interlining to the valance fabric along the pinned sides. From this point on, *handle both layers together as one fabric (p. 191).*

TIP Most machines have a handy thread cutter located within a few inches (centimeters) of the presser foot. By using this thread cutter, you are also pulling enough thread through the needle and up from the bobbin to help you prevent a **THREAD JAM** at the start of your next seam.

5 Place the lining over the valance fabric, right sides together. Pin the fabrics together along the sides and lower edge, inserting the pins perpendicular to the edge.

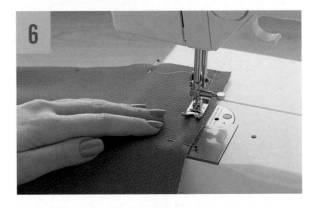

6 Place the pinned fabric under the presser foot, with the upper edge aligned to the back of the presser foot and the cut edges to the 1/2" (1.3 cm) seam allowance guide on the bed of your machine. The bulk of the fabric will extend to the left of the machine. *Backstitch (p. 19)* a few stitches. Then, stitching forward, stitch the **SEAM,** guiding the cut edges along the 1/2" (1.3 cm) seam allowance guide. *Remove pins as you come to them (p. 19).*

CONTINUED

QUICK REFERENCE

Machine-baste. Set the stitch length on your machine to sew long stitches. This is done to hold the two fabrics together until they are secured in a seam. Because the stitches are long, the fabric may want to pucker. To avoid this, hold the fabric taut, with one hand in front of the presser foot and the other hand behind it.

CONTINUED

----

7 Stop stitching ½" (1.3 cm) from the first corner, leaving the needle down in the fabric. (Turn the handwheel until the needle is down.) Raise the presser foot and turn the fabric a quarter turn. Lower the presser foot and continue stitching, **PIVOTING** in this manner at the other corner. Stitch the opposite side, backstitching a few stitches at the upper edge. *Remove the fabric from the machine (p. 19).*

8 *Trim the seam allowances diagonally (p. 193)* at the two corners. **PRESS** the seams flat to set the stitching line in the fabric. Insert a seam roll or heavy cardboard tube into the open end, and press the seam allowances open.

9 Turn the valance right side out. Insert a point turner or other tool into the valance through the opening to form *perfect corners (p. 193)*. Press the entire valance. Pin the upper edges together. Stitch ⅜" (1 cm) from the edges.

10 Cut two strips of fabric, 4" (10 cm) wide, from the **CROSSWISE GRAIN**, for the straps. The cut length of the straps is equal to twice the desired finished length plus 4" (10 cm). Fold one strap in half lengthwise, with the right sides together. Pin the layers together along the long raw edges. Stitch a ½" (1.3 cm) seam down the long side, backstitching a few stitches at the beginning and end of the seam.

11 Press the seam flat, keeping the iron away from the folded edge. Insert a ¾" (2 cm) wood dowel into the tube, centering it under the seam. Press the seam allowances open over the dowel. The dowel helps you press only the seam without pressing unwanted creases into the rest of the strap.

12 Tie a safety pin to a string, cut longer than the strap. Insert the safety pin into one end of the strap, allowing the weight of the pin to pull the string through the strap. Then secure the pin to the inside of the strap at the opposite end.

13 Pull on the string to turn the strap right side out, gently working the fabric over the safety pin. Remove the pin.

CONTINUED

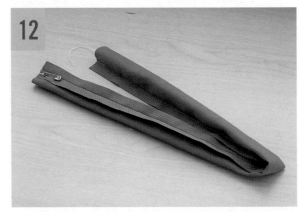

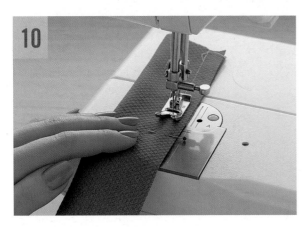

How to Sew a STRAP-TIED VALANCE

CONTINUED

14 Press the strap flat, centering the seam on the back of the strap.

15 Pin the straps, right side up, to the upper edge of the valance, placing them a distance from the sides equal to about one-sixth the total width of the valance. Wrap the straps under the valance, and pin the opposite ends in place. Stitch the straps in place, 3/8" (1 cm) from the edges.

16 *Finish the raw edges* together across the top of the valance, using a **ZIGZAG** stitch set at medium width and medium length. Stitch so the right swing of the needle just clears the fabric edge.

17 Cut the mounting board 1/2" (1.3 cm) shorter than the inside width of the window frame; cover it with fabric, if desired. Holding the board against the top inside of the window frame, flush with the frame front, predrill mounting holes through the board and into the frame. Center the valance over the top of the mounting board, with the finished edge along the back of the board.

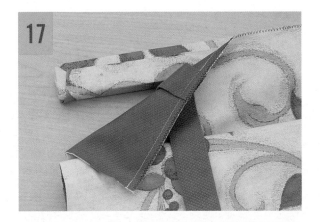

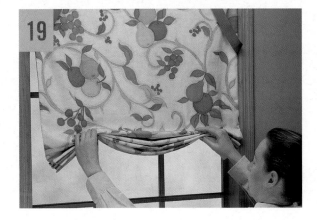

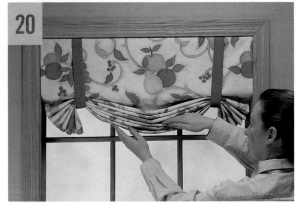

18 Staple the valance to the mounting board, inserting the staples near the back of the board. Begin in the center and work toward the ends, spacing the staples 4" to 6" (10 to 15 cm) apart. Apply two staples at each strap.

19 Mount the valance inside the window frame, inserting screws through the predrilled holes. Fanfold the lower 24" (61 cm) of the valance into five or six even pleats, beginning by folding under the lower edge toward the lining. Slip the pleats into the straps.

20 Pull the pleats into a gentle swag at the center. Adjust the folds as necessary near the straps.

QUICK REFERENCE

Finish the raw edges. Abrasion and laundering will cause yarns to ravel off the raw edges of any woven fabric unless you do something to prevent it. Zigzag stitches sewn over the edge lock the outer yarns in place. This is a suitable way to finish edges that normally don't show.

MORE IDEAS

Make three lightweight to sheer valances in lengths that vary by 2" (5 cm). Stack and mount them for a delicate layered look.

Convert this style into a coach valance. Reduce the excess length to 12" (30.5 cm) instead of 24" (61 cm). Roll the lower edge around a 1" (2.5 cm) wooden dowel, rolling from the right side, to expose the lining. Apply double-stick tape inside the straps, if necessary, to keep the fabric from unrolling. Paint the dowel ends to match the lining. Make four straps instead of two. Cut the straps 30" (76 cm) long, and stitch across one end before turning them right side out. Or use four lengths of sturdy ribbon. Tie them in bows or simple knots at the bottom of the valance.

Sew tent flap curtains, following steps 2 to 9 and 16 to 19; disregard the references to the straps and fanfolding. Determine the cut length of the fabric, lining, and interlining by adding $1/2"$ (1.3 cm) seam allowance and the width of the mounting board to the desired finished length of the curtain. For example: $45" + 1/2" + 1 1/2" = 47"$ (115 cm + 1.3 cm + 3.8 cm = 120 cm) Hand-stitch a decorative ring to one corner of the curtain. Pull back the curtain, and hook the ring on a decorative hook installed on the window frame or wall.

Knot two chair ties together to form a cord-and-tassel swag. Attach it to the valance as shown, using hand stitches.

Window TOPPER

This easy stylish window topper has lots of creative possibilities. Designed as a decorative accent over a shade or blinds, it is simply a flat **LINED-TO-THE-EDGE** shape that flips over a decorative rod. Buttonholes and buttons secure the topper and add splashes of color. A layer of lining fabric between the front and back fabrics, called **INTERLINING**, adds body and support for the buttonholes. Because you first create a paper pattern, you can design the topper with straight, curved, or pointed lower edges. Select firmly woven fabrics in two coordinating colors or a **NONDIRECTIONAL PRINT** and a solid color, one for the front and one for the back.

WHAT YOU'LL LEARN

If you can measure, draw lines, and cut paper, you can design a window topper!

How to sew buttonholes and buttons

How to shape perfect points and corners

WHAT YOU'LL NEED

Decorative curtain rod

Two coordinating firmly woven fabrics, amount determined after making pattern

Drapery lining fabric, amount determined after making pattern

Wide craft paper

Quilting ruler or carpenter's square

Thread to blend with the fabrics

Paper-backed fusible web

Buttons in desired sizes and colors

Liquid fray preventer

Buttonhole cutter

How to Sew a WINDOW TOPPER

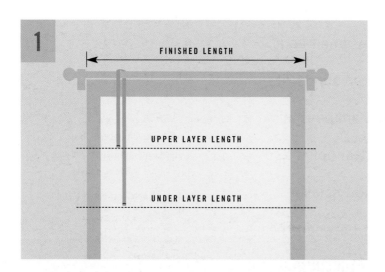

FINISHED LENGTH

UPPER LAYER LENGTH

UNDER LAYER LENGTH

LET'S BEGIN

1 Mount the rod so that the top is even with the top of the window frame or slightly higher. The brackets should be just outside the frame or at least 1" (2.5 cm) beyond any existing treatment. Measure from bracket to bracket to determine the width of the topper pattern. Hang a tape measure over the rod to determine the length of the pattern.

TIP The topper should be at least long enough to cover a raised blind or shade. For a pleasing proportion, it should cover no more than one-third of the window.

2 Cut a paper pattern to these dimensions, using a quilting ruler or carpenter's square for accuracy. Shape the lower edges into one or more shallow curves or points, if you desire, and hang it over the rod. Stand back for a look, and make any final adjustments. Draw a line where the pattern crosses the rod. Measure the pattern and buy equal amounts of both fabrics and the interlining. Preshrink (page 33) all three fabrics if you intend to launder the topper.

QUICK REFERENCE

Leave the pins in the fabric. The layers are already aligned and pinned to begin sewing.

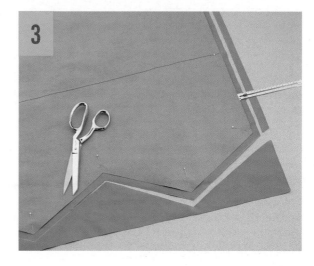

TIP If the window is narrower than the fabric, purchase slightly more fabric than the pattern length. You will align the pattern vertically to the **LENGTHWISE GRAIN** of the fabric. If the window is wider than the fabric, purchase slightly more fabric than the pattern width. You will align the pattern vertically to the **CROSSWISE GRAIN**.

3 Pin the pattern over one of the fabrics. The outer edge of the pattern is the stitching line for the topper. Mark the cutting line on the fabric, 1/2" (1.3 cm) beyond the pattern edge. Cut out the fabric. Remove the pattern.

4 Place the other fabric faceup over the interlining. Pin the cut fabric facedown over both layers, aligning all grainlines. *Insert the pins* near and *perpendicular to the cut edges (p. 19).* Cut the other layers. *Leave the pins in the fabric.*

CONTINUED

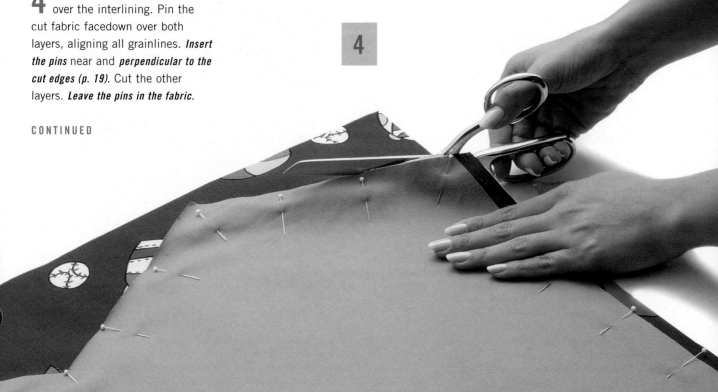

How to Sew a **WINDOW TOPPER**

CONTINUED
----

5 Set the machine for a straight stitch of 12 stitches per inch, which equals 2 mm. Place the fabric under the presser foot near the center of one long edge, so that the cut edges are aligned to the 1/2" (1.3 cm) *seam allowance guide (p. 19). Backstitch (p. 19)* a few stitches. Then stitch forward, guiding the cut edges along the 1/2" (1.3 cm) seam allowance guide. *Remove pins as you come to them (p. 19).*

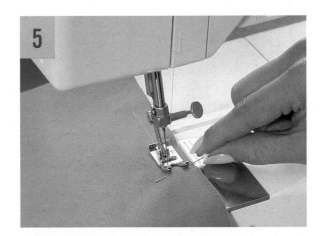

6 Stop stitching at the first corner, leaving the needle down in the fabric. (Turn the handwheel until the needle is down.) Raise the presser foot, and turn the fabric. Lower the presser foot, and continue stitching. **PIVOT** in the same way at each corner.

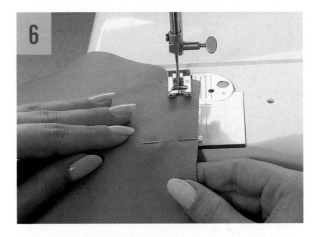

7 Stop stitching about 10" (25.5 cm) from where you began; backstitch, leaving an opening for turning the topper right side out. *Remove the fabric from the machine (p. 19). Trim the seam allowances diagonally at outer corners (p. 193). Clip to, but not through,* the stitches at any inner corners.

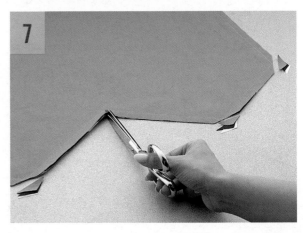

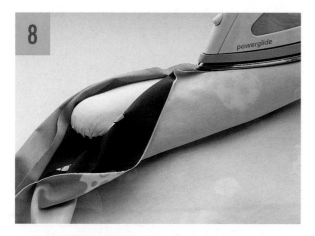

QUICK REFERENCE

Clip to, but not through. This will allow the fabric to lay smoothly without puckering when the topper is turned right side out. Be careful not to cut the stitches, or a hole will develop in the seam.

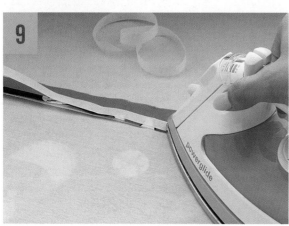

8 **PRESS** the seams flat to set the stitching line in the fabric. Insert a heavy cardboard tube or a seam roll (page 31) into the opening. Press the seam allowances open, applying light pressure with the tip of the iron down the crease of the seam.

9 Turn back the seam allowances 1/2" (1.3 cm) along the opening, and press. (On one side you will also be turning back the interlining.) Cut a 10" (25.5 cm) strip of 3/8" (1 cm) paper-backed fusible web (page 34). Place the strip over the seam allowance at the opening, just inside the folded edge. Press over the strip to fuse it to the seam allowance, following the manufacturer's directions.

CONTINUED

How to Sew a WINDOW TOPPER

CONTINUED

10 Turn the valance right side out through the opening. Insert a point turner or similar tool into the opening and gently push any pivot points out to form **perfect corners (p. 193).** Push the seam out so that it is centered all around the outer edge. Press the entire valance. Remove the protective paper backing from the fusible web at the opening. Align the folded edges of the opening. Press over the opening to fuse it closed.

11 Place the topper on a flat surface. Using the marked line on the pattern as a guide, fold the upper flap down. Plan and mark the placement for vertical buttonholes, keeping the lower ends of the buttonholes at least 1" (2.5 cm) above the lower edge of the flap. Mark lines that equal the diameter plus the thickness of the buttons.

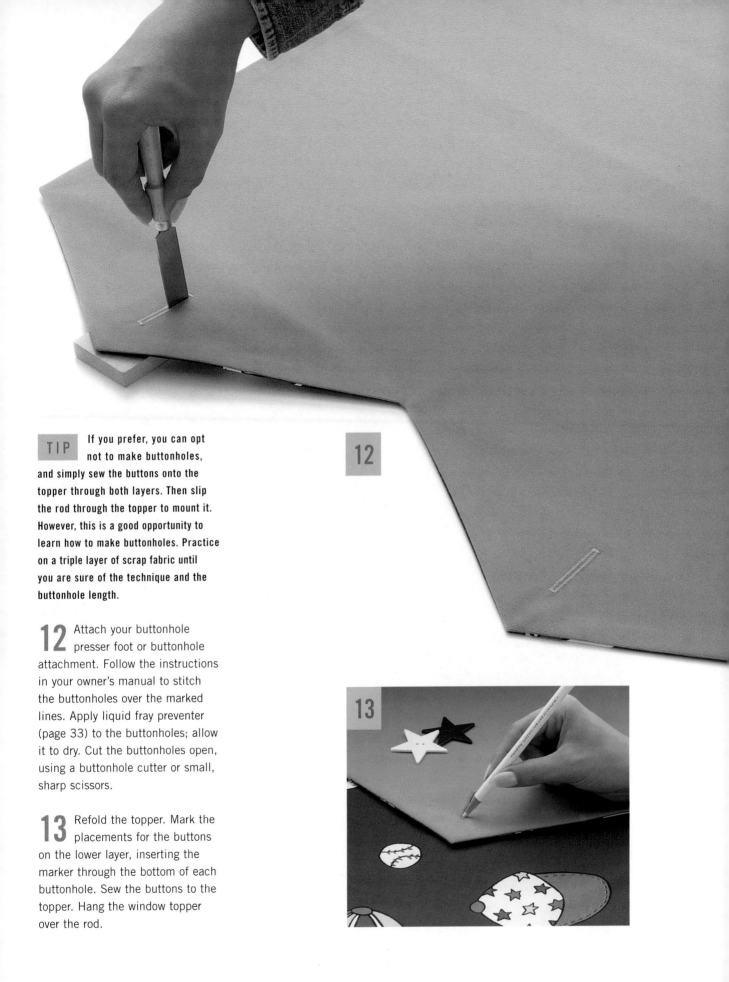

TIP   If you prefer, you can opt not to make buttonholes, and simply sew the buttons onto the topper through both layers. Then slip the rod through the topper to mount it. However, this is a good opportunity to learn how to make buttonholes. Practice on a triple layer of scrap fabric until you are sure of the technique and the buttonhole length.

12 Attach your buttonhole presser foot or buttonhole attachment. Follow the instructions in your owner's manual to stitch the buttonholes over the marked lines. Apply liquid fray preventer (page 33) to the buttonholes; allow it to dry. Cut the buttonholes open, using a buttonhole cutter or small, sharp scissors.

13 Refold the topper. Mark the placements for the buttons on the lower layer, inserting the marker through the bottom of each buttonhole. Sew the buttons to the topper. Hang the window topper over the rod.

MORE IDEAS

Dragonflies dart about in this cheerful
cotton print. Large buttons covered in the
striped fabric line up under the rod. The
pattern for this topper (diagram) is actually
a parallelogram. The sides are aligned
to the grain of the fabric; the angled lower
edges are sewn on the BIAS.

FOLD

GRAIN

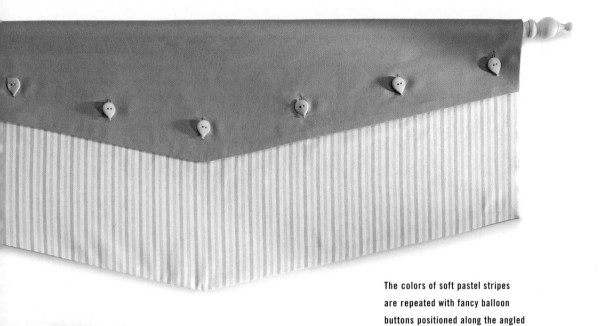

The colors of soft pastel stripes are repeated with fancy balloon buttons positioned along the angled lower edges. Sew buttonholes along the grainline, even though the edge runs on the bias.

Curved seam allowances are trimmed to ¼" (6 mm) for ease in turning right side out. Ribbon ties are cut 18" (46 cm) long and stitched to the under layer instead of buttons. The ribbon ends are then pulled through small buttonholes and tied into bows, anchoring the topper over the pole.

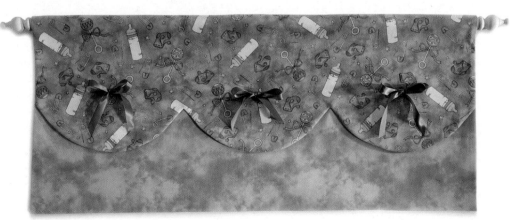

Rod-pocket TREATMENTS

Many window fashions are hung from a pole or rod by means of a "pocket" sewn along the upper edge. Thus the name, "rod-pocket" treatments. Styles vary depending on the rod or pole used, the depth of the **HEADING**, the length of the curtain or top treatment, the **FULLNESS** of the style, and the way the style is arranged once it has been mounted over the window. There are also added embellishments, such as decorative trims or tie-backs, that can give the treatment a distinctive look.

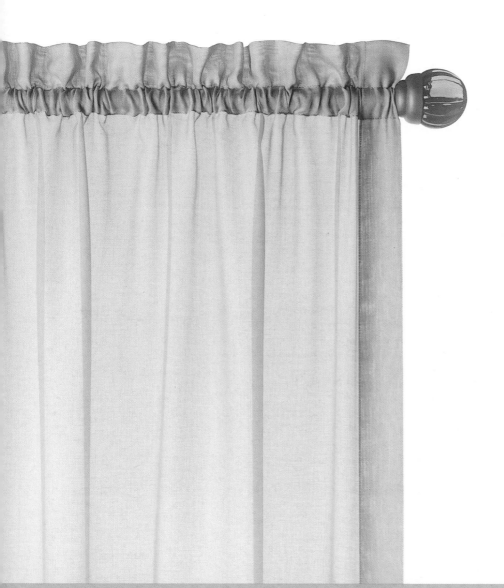

WHAT YOU'LL LEARN

How to determine the amount of fabric needed for any rod-pocket treatment

Basic steps for sewing any rod-pocket treatment

There are lots of rod-pocket styles to choose from

WHAT YOU'LL NEED

Fabric, amount determined by working through the chart on page 216

Thread to match fabric

Curtain rod or pole

Drapery weights (page 235) if sewing curtains

For now, though, let's just focus on a basic rod-pocket valance and identify its parts. The diagram below shows that the valance is really a flat rectangle of fabric. The sides and bottom of the rectangle are hemmed with *double-fold hems (p. 101)*. The top is folded to the back and sewn with two stitching lines. The heading, from the top fold to the top stitching line, forms a ruffle above the rod when the valance is mounted. The area between the stitching lines is the **ROD POCKET**. Designed to have two times fullness, the rectangle is made twice as wide as the desired **FINISHED WIDTH** of the valance. Note that this valance required two widths of fabric. One is centered and the other is cut in half and sewn to each side, thus avoiding a distracting center seam.

		HEADING		
		ROD POCKET		
SIDE HEM	SEAM		SEAM	SIDE HEM
		BOTTOM HEM		

To determine the rod-pocket depth **(A)**, measure around the widest part of the rod or pole. In some cases this may mean measuring in the crook of an elbow. Add ½" (1.3 cm) **EASE** to this measurement, and divide the result by 2. This measurement will be the distance between stitching lines.

The height of the heading **(B)** can be adjusted to suit your taste, from very short at ½" (1.3 cm) to quite high at 4" (10 cm). Sometimes the heading is made extremely long so that it falls forward over the rod pocket, forming an attached valance (page 223) along the top of a rod-pocket curtain.

How to Sew a ROD-POCKET TREATMENT

1

Finished length, measured from the bottom of the rod to the bottom of the treatment:	12" (30.5 cm)
Add the total hem depth	+ 4" (10 cm)
Add the rod pocket depth twice	+ 1¾" (4.5 cm)
	+ 1¾" (4.5 cm)
Add the heading height twice	+ 2½" (6.5 cm)
	+ 2½" (6.5 cm)
Add ½" (1.3 cm) to turn under bottom of rod pocket	+ ½" (1.3 cm)
Add ½" (1.3 cm) for ease	+ ½" (1.3 cm)
to find the CUT LENGTH of each piece	=*25½" (64.8 cm)
Multiply the window width	36" (91.5 cm)
by the desired fullness	× 2½
to find the finished width	= 90" (229 cm)
Add the total side hem depth twice	+ 2" (5 cm)
	+ 2" (5 cm)
To find the total CUT WIDTH needed	= 94" (239 cm)
Divide the total cut width by the fabric width	÷ 54" (137 cm)
Round the number up to the nearest whole number	= 1.74
to find the number of fabric widths needed	2
Multiply this number by the cut length	× 25½" (64.8 cm)
to find the length to buy	= 51" (129.5 cm)

Because fabric stores sell fabric in whole yards (meters) or eighths of a yard (fractions of a meter), purchase the next largest amount. If you buy a fabric with a **PATTERN REPEAT**, follow the chart until you have determined the cut length*. Your actual cut length must be rounded up to the next number evenly divisible by the pattern repeat. For instance, if the pattern repeat is 15" (38 cm), your cut length will be 30" (76 cm), not 25½" (64.8 cm), because 30 (76) can be evenly divided by 15 (38). Proceed with the chart using this revised cut length measurement.

LET'S BEGIN

1 Measure the window and calculate the length of fabric needed for your valance or curtain, working with the formula, opposite: (We used these numbers for our valance on page 215; your numbers will probably be different.)

2 **PRESHRINK** your fabric (page 31). Measure and mark the location of each cut along the **SELVAGE**. Cut the pieces, following the cutting guidelines on page 44. If you do not have to match a pattern (page 46), cut away the selvages, cutting just beyond the tightly woven area.

3 Pin two pieces together along the vertical edges, inserting the *pins perpendicular to the edges (p. 19).* Match the pattern, if necessary, following the guidelines on page 46. Stitch ½" (1.3 cm) **SEAM**, *backstitching (p. 19)* at the beginning and end of the seam for about ½" (1.3 cm). *Remove pins as you come to them (p. 19).*

QUICK REFERENCE

Finished length. Valances are not only decorative, they also "cap" the window visually and hide mechanical workings of any undertreatments. As a general proportion guideline, the valance length is about one-fifth of the total distance from the top of the window to the floor. You can make your valance longer or shorter, if you prefer. Sketch the total window treatment to scale to help you make this decision.

Measure from the bottom of the rod. If you have not yet installed the rod, or even selected a rod, plan to install it so that the bottom of the rod is even with the top of the window frame. Then you can measure from the top of the frame to where you want the bottom edge of the valance or curtain to be.

Round up to the nearest whole number. Most window treatments that have some amount of fullness in them, including rod-pocket treatments, are sewn using full and half widths of fabric. Even if your treatment requires two-and-one-half widths of fabric, you have to purchase three full widths, and your yardage requirements have to be determined by rounding up to the nearest whole number.

CONTINUED

How to Sew a ROD-POCKET TREATMENT

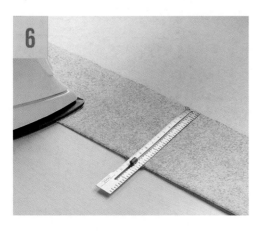

CONTINUED

4 Finish the raw edges together, using a zigzag stitch (page 21) set at medium width and medium length. Stitch so the right-hand swing of the needle just clears the fabric edge.

5 Repeat steps 3 and 4 until you have sewn all the pieces together across the valance or curtain width. If there are any *half widths*, sew them onto an end. **PRESS** all of the seam allowances to one side.

6 Place the valance or curtain facedown on an ironing surface. *Press under (p. 185)* the lower edge 4" (10 cm), for the hem.

7 Unfold the pressed edge. Turn the cut edge back, aligning it to the pressed foldline; press the outer fold.

8 Refold the hem along the pressed foldlines, encasing the raw edge to form a 2" (5 cm) *double-fold hem (p. 101)*. Pin the hem, inserting the pins perpendicular to the foldlines.

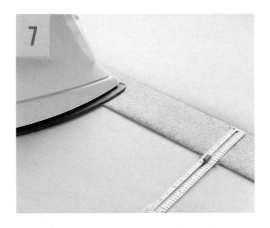

QUICK REFERENCE

Half widths are always added at the outer edge of a valance or curtain panel. The seam is sewn along the edge that had the selvage; the side hem is sewn along the edge that was the center of the fabric width. (This is the only way you are able to match the pattern, if there is one.) Also, half panels go on the side of the treatment nearest the **RETURN**.

9 Place the hem under the presser foot of the machine, with the wrong side of the valance or curtain facing up. The bulk of the fabric is positioned to the left of the machine. The side edge should be even with the back of the presser foot, with the needle aligned to enter the fabric just inside the inner fold.

10 Stitch the hem along the inner fold, backstitching at the beginning and the end about ½" (1.3 cm). Remove pins as you come to them.

TIP Double-fold side hems measure a total of 2" (5 cm): 1" (2.5 cm) turned under twice. Double-fold bottom hems on valances measure a total of 4" (10 cm): 2" (5 cm) turned under twice. Double-fold bottom hems on curtains measure a total of 8" (20.5 cm): 4" (10 cm) turned under twice.

CONTINUED

How to Sew a **ROD-POCKET TREATMENT**

C O N T I N U E D

11 Repeat steps 6 to 10 for the side hems, pressing under 2" (5 cm) first, instead of 4" (10 cm).

12 Press under ½" (1.3 cm) along the upper edge. Then, measuring from the pressed foldline, press under an amount equal to the heading height plus the rod-pocket depth. (Check your chart.) Insert pins along the lower foldline.

13 Place the folded upper edge under the presser foot of the machine, with the wrong side of the valance or curtain facing up. The bulk of the fabric is positioned to the left of the machine. The side hem should be even with the back of the presser foot, with the needle aligned to enter the fabric along the lower fold.

14 Stitch along the lower fold, across the entire width; backstitch about ½" (1.3 cm) at the beginning and the end. Remove pins as you come to them. This stitching line is the bottom of the rod pocket.

15 Measure the heading height, measuring on the wrong side, from the upper fold. Mark the stitching line, using chalk or an erasable marking pen. Pin frequently through both layers along the stitching line, inserting pins perpendicular to the line.

16 Stitch along the marked line across the entire width; backstitch at the beginning and end of the line. Remove pins as you come to them. This stitching line is the top of the rod pocket.

17 Press the valance or curtain one more time. Insert the rod into the rod pocket. Mount the rod on the brackets, following the instructions that came with the rod. Distribute the fullness evenly along the rod.

TIP Tape a small plastic bag over the end of the rod to make it slide more easily into the rod pocket.

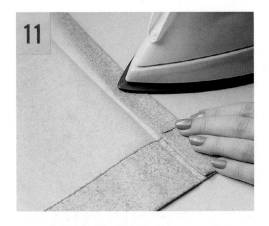

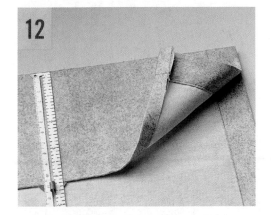

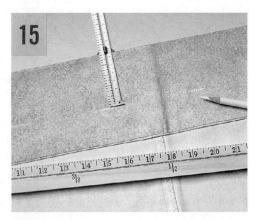

Rod-pocket VARIATIONS

Using this basic information about rod-pocket window fashions, you
can make any of the styles shown on these pages.

Straight side panels
are sewn with two
times fullness and
given a 3" (7.5 cm)
heading. They are
mounted on a wooden
pole with elbows that
have a 5" (12.5 cm)
PROJECTION.

Café curtains and
valances, mounted on
standard curtain rods,
have a 1½" (3.8 cm)
heading depth and
two times fullness.

Single panel drawn to one side is sewn with three times fullness. The 16" (40.5 cm) heading falls forward over a standard curtain rod to form an attached valance.

Floor-length sheers (below), are made from **RAILROADED** lace fabric and mounted on a standard curtain rod. They are sewn with two-and-one-half times fullness and a 2½" (6.5 cm) heading.

Print panel on a decorative rod is mounted over a sheer panel, mounted on a standard curtain rod. The panels, each with three times fullness, are pulled back at different heights to create a stunning decorator look.

Relaxed Rod-pocket CURTAINS

Many window fashions are hung from a pole or rod by means of a "pocket" or **CASING** sewn along the upper edge. These contemporary curtains are designed with deep, loose rod pockets. They look great hanging from narrow metal rods with decorative finials. Because rod-pocket styles are intended to be stationary, they can be designed as two separate panels hung at the sides of a window or as two panels that touch at the top center and are parted and pulled back to the sides. One continuous panel may cover the window or be pulled to one side or even tied in the center. For a luxurious look, the curtains can be made with extra length so that the hem brushes or puddles on the floor.

WHAT YOU'LL LEARN

How fullness affects the look of the curtain, and how to use fullness in calculating the amount of fabric to buy

How to match the design in a decorator print

How to make a rod pocket or casing

How to make deep double-fold hems

Where to put drapery weights and how to attach them

WHAT YOU'LL NEED

Decorator fabric, amount determined by working through the chart in step 1

Thread to match the fabric

Drapery weights, one for each lower corner and one for each vertical seam

Curtain rod and mounting hardware

How to Sew a RELAXED ROD-POCKET CURTAIN

1

FINISHED LENGTH, measured from the top of the rod to the bottom of the treatment:	84"	(213.5 cm)
Add 8" (20.5 cm) for the total hem depth	+ 8"	(20.5 cm)
Add 5½" (14 cm) for the rod pocket depth	+ 5½"	(14 cm)
Add ½" (1.3 cm) for ease	+ ½"	(1.3 cm)
to find the **CUT LENGTH** of each piece (see note below)	= 98"	(249 cm)
Multiply the total desired width of coverage	45"	(115 cm)
by the desired **FULLNESS**	× 2	
to find the total finished width	= 90"	(229 cm)
Add 3" (7.5 cm) for each side hem depth	+ 3"	(7.5 cm)
	+ 3"	(7.5 cm)
	+ 3"	(7.5 cm)
	+ 3"	(7.5 cm)
To find the total **CUT WIDTH** needed	= 102"	(259 cm)
Divide the total cut width by the fabric width	÷ 54"	(137 cm)
Round the number up to the nearest whole number	= 1.9	
to find the number of fabric widths needed	2	
Multiply this number by the cut length	× 98"	(249 cm)
to find the length to buy	= 196"	(498 cm)

If you buy a fabric with a **PATTERN REPEAT,** follow the chart until you have determined the cut length. Your actual cut length must be rounded up to the next number evenly divisible by the pattern repeat. For instance, if the pattern repeat is 15" (38 cm), your cut length will be 105" (267 cm), not 98" (249 cm), because 105" (266) can be evenly divided by 15 (38). Proceed with the chart using this revised cut length measurement. Because fabric stores sell fabric in whole yards (meters) or eighths of a yard (fractions of a meter), purchase the next largest amount.

LET'S BEGIN

1 Install the rod just above the window frame, following the manufacturer's directions. Measure the window and calculate the length of fabric needed for your curtain, working with the formula at left. (We used these numbers for our curtain on page 224; your numbers will probably be different.)

TIP A single width of 54" (137 cm) decorator fabric, hemmed and gathered onto a rod at one-and-one-half times fullness, will cover 32" (81.5 cm). The same panel gathered onto the rod at two times fullness will cover 24" (61 cm). Use less fullness for heavier fabrics or to allow a large pattern to be more apparent. Use more fullness for lighter-weight fabrics to create more body.

2 Preshrink your fabric (page 31). Measure and mark the location of each cut along the selvage. Cut the pieces, following the cutting guidelines on page 44. If your fabric has a pattern to match, follow the steps on page 46 to join fabric widths, and then jump to step 4, opposite. If you do not have to match a pattern, cut away the selvages, cutting just beyond the tightly woven area.

3 Pin two pieces together along the vertical edges, *inserting the pins perpendicular to the edges (p. 19)*. Stitch ½" (1.3 cm) **SEAM**, *backstitching (p. 19)* a few stitches at the beginning and end of the seam. *Remove the pins as you come to them (p. 19)*. Repeat this step until you have sewn all the pieces together for each curtain panel. If there are any *half widths,* sew them onto outer sides of panels.

4 For each seam, *finish the raw edges (p. 201)* together, using a **ZIGZAG STITCH** set at medium width and medium length. Stitch so the right-hand swing of the needle just clears the fabric edges. **PRESS** all of the seam allowances *to one side.*

5 Place the curtain facedown on an ironing surface. *Press under (p. 185)* lower edge 8" (20.5 cm), for hem. Unfold the pressed edge. Turn the cut edge back, aligning it to the pressed foldline; press outer fold.

QUICK REFERENCE

Round up to the nearest whole number. Most window treatments that have some amount of fullness in them, including rod-pocket treatments, are sewn using full and half widths of fabric. Even if your treatment requires two and one-half widths of fabric, you have to purchase three full widths, and your yardage requirements have to be determined by rounding up to the nearest whole number.

Half widths are always added at the outer edge of a curtain or valance panel. The seam is sewn along the edge that had the selvage; the side hem is sewn along the edge that was the center of the fabric width. (This is the only way you are able to match the pattern, if there is one.)

To one side. If there are two curtain panels, the seams of each panel are pressed away from the center.

How to Sew a RELAXED ROD-POCKET CURTAIN

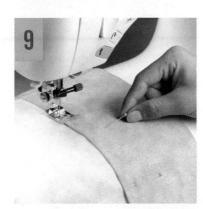

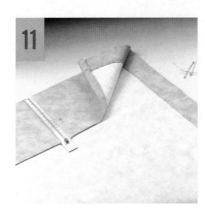

- -

CONTINUED

- -

6 Thread a hand needle with a double strand of thread (page 22). Place a drapery weight over the seam allowances, aligning the bottom of the weight to the bottom of the curtain. Hand-tack the upper flap of the weight to the seam allowances. Repeat at the bottom of all the seams.

7 Refold the hem along the pressed foldlines, encasing the raw edge to form a 4" (10 cm) *double-fold hem (p. 101)*. Pin the hem, inserting the pins perpendicular to the foldlines.

8 Place the hem under the presser foot of the machine, with the wrong side of the curtain facing up. The bulk of the fabric is positioned to the left of the machine. The side edge is under the presser foot, with the needle aligned to enter the fabric just inside the inner fold.

9 Stitch the hem along the inner fold, backstitching a few stitches at the beginning and end. Remove pins as you come to them.

TIP Double-fold bottom hems on floor-length curtains and curtains that brush on the floor measure a total of 8" (20.5 cm): 4" (10 cm) turned under twice. Double-fold hems on curtains that puddle on the floor measure a total of 2" (5 cm): 1" (2.5 cm) turned under twice. Double-fold side hems on curtains measure a total of 3" (7.5 cm): 1½" (3.8 cm) turned under twice. Double-fold bottom hems on valances measure a total of 4" (10 cm): 2" (5 cm) turned under twice.

10 Repeat steps 5 to 9 for the side hems, pressing under 3" (7.5 cm) first, instead of 8" (20.5 cm). Before refolding the side hems, slip a drapery weight into the space between the layers of the lower hem. It will be locked in place when you stitch.

TIP You may have difficulty sewing past the weight because of its thickness. Just as the presser foot toes reach the weight, stop with your needle down in the fabric and raise the presser foot. Slip another weight under the foot on the opposite side so the foot can ride on an even surface. Stitch slowly past the weight. Then stop with the needle down in the fabric, remove the loose weight, and continue on.

11 Press under ½" (1.3 cm) along the upper edge. Then, measuring from the pressed fold-line, press under 5" (12.7 cm) for the rod pocket. Insert pins along the lower foldline.

12 Place the folded upper edge under the presser foot of the machine, with the wrong side of the curtain facing up. The bulk of the fabric is positioned to the left of the machine. The side hem should be under the presser foot, with the needle aligned to enter the fabric along the lower fold.

13 Stitch along the lower fold, across the entire width; backstitch a few stitches at the beginning and the end. Remove pins as you come to them. This stitching line is the bottom of the rod pocket.

14 Press the curtain one more time. Insert the rod into the rod pocket. Mount the rod on the brackets, following the instructions that came with the rod. Distribute the fullness evenly along the rod, taking up the desired finished width.

TIP Tape a small plastic bag over the end of the rod to make it slide more easily into the rod pocket.

Grommet CURTAINS

This easy-to-sew unlined curtain boasts an unexpected design feature: grommets. Surely no one will suspect you made them yourself, with such a high-tech look. Yet the grommets and the proper fastening tools are readily available at fabric stores, and they are surprisingly easy to use. Because this involves cutting holes in your curtain panel, always test the technique first on a sample of your fabric folded to the same thickness as the finished curtain!

Use one full width of fabric for each curtain panel. For best results, select lightweight to mediumweight fabric. This is a great opportunity to use an eye-catching decorative rod, since the curtain style is relatively simple.

WHAT YOU'LL LEARN

How to install grommets

How to use drapery weights (page 235)

How to minimize bulk in multiple fabric layers

WHAT YOU'LL NEED

Decorator fabric

Thread to match

Grommets, size 0, or ¼" (6 mm), and attaching tool kit

Decorative rod and S-hooks

Drapery weights

How to Sew a GROMMET CURTAIN

1

FINISHED LENGTH, measured from ½" (1.3 cm) above the bottom of the hooks to the bottom of the treatment:		48" (122 cm)
Add the total bottom hem depth	+	8" (20.5 cm)
Add 3" for the total upper hem	+	3" (7.5 cm)
to find the CUT LENGTH of each piece	=	59" (149.8 cm)
If your treatment has two curtain panels, multiply the cut length of each piece by 2		59" (149.8 cm)
	×	2
to find the length to buy		= 118" = 3 yd. 10" (3 m)

Purchase the next largest amount possible. If you buy a fabric with a **PATTERN REPEAT,** follow the chart until you have determined the cut length (59" [149.8 cm]). Your actual cut length must be rounded up to the next number evenly divisible by the pattern repeat. Proceed with the chart using this revised cut length measurement.

LET'S BEGIN

1 Mount the rod so the bottom of the hooks will be above the window frame. Calculate the length of fabric needed for your curtain, working with the formula shown at left. (We used these numbers for our curtain on page 230; your numbers will probably be different.)

2 PRESHRINK your fabric (page 31). Measure and mark the location of each cut along the **SELVAGE.** Cut the curtain pieces, following the cutting guidelines on page 44. Cut away the selvages, cutting just beyond the tightly woven area.

3 Place the curtain facedown on a pressing surface. *Press under (p. 185)* the lower edge 8" (20.5 cm) for the hem. Unfold the pressed edge. Turn the cut edge back, aligning it to the pressed foldline; press the outer fold.

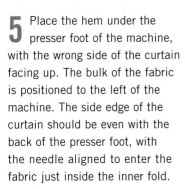

4 Refold the hem along the pressed foldlines, encasing the raw edge to form a 4" (5 cm) *double-fold hem (p. 101).* Pin the hem, *inserting the pins perpendicular to the foldlines (p. 19).*

5 Place the hem under the presser foot of the machine, with the wrong side of the curtain facing up. The bulk of the fabric is positioned to the left of the machine. The side edge of the curtain should be even with the back of the presser foot, with the needle aligned to enter the fabric just inside the inner fold.

6 Stitch the hem along the inner fold, *backstitching (p. 19)* a few stitches at the beginning and end. *Remove pins as you come to them (p. 19).*

CONTINUED

How to Sew a GROMMET CURTAIN

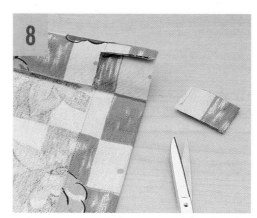

CONTINUED

---

7 Repeat steps 3 to 6 for the side hems, pressing under 3" (7.5 cm) first, instead of 8" (20.5 cm). *Insert drapery weights* into the space between the layers of the lower hem before refolding side hem.

TIP When you stitch past the drapery weight, half of the presser foot will probably travel over the weight. Place another weight under the presser foot on the opposite side to help you guide the fabric and keep your stitches even.

8 Repeat step 3 for the top hem, pressing under 3" (7.5 cm) first, instead of 8" (20.5 cm). Unfold the fabric at the corners. *Trim out excess fabric* from the inner layer, as shown, trimming to within ⅜" (1 cm) of the fold.

9 Refold the upper edge, and pin. Stitch along the inner fold, backstitching a few stitches at the beginning and end. Remove pins as you come to them.

10 Mark the placement for the grommets along the top hem, placing the end marks ¾" (2 cm) from the sides. Space the remaining marks evenly 6" to 10" (15 to 25.5 cm) apart.

TIP Closer spacing provides a more controlled upper edge, and consequently, a more even lower hem. When the grommets are spaced farther apart, the upper edge is allowed to droop gently between grommets and the lower hem will appear more uneven. To discover which look you prefer, hang your curtain panel, using safety pins, at various spacing patterns.

11 Read the manufacturer's directions for attaching the grommets, and test the technique on a sample. Attach the grommets at the marks, centering them between the fold and the stitching line of the top hem.

12 Insert decorative S-hooks through the grommets, and hang the curtain from the rod. Distribute the fullness evenly, and arrange the upper edge as desired between the hooks.

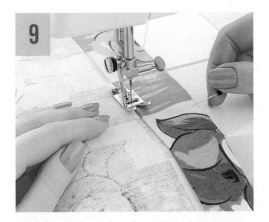

QUICK REFERENCE

Insert drapery weights. Drapery weights make your curtains hang better at the sides, by pulling gently and constantly on the side hems. Inserted between the layers of the bottom hem, they are "trapped" in place when you stitch the side hem. Because they are made of metal, avoid hitting them with the needle.

Trim out excess fabric. Eliminating some of the bulk from this area will make it easier to install the end grommets. The cutting tool will have to go through only six layers of fabric, instead of nine.

Expanding the IDEA

If the totally relaxed, spilling-onto-the-floor look is what you're after, space the grommets up to 15" (38 cm) apart. Instead of 8" (20.5 cm) for a bottom hem, allow 20" (51 cm) of extra fabric, and sew a 1" (2.5 cm) double-fold bottom hem. Turn under the hem, and arrange the curtain in dramatic puddles on the floor.

String your curtain
to the rod, using
decorative cording
or leather lacing.

For a more
decorative look,
or perhaps if
you don't care
to use grommets,
substitute clip-on
or sew-on hooks.

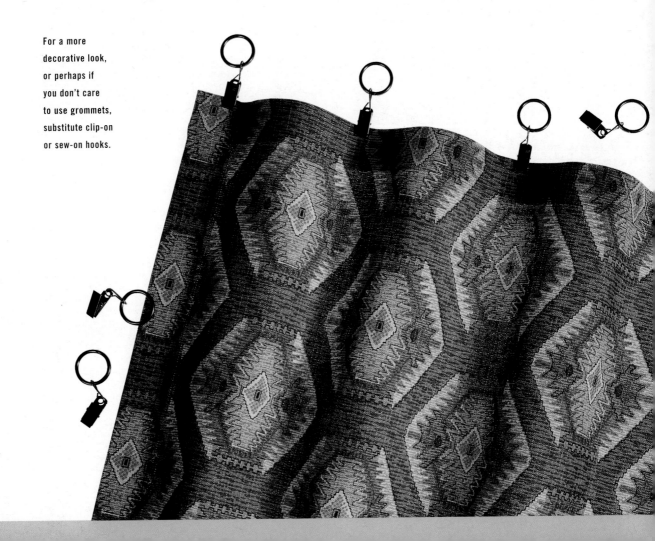

Sewing
LINENS AND MORE

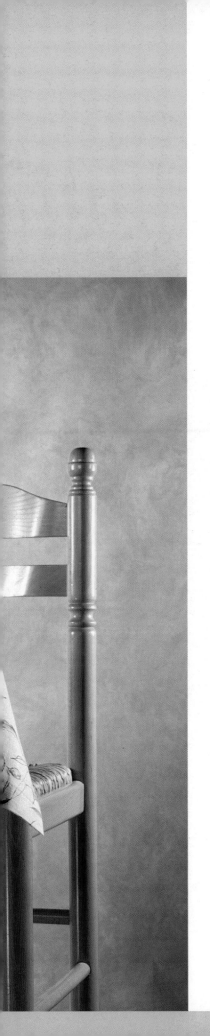

Pillow CASES

Brighten up your bedding ensemble with easy-to-sew pillow cases. Choose three coordinating fabrics: one for the main body of the case, one for the contrasting **HEM** band, and a striped fabric to make a **BIAS** trim. Look for washable cotton or cotton/polyester blend fabrics that will feel comfortable against your skin. The chart in step 1 shows the dimensions of bed pillows and the sizes to cut the pillow case body pieces for each.

WHAT YOU'LL LEARN

How to machine-baste

How to make a bias trim

How to finish raw edges with a ZIGZAG STITCH

How to encase a raw edge in a hem band

WHAT YOU'LL NEED

1¼ yd. (1.15 m) fabric for the pillow case body

⅜ yd. (0.35 m) fabric for the hem band

½ yd. (0.5 m) striped fabric for the bias trim

Rotary cutter and mat, heavy plastic quilter's ruler (optional for cutting bias trim)

Thread to blend with the fabrics

How to Sew a PILLOW CASE

LET'S BEGIN

1 Preshrink the fabrics (page 31). Cut a rectangle of fabric for the pillow case body, according to the chart, running the longer sides parallel to the **LENGTHWISE GRAIN**. Cut a rectangle of fabric for the hem band 41" × 10" (104 × 25.5 cm), running the longer sides parallel to the **CROSSWISE GRAIN**. Do not use a **SELVAGE** as an edge.

2 Cut the selvages from the striped fabric. Place the fabric on an ironing surface. Fold the fabric diagonally, turning the left side over to align to the upper edge. The lengthwise grain of the upper layer should be parallel to the crosswise grain of the lower layer. **PRESS** the fold, *taking care not to distort it.* The foldline lies on the true bias.

3 Mark a line 2" (5 cm) from the fold. Cut both layers. Then cut this bias strip in half along the foldline.

TIP If you have a rotary cutter, cutting mat, and quilter's ruler, you can easily cut these bias strips by aligning the 45° angle line on the ruler to the fabric edge and cutting the fabric diagonally along the edge of the ruler.

4 Trim the ends of both strips parallel to the stripes. Draw a line 1/4" (6 mm) from the cut ends on the wrong side of the fabric; this will be the seamline. Place the strips, right sides together, aligning the raw edges on one end. The ends of the marked lines should align, so a small triangle of fabric extends on each side. Pin, *inserting the pins perpendicular to the edges (p. 19).* Stitch on the seamline, *removing the pins as you come to them (p. 19).*

5 Press the seam allowances open. Trim off the triangular points. Press the bias strip in half, taking care not to distort the width of the strip. Cut the strip 41" (104 cm) long, cutting both ends straight across.

CONTINUED

1

PILLOW SIZE	CUT SIZE OF CASE BODY
Standard 20" × 26" (51 × 66 cm)	41" × 27" (104 × 68.5 cm)
Queen 20" × 30" (51 × 76 cm)	41" × 31" (104 × 78.5 cm)
King 20" × 36" (51 × 91.5 cm)	41" × 37" (104 × 94 cm)

2

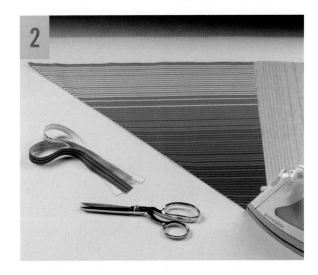

3

4

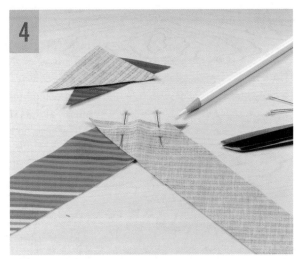

5

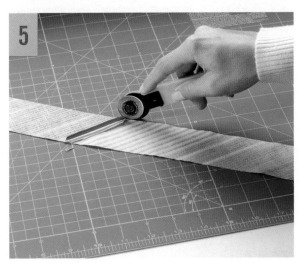

QUICK REFERENCE

Taking care not to distort it. Fabric has a lot of "give" in the bias direction, so it is easily distorted. If you simply slide the iron along the fold, it will probably grow in length and get wavy. Instead, lift and move the iron to press the fold, and continually check that to see that it lies flat.

How to Sew a PILLOW CASE

CONTINUED

---

6 Pin the bias trim to one long edge of the pillow case body. If you have selected a **DIRECTIONAL PRINT** for the body, pin the trim to the side where you want the hem. Insert the pins perpendicular to the edges, and check that the trim width is always 1" (2.5 cm). Set the machine for a long straight stitch, and **BASTE** the trim to the pillow case body, guiding the raw edges along the 3/8" (1 cm) *seam allowance guide (p. 19).* Remove pins as you come to them.

TIP If you baste the trim to the pillow case body with the trim on the underside, the trim width is less likely to become distorted. It is harder to see the pins this way, so leave the pin heads extending off the edge.

7 Press the hem in half, wrong sides together, lengthwise; unfold. Press under 1/2" (1.3 cm) on one long edge. Pin the plain edge of the hem, right side down, to the wrong side of the pillow case body. Reset the machine to a stitch length of 10 stitches per inch, which equals 2.5 mm. Stitch, guiding the raw edges along the 1/2" (1.3 cm) seam allowance guide.

8 Place the pillow case facedown on the ironing surface. Turn the hem away from the body and press along the seamline.

9 Turn the pillow case over. Turn the hem back along the foldline, just covering the inner stitching line with the folded edge of the hem. Pin. *Edgestitch (p. 309)* close to the fold, removing the pins as you come to them.

10 Fold the pillow case in half, right sides together, aligning the unfinished edges. Pin. Stitch a 1/2" (1.3 cm) seam, beginning at the fold. *Backstitch (p. 19)* a few stitches at the beginning, and **PIVOT** 1/2" (1.3 cm) from the corner. Backstitch a few stitches at the end. *Trim the seam allowances diagonally (p. 193)* at the corner where you pivoted.

11 Set the machine for a **ZIGZAG STITCH** of medium length (2.5 mm) and near maximum width (4 mm). Finish the edges of the seam allowances by stitching so that the right-hand stitches go just over the edges and the left-hand stitches go into the fabric. Turn the pillow case right side out, and give it a final pressing.

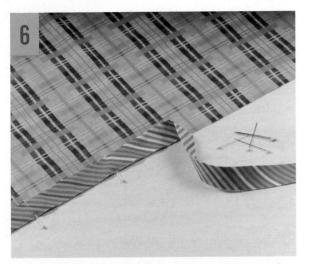

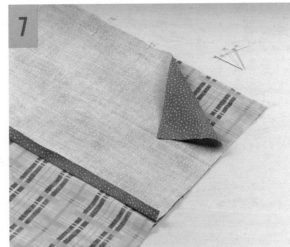

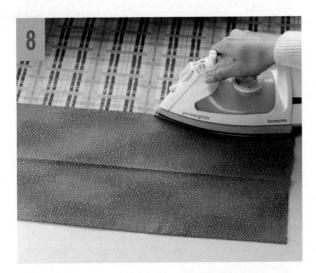

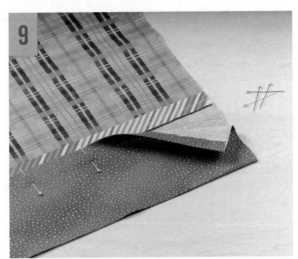

Flanged PILLOW SHAMS

FLANGED shams transform ordinary bed pillows into custom designer pillows. Because there are few measurements to take and the straight **SEAMS** and **HEMS** are easy to sew, a sham is a good beginning sewing project. Flanged shams can be made to fit standard-size, queen-size, or king-size pillows. An overlapping closure in the center of the back makes it easy to insert and remove the pillow. Select decorator fabric to coordinate with your duvet or bedspread.

WHAT YOU'LL LEARN

How to PIVOT the stitching line to make perfect square corners

How to guide your stitching line at a depth beyond the seam allowance guides

How to make a flange

How to make a lapped opening

WHAT YOU'LL NEED

1⅝ yd. (1.5 m) of 54" (137 cm) decorator fabric for each pillow sham

Thread

Masking tape

How to Sew a PILLOW SHAM

1		
PILLOW SIZE	**CUT SIZE OF FRONT**	**CUT SIZE OF EACH BACK**
Standard 20" × 26" (51 × 66 cm)	27" × 33" (68.5 × 84 cm)	27" × 19" (68.5 × 48.5 cm)
Queen 20" × 30" (51 × 76 cm)	27" × 37" (68.5 × 94 cm)	27" × 21" (68.5 × 53.5 cm)
King 20" × 36" (51 × 91.5 cm)	27" × 43" (68.5 × 109 cm)	27" × 24" (68.5 × 61 cm)

LET'S BEGIN

1 Cut a sham front and two sham back pieces according to the measurements given in the chart.

TIP Make tissue paper patterns of the pieces for easier cutting. If your fabric has a large design or stripes, you can see through the tissue paper to center the design on the sham front piece.

2 PRESS under 1" (2.5 cm) on one long edge of a back piece. Unfold the pressed edge and fold the cut edge in, aligning it to the first fold line; press the outer fold.

3 Refold the hem along the pressed foldlines, encasing the raw edge to form a 1/2" (1.3 cm) *double-fold hem (p. 101)*. Pin the hem, *inserting the pins perpendicular to the folds (p. 19)*.

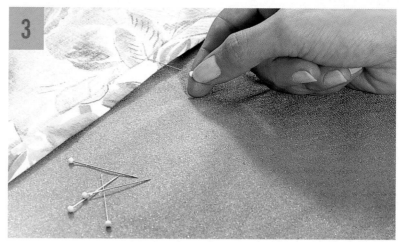

4 Set the machine for a straight stitch of 10 stitches per inch which equals 2.5 mm. Place the hem under the presser foot with the wrong side of the fabric up. Align the needle to enter the fabric just inside the inner fold. *Edgestitch (p. 309)* along the inner folded edge, *removing the pins as you come to them (p.19).*

5 Repeat steps 2 to 4 for one long edge of the other back piece. Place the sham back pieces over the sham front, right sides together, aligning the cut edges and overlapping the back hemmed edges 3" (7.5 cm). Pin the layers together around the outer edge.

TIP Pin the layers together along the back opening using safety pins. This will keep the overlapped edges in place while you sew.

6 Mark pencil dots ½" (1.3 cm) from the edges in each corner. Beginning anywhere along the outer edge, place the fabric under the presser foot, aligning the cut edges to the ½" (1.3 cm) *seam allowance guide (p. 19).* Stitch forward until you come to the dot at the first corner.

CONTINUED

How to Sew a PILLOW SHAM

CONTINUED

7 Stop the machine with the needle completely down in the fabric at the dot; lift the presser foot and turn the fabric so the next side aligns to the ½" (1.3 cm) seam guide. Lower the presser foot and continue stitching around all four sides, pivoting in this manner at each corner. Overlap the stitches ½" (1.3 cm) where they meet.

8 *Remove the fabric from the machine (p. 19)* and trim the threads close to the fabric. Press the outer edges flat to set the stitches in the seam. *Trim the seam allowances diagonally (p. 193)* at the four corners to remove excess bulk.

9 Insert a heavy cardboard tube or a seam roll (page 31) into the opening and place it under the seam. Press the seam allowances open, applying light pressure with the tip of the iron down the crease of the seam.

10 Turn the pillow sham right side out, reaching in through the overlap to pull out each corner. Insert a point turner or similar tool into the sham, gently pushing the points out to form *perfect corners (p. 193)*.

QUICK REFERENCE

Place a piece of masking tape on the bed of your machine. Whenever you want to sew a straight seam at a depth beyond the marked seam allowance guides on the throat plate, this method is handy. Use masking tape that can be easily removed.

11 Press the seamed edges lightly, centering the seamline around the outer edge. With the front facing up, pin the layers together about 3" (7.5 cm) from the four sides, inserting the pins perpendicular to the edges.

TIP Tape the back overlapped edges closed in the area of the outer flange. You can remove the tape after stitching.

12 Mark small dots 3" (7.5 cm) from the corners of the shams to help you know when to pivot. *Place a piece of masking tape on the bed of your machine* 3" (7.5 cm) to the right of the needle, parallel to the seam allowance guide.

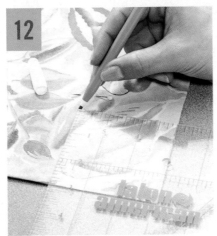

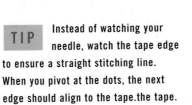

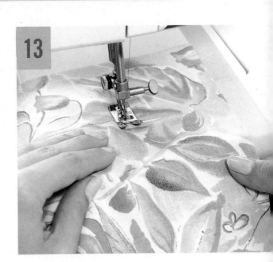

TIP Instead of watching your needle, watch the tape edge to ensure a straight stitching line. When you pivot at the dots, the next edge should align to the tape.the tape.

13 Stitch the pillow sham flange, guiding the seamed edge along the tape. Remove the pins as you come to them. Stop stitching with the needle down to pivot at each corner. Overlap the stitches 1/2" (1.3 cm) where they meet.

Duvet COVER

A duvet cover keeps a duvet or comforter clean and is easily removed for laundering. The sewing steps are fairly simple; the difficulty comes in handling large expanses of fabric. Set up a card table next to your sewing machine station to help with the task. Duvet covers usually require two or more widths of fabric sewn together for the front and back: one full width down the center with equal partial widths along the sides. Choose a lightweight, firmly woven, washable fabric. Be aware that fabrics with large **PATTERN REPEATS** could result in a lot of wasted fabric.

WHAT YOU'LL LEARN

How to match a pattern when using more than one width of decorator fabric in a project

How to make a lapped button closure

How to sew a buttonhole

WHAT YOU'LL NEED

Fabric for top and underside of duvet cover, amount determined in step 1

Thread

Buttons, 1/2" to 5/8" (1.3 to 1.5 cm) diameter

Twill tape (page 36)

Four small plastic rings

How to Sew a DUVET COVER

1

FINISHED LENGTH of the duvet cover		86" (218.5 cm)
Add 1" (2.5 cm) for seam allowances	+	1" (2.5 cm)
to find the cut length of the front	=	87" (221 cm)
Finished length of the duvet cover		86" (218.5 cm)
Add 8½" (21.8 cm)	+	8½" (21.8 cm)
to find the cut length of the back	=	94½" (240 cm)
FINISHED WIDTH of the duvet cover		86" (218.5 cm)
Add 1" (2.5 cm) for seam allowances	+	1" (2.5 cm)
to find the cut width of the cover	=	87" (221 cm)
Divide the cut width		87" (221 cm)
by the fabric width	÷	54" (137 cm)
Round up to the next whole number		1.6
to find the number of widths needed		2
Multiply the number of widths		2
by the cut length of the front	×	87" (221 cm)
to find the amount needed for the front	=	174" (442 cm)
Multiply the number of widths		2
by the cut length of the back	×	94½" (240 cm)
to find the amount needed for the back	=	189" (480 cm)
Add the amount needed for the front		174" (442 cm)
to the amount needed for the back	+	189" (480 cm)
to find the total amount needed	=	363" (922 cm)
Convert to yards (meters); round up		=10⅛ yd. (9.25 m)

If you buy a fabric with a pattern repeat, the cut lengths must be rounded up to the next number evenly divisible by the pattern repeat length. In our example, if the repeat length is 7" (18 cm) the cut lengths are 91" and 98" (231 and 249 cm) instead of 87" and 94½" (221 and 240 cm). Proceed with your figures using the revised cut lengths.

LET'S BEGIN

1 Measure your duvet or comforter to determine the *finished size* of the cover. Use this formula to determine the **CUT LENGTH** and **CUT WIDTH** of the pieces and the amount of fabric you will need. We are using numbers for a queen-size duvet cover; yours may be different.

2 Prepare your fabric (page 31). *Measure and mark the location of each cut* along the **SELVAGE**. Cut the pieces, following the cutting guidelines (pages 44 and 45). If you do not have to match a pattern (page 46), cut away the selvages, cutting just beyond the tightly woven area. Cut one front and one back piece in half lengthwise.

3 Pin a half-width piece to the full-width front piece, right sides together, along the lengthwise edges, *inserting the pins perpendicular to the edges (p. 19).* Match the pattern, if necessary, following the guidelines on page 46. Place the pinned edges under the presser foot with the edges aligned to the ½" (1.3 cm) *seam allowance guide (p. 19).* The bulk of the fabric is to the left of the machine.

FRONT   BACK

| HALF WIDTH | FULL WIDTH | HALF WIDTH | HALF WIDTH | FULL WIDTH | HALF WIDTH |

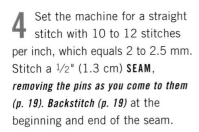

4 Set the machine for a straight stitch with 10 to 12 stitches per inch, which equals 2 to 2.5 mm. Stitch a ½" (1.3 cm) **SEAM**, *removing the pins as you come to them (p. 19). Backstitch (p. 19)* at the beginning and end of the seam.

5 Stitch the second half-width piece to the opposite side of the full-width piece, following steps 3 and 4. Set the machine for a wide **ZIGZAG STITCH** with a length of 10 stitches per inch, which equals 2.5 mm. Stitch close to the edge of each **SEAM ALLOWANCE** so that the right-hand stitches go just over the edge. This step, called a seam finish, keeps the edges from raveling.

CONTINUED

QUICK REFERENCE

Finished size. The finished size of the cover is usually the same size as the duvet measurements. For a snug fit over a down comforter, the cover may be up to 2" (5 cm) shorter and narrower than the comforter.

Measure and mark the location of each cut. Use pins or pencil marks on the selvage to mark off all the cut lengths of the pieces. Double-check your measurements before you begin cutting to avoid costly mistakes.

How to Sew a DUVET COVER

CONTINUED

6 **PRESS** over the stitching line of the closed seams; then open the seam allowances and press them again. Measure and cut the duvet front to the exact cut width, as determined in the chart on page 255.

TIP It may be easier to fold the pieced top in half lengthwise and measure one-half the width plus ½" (1.3 cm) from the fold line. Remember the partial widths on the sides should be equal.

7 Repeat steps 3 to 6 for the duvet cover back. Mark a line 12" (30.5 cm) from the lower edge of the back. Cut on the marked line.

8 Press under 3" (7.5 cm) along the upper edge of the small back piece. Unfold and turn the cut edge in, aligning it to the first fold line. Press outer fold.

9 Refold on the first fold line encasing the raw edge to form a 1½" (3.8 cm) *double-fold hem (p. 101).* Pin the hem in place, inserting the pins perpendicular to the folds. *Edgestitch (p. 309)* along the inner fold line. (Remember to set the machine back to a straight stitch.)

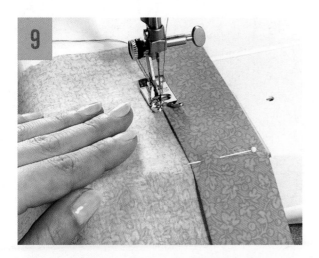

QUICK REFERENCE

Length for buttonholes. The correct buttonhole length is equal to the diameter of the button plus the thickness of the button. Wrap a tape measure around your button, note the length, and divide by 2 to determine the correct length of the buttonhole. Practice on a scrap of fabric before sewing buttonholes into your duvet cover.

10 Press and stitch 1½" (3.8 cm) double-fold hem on the lower edge of the large back piece. Mark the placement and *length for buttonholes* on the hem of the large back piece, centered between the fold and stitching line. Place outer marks 6" (15 cm) from each side and the others spaced about 10" to 12" (25.5 to 30.5 cm) apart. Run the marks perpendicular to the hem edge.

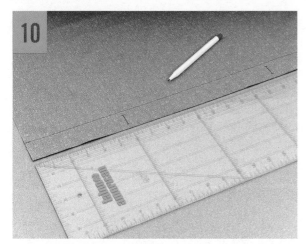

11 Attach your buttonhole presser foot or buttonhole attachment. Follow the instructions in your owner's manual to sew buttonholes over the marked lines. Apply liquid fray preventer (page 33) to the buttonholes; allow to dry and then cut the buttonholes open.

TIP Use a small, sharply pointed scissors to cut the button-holes open. Insert pins across the buttonhole ends to prevent clipping too far. Clip from the center into each end.

CONTINUED

CONTINUED

12 Overlap the hemlines of the back pieces 1½" (3.8 cm), and pin them together at the outer edges. Mark the placement for the buttons on the hemline of the small back piece. Sew buttons over the marks, following the steps on page 95.

13 Button the back pieces together; place the duvet cover back over the front, right sides together, aligning the outer edges. Pin the layers together, inserting the pins perpendicular to the edges. Mark dots ½" (1.3 cm) from each corner.

14 Fold a 20" (51 cm) piece of twill tape (page 27) in half. Align the folded edge to the outer edge of the duvet cover ½" (1.3 cm) from each corner, and pin in place.

15 Stitch a ½" (1.3 cm) seam around the edge of the duvet cover, **PIVOTING** at each corner and catching the folded end of the twill tape in the stitching. Overlap the stitches ½" (1.3 cm) where they meet.

12

16 *Remove the fabric from the machine (p. 19)* and trim the threads close to the fabric. Press the outer edges flat to set the stitches in the seam. *Trim the seam allowances diagonally (p. 193)* at the four corners to remove excess bulk. Avoid cutting through the twill tape.

17 Unbutton the opening. Insert a heavy cardboard tube or a seam roll (page 31) into the opening and place it under the seam. Press the seam allowances open, applying light pressure with the tip of the iron down the crease of the seam.

18 Hand-stitch a plastic ring at each corner of your duvet or comforter. Spread the duvet or comforter out over your new duvet cover and tie the twill tape to the rings at each corner. Now turn the duvet cover right side out, encasing the duvet or comforter inside.

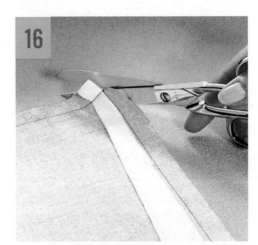

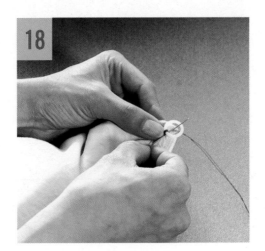

Shower CURTAIN

An easy-to-sew bathroom shower curtain adds a decorator touch. You can choose fabric to coordinate with your fixtures, tile color, and window treatment fabric. Grommets attached along the upper hem align to the grommets in a standard shower curtain liner. The **FRENCH SEAM** gives the curtain a neat appearance from both sides and keeps raw edges hidden. To make the shower curtain washable, select a washable fabric and preshrink it before you cut it.

WHAT YOU'LL LEARN

How to sew a French seam

How to sew double-fold hems

How to minimize bulk in multiple fabric layers

How to install grommets

WHAT YOU'LL NEED

4⅝ yd. (4.25 m) fabric

Water-soluble fabric marker

Twelve grommets, size 0 or ¼" (6 mm), and attaching tool

Thread to match the fabric

How to Sew a SHOWER CURTAIN

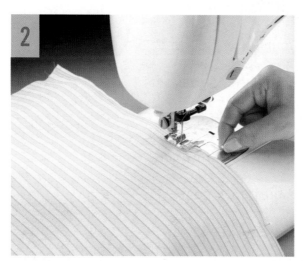

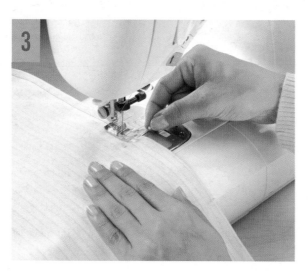

LET'S BEGIN

1 Preshrink the fabric (page 31). Cut two full-width pieces 82" (208.5 cm) long, following the cutting guidelines on page 44. Cut away the **SELVAGES** evenly, cutting just beyond the tightly woven area. Pin two vertical edges, wrong sides together, *inserting the pins perpendicular to the edges (p. 19).*

2 Place the fabric under the presser foot, aligning the raw edges to the ¹⁄₄" *(6 mm) seam allowance guide.* Stitch ¹⁄₄" (6 mm) **SEAM**, *backstitching (p. 19)* at the beginning and end of the seam. *Remove the pins as you come to them (p. 19). Remove the fabric from the machine (p. 19).*

3 **PRESS** the seam allowances to one side. Then fold the fabric, right sides together, with the seam exactly on the fold; press. Pin, inserting the pins perpendicular to the fold. Stitch again, guiding the folded edge along the ³⁄₈" (1 cm) seam allowance guide, and removing the pins as you come to them. This encases the raw edges in what is known as a French seam. Press the seam allowances to one side.

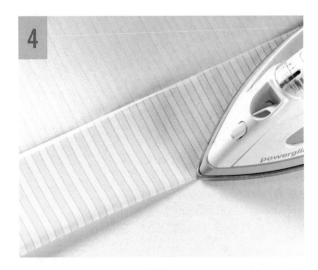

4 Cut one vertical edge of the shower curtain so the total width is 76" (193 cm). The finished width of a standard shower curtain is 72" (183 cm). This allows 2" (5 cm) on each side for hemming. Place the curtain facedown on a pressing surface. *Press under (p. 185)* the lower edge 6" (15 cm) for the hem. Unfold the pressed edge. Turn the cut edge back, aligning it to the pressed foldline; press the outer fold.

5 Refold the hem along the pressed foldlines, encasing the raw edge to form a 3" (7.5 cm) *double-fold hem (p. 101).* Pin the hem, inserting the pins perpendicular to the foldlines.

6 Stitch the hem, guiding the presser foot along the inner fold of the hem. Backstitch a few stitches at the beginning and end. Remove pins as you come to them.

CONTINUED

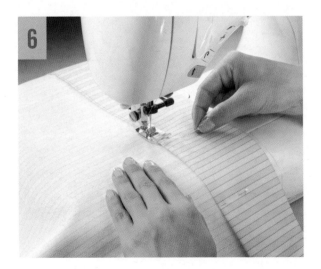

QUICK REFERENCE

¼" (6 mm) seam allowance guide. The seam allowance guide on the throat plate may not have a line for ¼" (6 mm). On some machines, the distance from the tip of the needle to the right edge of the presser foot measures exactly ¼" (6 mm). If this is not true of your machine, mark a ¼" (6 mm) seam guide on the bed of the machine with tape.

How to Sew a SHOWER CURTAIN

CONTINUED

7 Repeat steps 4 to 6 for the side hems, pressing under 2" (5 cm) first, instead of 6" (15 cm). Follow step 4 for the top hem, pressing under 4" (10 cm) first. Unfold the fabric at the corners. *Trim out the excess fabric* from the inner layer, as shown, trimming to within 3/8" (1 cm) of the fold.

8 Refold the upper edge, and pin. Stitch along the inner fold, backstitching a few stitches at the beginning and end. Remove pins as you come to them.

9 Mark the placement for 12 evenly spaced grommets along the upper hem, using a fabric marker. Position them 3/4" (2 cm) from the upper edge with the outer marks centered in the side hems. Read the manufacturer's directions for attaching the grommets, and test the technique on a sample of fabric folded several times. Attach the grommets.

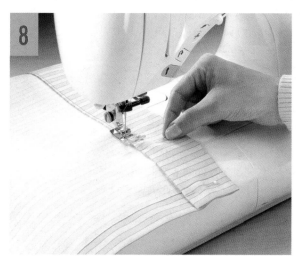

QUICK REFERENCE

Trim out the excess fabric. Eliminating some of the bulk from this area will make it easier to install the end grommets. The cutting tool will have to go through six layers of fabric instead of nine.

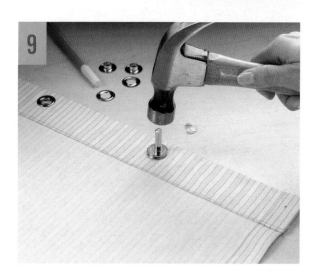

MORE IDEAS

Make a coordinating valance for your
shower curtain, following the directions for a
self-lined rectangle valance on page 188.
Plan the valance to have a finished width of
72" (18 cm) and a finished length of
10" (25.5 cm). Instead of grommets, stitch
buttonholes along the upper hem of the shower
curtain and the upper edge of the valance.

Button-tufted CUSHION

Button-tufted cushions can be custom shaped to fit chairs, benches, or window seats. They have inner cores of batting-wrapped foam and can be anchored to the furniture with fabric ties. Buttons keep the filling from shifting and accent the "stuffed" appearance of the cushion. Since tufted cushion covers are not usually removed, zippers or other closures are not necessary. Tightly woven decorator fabric with a stain-resistant finish, available in endless colors and designs, is a great choice for this project.

WHAT YOU'LL LEARN

How to make a simple foam and batting cushion and a cover to fit it

How to make ties

How to button-tuft a cushion

WHAT YOU'LL NEED

Fabric, amount determined after making pattern

Polyurethane foam (page 37), 1" (2.5 cm) thick

Polyester upholstery batting (page 35)

Thread to match

Buttons to cover (page 28); two for each button tuft

Button and carpet thread (page 36)

Long needle with a large eye

How to Sew a BUTTON-TUFTED CUSHION

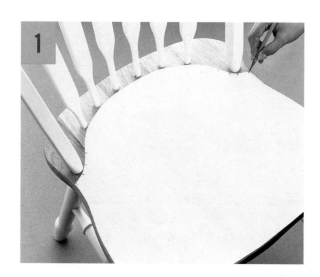

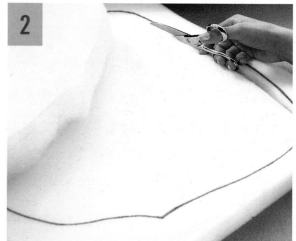

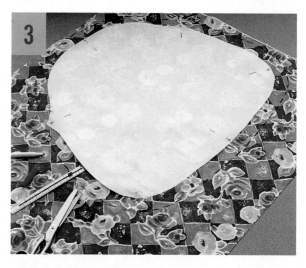

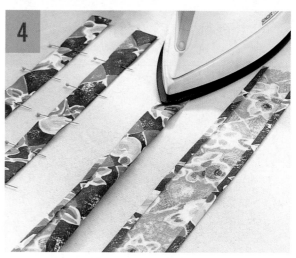

LET'S BEGIN

1 Make a paper pattern of the seat to be covered by the cushion, rounding any sharp corners. Simplify the shape as much as you can. Cut out the pattern and check it for *symmetry* and fit. Mark the pattern where the ties would be placed.

TIP A piece of wrapping paper or newsprint will make a sturdy pattern. You will be using this pattern for the foam, the batting, and the fabric.

2 Cut two pieces of polyester upholstery batting, using the pattern for size. Place the pattern on the foam and trace around it, using a felt-tip pen. *Cut the foam* 1/4" (6 mm) inside the marked line.

3 Place the pattern on the right side of the decorator fabric. Mark the cutting line 1" (2.5 cm) from the edge of the pattern; this allows for ¹⁄₂" (1.3 cm) **SEAM ALLOWANCES** and ¹⁄₂" (1.3 cm) for the thickness of the foam and batting. Cut the cushion top out on the marked line. Cut the cushion bottom, using the top as a pattern. Remember to *cut the covers on straight grain*. Transfer any marks for ties from the pattern to the cushion front. Omit steps 4 to 6 if your cushion will not have ties.

4 Cut two 2¹⁄₂" × 16" (6.5 × 40.5 cm) fabric strips for each tie, following fabric grainlines. **PRESS** under ¹⁄₄" (6 mm) on the long edges of each strip. Then press them in half lengthwise, wrong sides together, aligning the pressed edges. Pin.

5 Set the machine for a straight stitch of 10 stitches per inch, which equals 2.5 mm. *Edgestitch (p. 309)* along the open edge of each tie. Leave both ends of the ties open. Tie a single knot at one end of each tie, enclosing the raw edges in the knot.

CONTINUED

QUICK REFERENCE

Symmetry. Hand-drawn patterns can easily turn out a bit askew. Fold the pattern in half to check that the edges are identical and make any necessary adjustments. Then recheck it on the seat.

Cut the foam. Polyurethane foam with a thickness of 1" (2.5 cm) can be easily cut with sewing shears. Other options include a serrated kitchen knife or an electric knife. Be sure to hold the blade perpendicular to the foam as you cut. Some fabric stores will cut the foam for you if you prepare your pattern before you go shopping.

Cut the covers on straight grain. Ideally, the center of the cushion, front to back, runs on the **LENGTHWISE GRAIN** of the fabric. If you are using a **DIRECTIONAL PRINT**, cut the pieces so the top of the design is at the back of the cushion. Center large design motifs.

How to Sew a BUTTON-TUFTED CUSHION

CONTINUED

6 Pin the unfinished ends of the ties to the right side of the cushion front at the marked positions. Stitch the ties in place 3/8" (1 cm) from the edge, *removing the pins as you come to them (p. 19)*.

TIP To make sure the ties don't get in the way when you stitch the outer seam, pin the free ends to the cushion front. Use safety pins to avoid scratching your hands when you turn the cover right side out.

7 Place the cushion top and bottom right sides together, aligning the outer edges; pin, *inserting the pins perpendicular to the edges (page 19). Leave an opening for inserting the foam.*

8 Place the pieces under the presser foot, just ahead of the opening. Align the cut edges to the 1/2" (1.3 cm) *seam allowance guide (p. 19)*. Remove the pin that marks the opening before lowering the presser foot.

9 *Backstitch (p. 19)* three or four stitches; stop. Then, stitching forward, stitch the seam on all sides. End the seam at the opposite side of the opening; backstitch three or four stitches.

QUICK REFERENCE

Leave an opening for inserting the foam. The size of
the opening depends on the size of the cushion. For chair
seats, leave at least 8" (20.5 cm) at the back of the cushion; for longer cushions, leave an entire short end open.

Clip the seam allowance. Before turning a curved
seam right side out, clip the seam allowance perpendicular to the stitches every 1/4" to 1/2" (6 mm to 1.3
cm). This allows the seam to open up for pressing or to
lie along the edge without any bubbles or folds. Clip up
to, but not through, the stitches. The sharper the curve,
the closer together the clips should be.

Turn back the top seam allowance. It is difficult to fit
a seam roll or hard cardboard tube into a cushion cover
to press the seam allowances open. Turning back and
pressing one seam allowance helps to separate them
and make the seam look neater from the right side.

10 ***Clip the seam allowances*** of
any curved areas. Press
the seam flat. ***Turn back the top seam
allowance***, and press, using light
pressure with the tip of your iron
down the crease of the seam. Press
back 1/2" (1.3 cm) seam allowance
on the cushion cover back in the
open area.

11 Reach in through the
opening to turn the cushion
cover completely right side out.
Press lightly, centering the seam
around the outer edge. Make sure
the ties are sewn securely into the
seam at the correct positions.

CONTINUED

How to Sew a BUTTON-TUFTED CUSHION

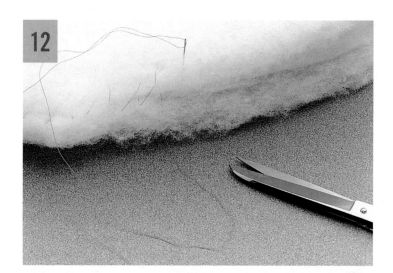

CONTINUED

12 Place the foam between the layers of upholstery batting. Hand-stitch the edges of the batting together, encasing the foam.

13 Fold the batted foam in half and insert it into the cushion cover. Unfold the foam, smoothing the fabric over the batting. Slipstitch (page 22) the opening closed. You can use your cushion like this if you prefer. However, if you want to add button tufting, continue with the next steps.

14 *Mark the button placement* on both sides of the cushion. Follow the manufacturer's directions for making covered buttons and the general guidelines on page 95. You will need two buttons for every tuft.

15 Cut two or three 18" (46 cm) strands of button and carpet thread (page 36); insert all the strands through the button shank, and secure at the middle of the thread with a double knot.

Mark the button placement. Button placements are usually equally spaced in all directions. Use the pattern piece to plan out the placement, trying different arrangements. A chair seat, for instance, can have four buttons arranged in a square or a fifth button in the center.

16 Insert the ends of the thread strands through the eye of a long needle. Insert the needle through the cushion to the back side. Remove the strands from the needle and divide them into two groups.

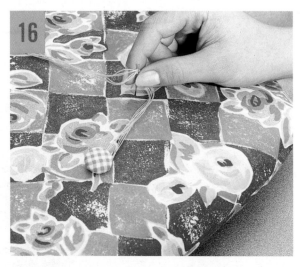

17 Thread a second button onto one group of threads. Tie a single knot, using both thread groups; pull the strands until the buttons are tight against the cushion, creating an indentation. Wrap the thread two or three times around the button shank and tie a double knot. Trim the thread tails so they are hidden under the button, but not so short that the knot could loosen. Repeat steps 15 to 17 for each tuft, keeping the indentations equal.

TIP A drop of liquid fray preventer (page 33) on the double knots would secure them permanently.

MORE IDEAS

Sew welting to the cushion front piece before adding ties or sewing it to the back. Follow pages 331 to 333, steps 4 to 10. (top left)

Sew pregathered ruffles or eyelet trim to the cushion front piece before sewing it to the back. Begin and end the trim at the ties, avoiding the cushion back. (top middle)

Make a removable cushion cover by eliminating the button tufting and adding a zipper along a straight side of the cushion. Follow the directions for zipper application on pages 134 to 137. (top right)

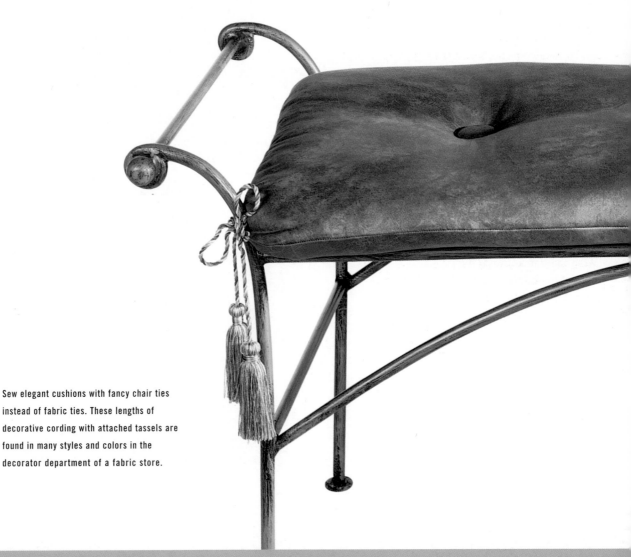

Sew elegant cushions with fancy chair ties instead of fabric ties. These lengths of decorative cording with attached tassels are found in many styles and colors in the decorator department of a fabric store.

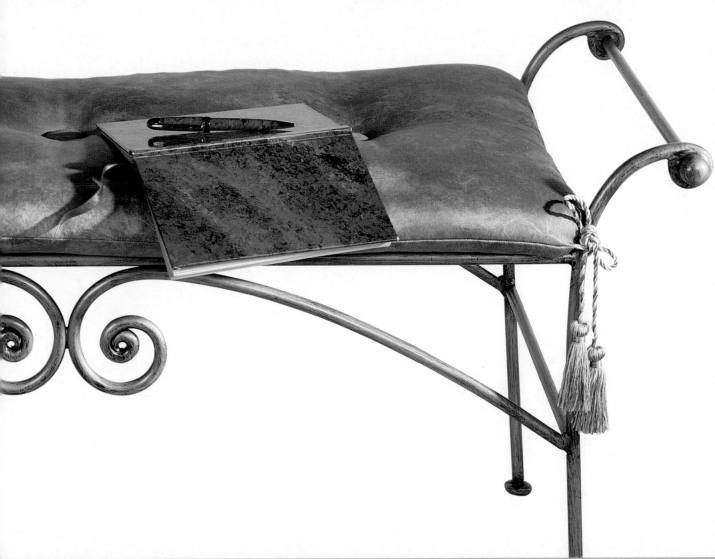

Reversible SEAT COVERS

Simple seat covers give your dining room or kitchen chairs a fresh look. These **LINED-TO-THE-EDGE** covers are made with two coordinating decorator fabrics, so they can be flipped over for an instant décor change. **DARTS** sewn at the front corners shape the covers to fit the chair seats smoothly. The back corners are held in place with a button tab that wraps around the back of the leg. These covers are suitable for armless chairs that have open backs and smooth, straight sides and fronts. Because the amount of fabric needed depends on your chair size and the fabric design size, it is a good idea to make the pattern first and take it with you when you shop for fabric.

How to Sew a REVERSIBLE SEAT COVER

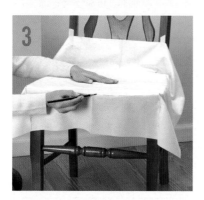

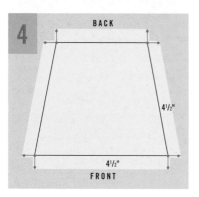

BACK

4½"

4½"

FRONT

LET'S BEGIN

1 Measure the chair seat side to side and front to back. Add 10" (25.5 cm) in each direction. *Cut or tear* a **MUSLIN** square to this size to make a pattern. Press the muslin pattern in half in both directions. Unfold. Center the pattern on the chair seat, allowing it to fall down over the front and sides. At the back, turn the pattern up along the legs. If necessary, tape the pattern in place.

2 Mark a dot at one front corner. Pinch the fabric together from the dot down, bringing the front to meet the side. Pin out the excess fabric, inserting the pins parallel to the chair leg, forming a dart. Mark lines on both sides of the dart from the dot down to the bottom. Repeat on the other front corner.

3 Mark dots at the back of the seat, at the inside front corners of the chair legs. (If your chair legs are round, mark each dot at a point in line with the front and side of the leg.) Trace the outline of the chair seat on the pattern.

4 Remove the pattern from the chair; remove the pins. Draw lines 4½" (11.5 cm) outside the traced seat lines. At the back corners, draw lines from the dots to the outer lines, forming squares. (These will be stitching lines.) Mark **PIVOT** points (shown in blue) on the stitching lines ½" (1.3 cm) from the outer edge. Draw cutting lines (shown in red) ½" (1.3 cm) outside the stitching lines at the legs and at the front darts. Fold the pattern in half to make sure it is symmetrical, and make any necessary corrections. Cut out the pattern on the outer lines.

5 Place the pattern on the printed (top) fabric, aligning the front-to-back crease with the **LENGTHWISE GRAIN** and the side-to-side crease with the **CROSSWISE GRAIN**. Position the pattern so that the intersection of the creases is at the exact *center of a design motif*. Cut out the seat cover top. *Transfer the pivot points and dart dots to the wrong side of the fabric.*

6 Cut out the remaining seat cover tops, using the first piece as a guide. This will make it easier to center the design motifs. Place each of the tops on the bottom fabric, right sides together. Pin near the outer edges. Cut them out; remove the pins.

7 Fold the dart on one front corner, right sides together, aligning the raw edges. Pin together, *inserting pins perpendicular to the edges (p. 19)*. Place the fabric under the presser foot, aligning the cut edges to the ½" (1.3 cm) *seam allowance guide (p. 19),* with the open end of the dart under the presser foot. Set the machine for a straight stitch of 12 stitches per inch, which equals 2 mm. *Backstitch (p. 19)* to the end. Then stitch forward, *removing the pins as you come to them (p. 19)*. Stitch to the edge of the fold, and back-stitch a few stitches. *Remove the fabric from the machine (p. 19).*

CONTINUED

QUICK REFERENCE

Cut or tear. Muslin is an inexpensive cotton fabric. If you make a small cut in the selvage and pull it apart, it will easily tear in a straight line across the fabric. You will have to cut again at the other selvage. Then repeat the procedure in the other direction to tear it to the desired size.

Center of a design motif. The designs of a decorator fabric are printed at regularly repeating intervals lengthwise and crosswise. For best results, you should center a design motif on each of the chair seat covers. Depending on the size of the design, you will probably be wasting some fabric. It is a good idea to make the pattern before you buy the fabric, and take the pattern along so you'll know exactly how much to buy.

Transfer the pivot points and dart dots to the wrong side of the fabric. Run a pin through each dot from the right side of the pattern. On the back side of the cover fabric, where the pins exit, mark the dots using pencil, chalk, or fabric marker.

How to Sew a REVERSIBLE SEAT COVER

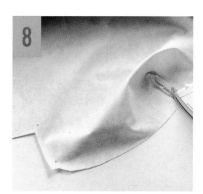

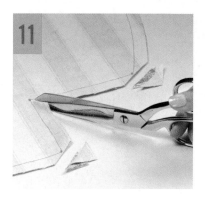

CONTINUED

8 Repeat step 7 for the remaining front corners on the top and bottom pieces. **PRESS** the seam allowances of the darts open.

TIP When you press the dart seam allowances open, the fabric at the end of the dart will fold down in a triangle shape, with the top of the triangle at the tip of the dart. Hold the corner so the right side of the dart is flat on the pressing surface. Press the triangle flat, using the tip of the iron.

9 Place the top and bottom seat covers right sides together aligning the raw edges; pin. Align the seams of the front darts, *inserting pins in the wells of the seams.* Place the fabric under the presser foot near the center of the back edge, so that the cut edges are aligned to the 1/2" (1.3 cm) seam allowance guide. Backstitch a few stitches. Then stitch forward, guiding the cut edges along the 1/2" (1.3 cm) seam allowance guide. Remove the pins as you come to them.

10 Stop stitching at the first corner, leaving the needle down in the fabric. (Turn the handwheel until the needle is down.) Raise the presser foot, and turn the fabric. Lower the presser foot, and continue. **PIVOT** in the same way at each corner. Stop stitching about 6" (15 cm) from where you began; backstitch a few stitches. This leaves an opening for turning the cover right side out.

11 *Trim the seam allowances diagonally (p. 193)* at the outer corners. *Clip to, but not through (p. 209)* the stitches at the inner corners

12 *Turn back the top seam allowance and press (p. 271),* applying light pressure with the tip of the iron down the crease of the seam. In the area of the opening, turn back and press the seam allowances 1/2" (1.3 cm).

13 Turn the cover right side out through the opening. Insert a point turner or similar tool into the opening and gently push the pivot points out to form *perfect corners (p. 193).* Push the seam out so that it is centered all around the outer edge; press. Align the folded edges of the opening and pin them closed. *Edgestitch (p. 309)* around the seat cover, stitching the opening closed; pivot at the corners. Overlap the stitches about 1/2" (1.3 cm) where they meet.

14 Mark placement lines for the buttonholes parallel to and 1" (2.5 cm) above the lower side edges. Mark lines that equal the diameter plus the thickness of the buttons, with one end 1" (2.5 cm) from the vertical edges. Attach your buttonhole presser foot or buttonhole attachment. Follow the instructions in your owner's manual to stitch the buttonholes over the marked lines. Apply liquid fray preventer (page 33) to the buttonholes; allow it to dry. Cut the buttonholes open, using a buttonhole cutter or small, sharp scissors.

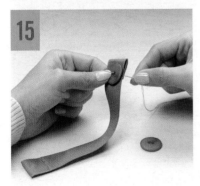

QUICK REFERENCE

Inserting pins in the wells of the seams. By pinning the darts together with a pin directly in the center of the seamlines, you are making sure that the darts will line up perfectly on the right side of the cover. Stitch up to these pins as close as you can before removing them.

15 Place the cover on the chair seat. At the back of one chair leg, measure the distance between buttonholes. Cut ribbon 4" (10 cm) longer than this measurement. Turn under 1" (2.5 cm) on each end of the ribbon; press. Turn the raw ends under again, aligning them to the pressed folds and encasing the raw edges. Stitch across the inner folds, forming *double-fold hems (p. 101).* Hand-stitch a button (page 95) to the center of each hem. Repeat for the other leg. Button the chair seat cover in place.

Synthetic Fleece THROW

When there's a chill in the air, you'll be cuddled up cozy in your synthetic fleece throw. Not just for cold-weather climates, synthetic fleece is a comfortable choice for cool southern mornings and evenings, too. The contemporary flowers are raw-edge APPLIQUÉS with fleece pompom centers. Because the cut edges of synthetic fleece don't ravel, a throw requires very little sewing, and edges can simply be cut into fringe.

WHAT YOU'LL LEARN

How to use a rotary cutter and mat

How to sew raw-edge appliqués

Quick and easy tricks for cutting fringe

Synthetic fleece might be your new favorite fabric

WHAT YOU'LL NEED

2 yd. (1.85 m) polyester fleece for the throw

¼ yd. (0.25 m) fleece for flower appliqués

⅛ yd. (0.15 m) fleece for flower centers

Paper for drawing the appliqué pattern

Rotary cutter and mat

Metal or heavy plastic straightedge

Temporary fabric adhesive

Narrow masking tape; pencil

Thread to match the fabrics

4" (10 cm) square of cardboard

How to Sew a SYNTHETIC FLEECE THROW

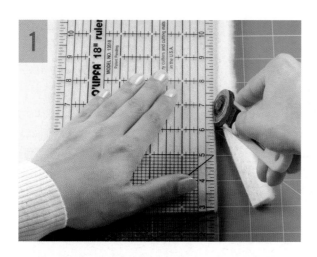

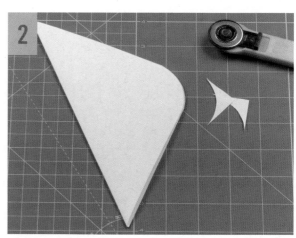

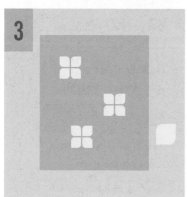

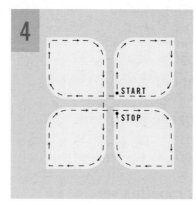

3 Position the flowers in blocks of four petals each, with the square corners at the centers and outer edges of the flowers. Space the petals evenly 3/8" (1 cm) apart. Spray the wrong side of the petals with **TEMPORARY FABRIC ADHESIVE**, following the manufacturer's directions. Adhere them in place.

TIP To protect your work surface from overspray, place the pieces in the bottom of a box.

4 Insert a ballpoint or universal point needle into the machine (page 10). Wind a bobbin with thread to match the throw fabric, and insert it into the machine. Thread the upper machine with a color that matches the petals. *Edgestitch (p. 309)* around petals of one flower in one continuous stitching line, beginning at the center point of one petal. Stitch slowly around the curves, stopping and turning fabric as needed. **PIVOT** fabric at the square corners. Overlap a few stitches where they meet. Repeat for each of the flowers.

LET'S BEGIN

1 Square off the ends of the fleece and trim off the **SELVAGES**, using a *rotary cutter and mat (p. 285)* with a metal or heavy plastic straightedge.

2 Cut out a 5" (12.7 cm) paper square for the appliqué pattern. Fold it in half diagonally, and round the two open corners. Unfold. Using the pattern, cut out 12 flower petals from the appliqué fleece.

TIP By threading the machine in this way, the stitches will be less visible on both sides of the throw. They will simply sink into the fleece. The back of the throw will look as if it has been quilted.

5 Place a strip of narrow masking tape 5" (12.7 cm) from one end of the throw. Mark the tape every 1/2" (1.3 cm). Using a rotary cutter and mat and a straightedge, cut fabric perpendicular to the tape at each mark, fringing the edge. Remove the tape. Repeat at the other end. Tie a knot at the top of each fringe strip, tying all of them in the same direction for best appearance.

TIP You may be able to use the same strip of tape on the opposite end. It only has to be slightly sticky to serve its purpose.

6 Cut the pompom fabric into four 1/2" × 30" (1.3 × 76 cm) strips on the crosswise grain; trim off the selvages at the ends. Stretch the strips to make them curl. Cut one of the strips into three pieces for the ties.

7 Wrap a long strip around a 4" (10 cm) square of cardboard. Slide the loops off the cardboard and tie them around the center with a short strip forming a pompom. Cut the loops, if desired. Repeat to make the other pompoms. Trim the tie ends to the same length as the other pieces. Hand-stitch a pompom to the center of each flower.

QUICK REFERENCE

Rotary cutter and mat. These time-saving tools for cutting fabric may take a little practice and serious precautions. The blade on a rotary cutter is extremely sharp. Cut slowly, guiding the blade along the straightedge. Watch your fingers, and always retract or cover the blade between cuts. The rotary cutter cannot be used without the special protective mat.

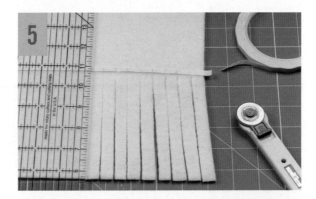

Baby BLANKET

Blankets serve many purposes in the day-to-day routine of baby care. Most often they provide comfort, warmth, and security for little tykes. A blanket also provides a soft surface for rolling around on the floor or a make-do pad for a quick change when you're on the go. With easy-to-apply blanket binding and synthetic fleece fabric, you can sew up new blankets in a jiffy. Because the following method involves the use of fabric glue, you'll want to launder the finished blanket before you use it.

WHAT YOU'LL LEARN

How to apply satin blanket binding

The secret to sewing MITERED corners

The importance of careful PRESSING

WHAT YOU'LL NEED

1 yd. (0.95 m) synthetic fleece

Satin blanket binding in color to match or coordinate with fabric

Quilting ruler or carpenter's square

Fabric glue stick (page 34)

Thread to match blanket binding

How to Sew a BABY BLANKET

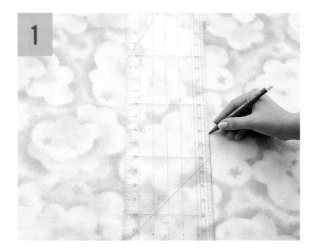

1 Cut a rectangle of fabric 36" × 45" (91.5 × 115 cm). Use a quilting ruler or carpenter's square to ensure square corners. In the following steps, unroll the binding from the package as you need it, and don't cut it until step 7.

TIP Synthetic fleece is actually a knit fabric and is usually 60" (152.5 cm) wide. Avoid using either of the SELVAGES as a side of your rectangle because they may be slightly stretched out of shape.

2 Beginning about 10" (25.5 cm) from one corner and working toward the corner in a clockwise direction, slip the blanket edge between the layers of the binding. Tuck the edge in as close as possible to the binding fold. Insert pins through all the layers, perpendicular to the edge. Space the pins about 2" (5 cm) apart with the heads outward.

TIP Be sure to keep the binding folded smooth and flat over the edge, so that the outer crease remains sharp. This will ensure that the finished binding edges on the front and back of the blanket are perfectly aligned.

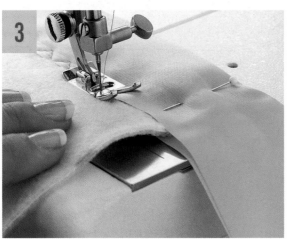

3 Set the machine to sew a multistitch zigzag (page 21) at maximum width and 12 stitches per inch, which equals 2 mm. Place the blanket under the presser foot at the binding end, with the inner edge of the binding aligned to the *left side of the presser foot opening.* Stitch to the fabric edge, removing pins as you come to them. Stop, and *remove the fabric from the machine (p. 123).*

4 Take the blanket to the ironing board. Open out the binding at the corner, and fold it down along the next side, so that the fabric edge aligns to the binding fold. A 45° angle will form in the binding. Press the angle lightly with the tip of the iron.

5 Fold the binding closed so that the angled fold forms a mitered corner. The fold runs diagonally from the outer corner to the inner corner, matching up perfectly.

QUICK REFERENCE

Left side of the presser foot opening. The opening in the center of the presser foot is more than wide enough to accommodate the widest stitch your machine can sew. Guide the fabric, keeping a tiny space between the binding edge and the left edge of the opening. The farthest left stitch of the needle should just stitch off the edge of the binding. Adjust the position slightly, if necessary.

CONTINUED

How to Sew a BABY BLANKET

CONTINUED

6 Flip the blanket over and miter the back of the binding so that the diagonal fold on the back also lines up perfectly. Using a fabric glue stick, secure the folds in place. This is called *glue-basting*.

7 Encase and pin the blanket edge to the next corner. Place the blanket under the presser foot, aligning the inner corner of the miter to the left side of the presser foot opening. *Backstitch (p. 19)* two or three stitches. Stitch forward to the fabric edge at the next corner. Stop, and remove the blanket from the machine.

8 Repeat steps 4 to 7 for the remaining corners. On the side where you started, cut the binding 4" (10 cm) beyond the beginning. Open the fold; press under 2" (5 cm) at the end.

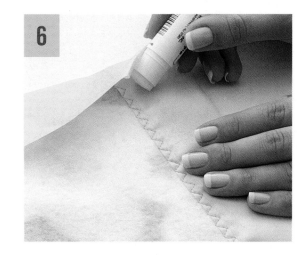

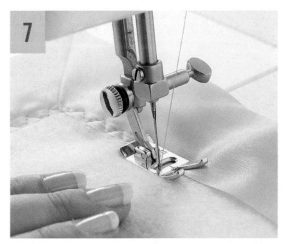

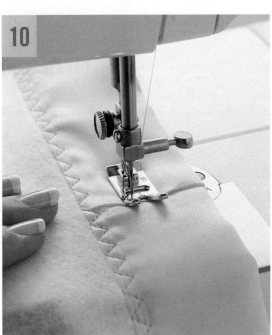

QUICK REFERENCE

Glue-basting. Use a fabric glue stick. This versatile product may become one of your favorite sewing tools. The temporary adhesive in a handy retractable tube can be applied in small dabs or continuous lines. It won't discolor the fabric and will wash out completely, if necessary.

Reset the stitch length to 0. The machine will still stitch side to side, as it is still set for multistitch-zigzag, but the fabric will not move forward.

9 Refold and finish encasing and pinning the blanket edge. The folded end should overlap the cut end 2" (5 cm). Glue-baste the folded end in place. Stitch the last side, stitching about 1" (2.5 cm) beyond the overlap. Remove the blanket from the machine, and clip the threads.

10 ***Reset the stitch length to 0.*** Place the overlapped binding ends under the presser foot so that the fold is about ¼" (6 mm) ahead of the presser foot opening. Stitch in place until the needle has traveled from left to right at least twice. This **TACKING** will keep the ends in place through many launderings.

NOW THAT WAS PRETTY EASY

Preliminary steps that include pinning, pressing, and glue-basting may seem tedious but they make a world of difference in the ease and precision of the final stitching.

Nap-time TOTE

When you take your baby for short visits, this convenient tote holds the essentials and zips open to provide a soft, cuddly surface for sleeping or playing. The tote is really a **LINED-TO-THE-EDGE** square. A handy lined pocket running from front to back provides extra cushion through the center. Purchase prequilted fabric for the outer layer and cotton flannel for the **LINING**. Be sure to **PRESHRINK** both fabrics before cutting and sewing. Look for a 30" (76 cm) molded **SEPARATING ZIPPER** in a color to coordinate with the fabric and lining.

WHAT YOU'LL LEARN

How to sew something that is lined to the edge

How to use paper-backed fusible web (page 34)

How to TOPSTITCH

Zippers aren't as scary as you think!

WHAT YOU'LL NEED

Quilting ruler or carpenter's square for measuring and cutting

1¼ yd. (1.15 m) prequilted fabric

1¼ yd. (1.15 m) cotton flannel for lining

Thread to match or blend with the fabrics

Paper-backed fusible web, ⅜" (1 cm) wide

30" (76 cm) molded separating zipper

Basting tape

Point turner (page 33)

How to Sew a **NAP-TIME TOTE**

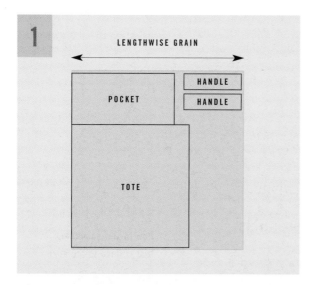

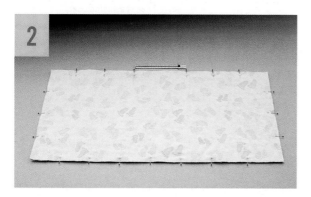

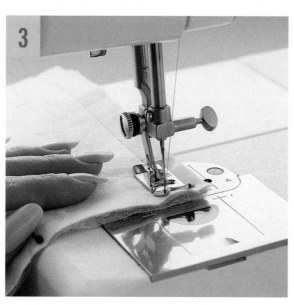

LET'S BEGIN

1 Preshrink the fabric and lining. Using a quilting ruler or a carpenter's square, mark out a perfect 31" (78.5 cm) square on the prequilted fabric, for the tote. Also measure and mark a 13" × 27" (33 × 68.5 cm) rectangle for the pocket and two 4" × 15" (10 × 38 cm) rectangles for the handles. *Do not use a selvage* as one of the sides. Cut out the pieces. Using the square and the pocket piece as patterns, cut matching pieces from the lining fabric.

2 Pin the lining over the pocket, right sides together, around the entire outer edge. *Insert the pins perpendicular to the edges (p. 19).* Leave a 6" (15 cm) opening unpinned along one side.

3 Set the machine for a straight stitch of 10 to 12 stitches per inch, or 2 to 2.5 mm. Place the pinned fabric under the presser foot just ahead of the opening. Align the cut edges to the ½" (1.3 cm) *seam allowance guide (p. 19)* on the bed of the machine. The bulk of the fabric will extend to the left of the machine. *Backstitch (p. 19)* to the opening; stop. Then, stitch forward, guiding the cut edges along the ½" (1.3 cm) seam allowance guide. *Remove pins as you come to them (p. 19).* Stop stitching ½" (1.3 cm) from the edge at the corner, leaving the needle down in the fabric. (Turn the handwheel until the needle is down.)

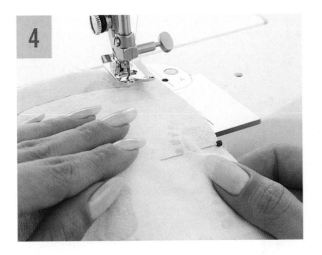

4 Raise the presser foot and turn the fabric a quarter turn. Lower the presser foot and continue stitching. **PIVOT** in this manner at each corner. Stop stitching when you reach the last pin before the opening. Backstitch two or three stitches. *Remove the fabric from the machine (p. 123).*

TIP Mark a dot ½" (1.3 cm) from each corner on the wrong side of the lining. As you stitch toward each corner, you will be able to see exactly where you should stop.

5 *Trim the seam allowance corners diagonally (p. 193).* **PRESS** the seams flat to set the stitching line in the fabric. Insert a seam roll or wooden dowel into the opening and press the **SEAM ALLOWANCES** open over the curved surface. In the area of the opening, turn back the seam allowances ½" (1.3 cm) and press.

6 Cut a 6" (15 cm) strip of paper-backed fusible web. Place the strip over the lining seam allowance at the opening, just inside the folded edge. Press over the strip to fuse it to the seam allowance, following the manufacturer's directions.

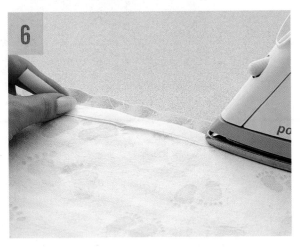

QUICK REFERENCE

Do not use the selvage. The tightly woven area along the outer edge of the fabric should be cut away in order to avoid puckering. Even if it looks flat, it will probably shrink and distort the sewn edge after laundering.

CONTINUED

How to Sew a NAP-TIME TOTE

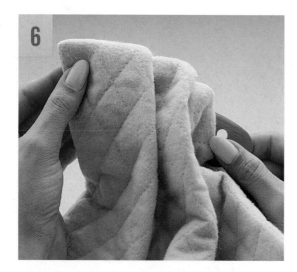

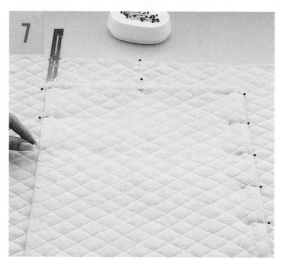

7 Turn the pocket right side out through the opening. Insert a point turner or similar tool into the opening and gently push the pivot points out to form *perfect corners (p. 193)*. Remove the protective paper backing from the fusible web at the opening. Align the folded edges of the opening. Press over the opening from the lining side to fuse it closed. Press the remaining outer edges.

8 MARK the centers of two opposite sides of the tote piece; also mark the centers of the two short ends of the pocket. Center the pocket over the tote, right sides up. The pocket ends should be 2½" (6.5 cm) from the tote ends. Pin the pocket in place along both long edges, inserting pins perpendicular to the pocket edges.

9 Place the fabric under the presser foot so that the right edge of the foot is aligned to the side of the pocket and the back of the foot is aligned to the pocket end. Backstitch to the pocket end. Then, stitch forward to the opposite end; backstitch a few stitches. This is called topstitching. Repeat for the opposite side of the pocket.

TIP On most machines the right edge of the presser foot is ¼" (6 mm) from the needle tip. If this is not true of your machine, determine a different way to guide the stitching line ¼" (6 mm) from the pocket edge.

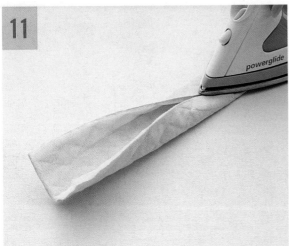

10 Mark two lines across the pocket, each 1" (2.5 cm) from the center. Stitch on the marked lines, backstitching at each end of each line. This will divide the pocket into two. Mark and stitch a line down the center of one pocket side, to divide it for carrying bottles.

11 Press a handle piece in half lengthwise. Open the fold and turn the long edges in, aligning them to the center crease; press. Refold the center, encasing the raw edges. Pin the layers together. Repeat for the other handle. Topstitch ¼" (6 mm) from both edges of each handle.

12 Pin the ends of one handle to the tote edge above one pocket, with the inner edges of the handle 3" (7.5 cm) from the center. Pin the other handle in the same position at the opposite edge. Stitch across the ends within the ½" (1.3 cm) seam allowance.

CONTINUED

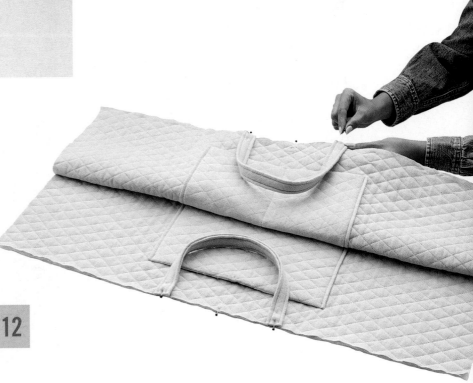

How to Sew a NAP-TIME TOTE

CONTINUED

13 Apply basting tape (page 34) to the right side of the zipper tape, running it along both outer edges. Remove the protective paper backing.

14 Place the closed zipper facedown along one of the sides that doesn't have a handle, aligning the edges. The *zipper stops* at the top and bottom of the zipper should be ½" (1.3 cm) from the ends of the tote. Attach the zipper foot to the sewing machine, and adjust the machine so that the *needle will be stitching on the left side of the foot.* Set the machine for long straight stitches. **BASTE** the zipper tape to the fabric, stitching ⅜" (1 cm) from the edge.

TIP Measure ⅜" (1 cm) from the outer edge of the zipper tape, and draw a guideline, using a pencil.

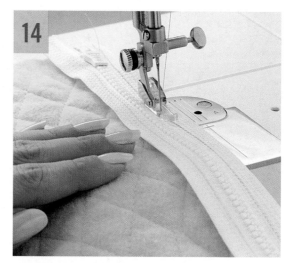

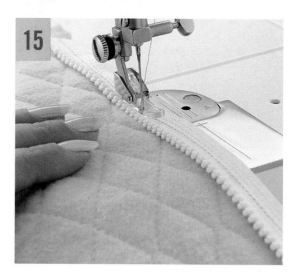

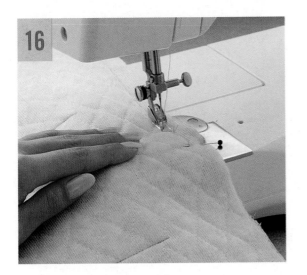

15 Adhere the other zipper tape edge to the opposite side of the tote as in step 14. Separate the zipper halves, and baste the other half in the same way. Pin the tote over the lining, right sides together, aligning all the edges and encasing the zipper and handles. Leave an opening between the handles on one end.

16 Place the fabric under the zipper foot, with the tote fabric on top, starting over one handle. Stitch ½" (1.3 cm) seam all around the tote, backstitching after and before the opening, and pivoting at the corners as in steps 2 and 3.

17 Trim the corners, press the seam allowances, turn the tote right side out, and close the opening as in steps 5 to 7 for the pocket. Attach the all-purpose presser foot. Topstitch ¼" (6 mm) from the edge all around the tote.

QUICK REFERENCE

Zipper stops. Tiny bars at the top of the zipper prevent the zipper slide from sliding right off the end. On a separating zipper, the larger stop at the bottom secures and aligns the zipper teeth.

Needle will be stitching on the left side of the foot. On some machines, the needle position is adjustable; on others, the foot position is adjustable. Check your owner's manual for the correct way to set your machine.

YOUR TOTE IS FINISHED

Simply zip it closed down the center, fold it in half, and get packing!

Round TABLECLOTH

A round table dressed with a floor-length tablecloth is an elegant accent in any room and also provides hidden storage space. This tablecloth features welting (page 35) at the outer edge which simplifies **HEMMING** and adds a designer touch. Single-fold bias tape (page 35) can also be used to sew a simple hem. Select fabric for the tablecloth that will drape in soft folds as it falls from the tabletop. To eliminate the need for matching a pattern at the **SEAM,** look for solid colors or small allover prints.

WHAT YOU'LL LEARN

How to measure and determine the amount of fabric needed for a round tablecloth

How to cut an accurate circle

Two easy ways to finish (page 21) a curved edge

WHAT YOU'LL NEED

Fabric, amount determined in step 1

Steel tape measure

Fabric marking pen

Fabric glue stick (page 34)

Thread

Fabric-covered welting or single-fold bias tape to match or contrast with tablecloth fabric, amount equal to 3½ times the diameter of the tablecloth

How to Sew a ROUND TABLECLOTH WITH A WELTED HEM

LET'S BEGIN

1 Measure the tabletop diameter and the desired **DROP LENGTH** for your tablecloth. Determine the amount of fabric needed, working with the following formula. (We used these numbers for our tablecloth on page 300; your numbers will probably be different.)

TIP Most decorator fabrics are 48" or 54" (122 or 137 cm) wide. You will probably have to sew together at least one full width and one or two partial widths of fabric to obtain the necessary diameter. The length of each piece will equal the diameter of your tablecloth.

2 Prepare your fabric (page 31). Measure and **MARK** the location of the cuts (equal to the tablecloth diameter) along the **SELVAGE**. Cut the lengths following the cutting guidelines on pages 44 and 45. Trim away the selvages, cutting just beyond the tightly woven area.

1

Table diameter		28" (71 cm)
Add the drop length twice	+	29" (73.5 cm)
	+	29" (73.5 cm)
to find the diameter of the tablecloth	=	86" (218.5 cm)
Divide by the fabric width	÷	54" (137 cm)
Round up to the nearest whole number	=	1.59
to find the number of fabric widths needed		2
Multiply by the tablecloth diameter (above)	×	86" (218.5 cm)
to find the amount of fabric needed	=	172" (437 cm)
Convert to yards (meters); round up		4⅞ yd. (4.5 m)

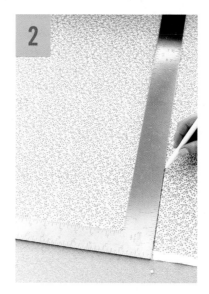

3 Determine where you want the seam(s) in your tablecloth, using the diagrams as a guide. Cut one of the fabric widths as directed for either option A or B.

Option A
Use one seam when the diameter of the tablecloth is less than one-and-one-half times the fabric width. Subtract the fabric width from the tablecloth diameter. Cut a strip on the **LENGTHWISE GRAIN** of one fabric piece that is 2" (5 cm) wider than this measurement.

Option B
Use two seams when the diameter of the tablecloth is more than one-and-one half times the fabric width. *Cut one fabric piece in half lengthwise.*

4 Pin a partial- or a half-width piece to the full-width piece, right sides together, along the lengthwise edges, *inserting the pins perpendicular to the edges (p. 19).* Place the pinned edges under the presser foot with the edges aligned to the ½" (1.3 cm) *seam allowance guide (p. 19).* The bulk of the fabric is to the left of the machine.

3

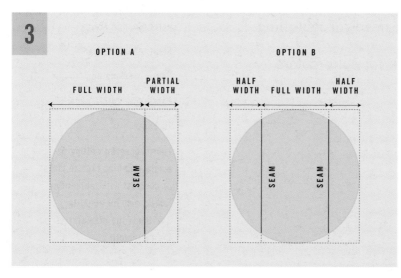

OPTION A

FULL WIDTH   PARTIAL WIDTH

SEAM

OPTION B

HALF WIDTH   FULL WIDTH   HALF WIDTH

SEAM   SEAM

QUICK REFERENCE

Cut one fabric piece in half lengthwise. Fold one width of fabric in half on the lengthwise grain. **PRESS** the fold and cut along the fold line.

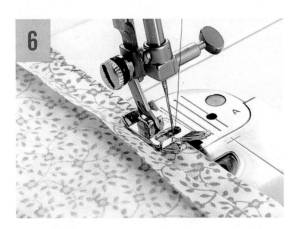

5 Set the machine for a straight stitch with 10 to 12 stitches per inch, which equals 2 to 2.5 mm. Stitch a ½" (1.3 cm) seam, *removing the pins as you come to them (p. 19).*

6 If you chose option B, stitch the second narrow piece to the opposite side of the full-width piece, following steps 4 and 5. Set the machine for a wide zigzag stitch (page 21) with a length of 10 stitches per inch, which equals 2.5 mm. Stitch close to the edge of each seam allowance so that the right-hand stitches go just over the edge. This step, called a seam finish, keeps the edges from raveling.

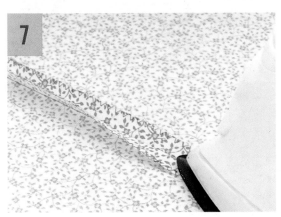

7 Press over the stitching line of the closed seams; then spread the layers apart, open the **SEAM ALLOWANCES,** and press them again.

TIP Pressing the seam flat before pressing it open sets the stitches in the seamline and ultimately makes a better looking seam.

CONTINUED

How to Sew a ROUND TABLECLOTH WITH A WELTED HEM

CONTINUED

8 Fold the fabric in half lengthwise, then crosswise, aligning the outer edges of the four layers. Pin the layers together to keep them from slipping. Using a steel tape measure and a fabric marking pen, mark an arc on the fabric, measuring the radius (one-half the diameter) of the tablecloth from the center folded corner of the fabric. Cut on the marked line through all four layers of fabric; remove the pins.

9 Pin the welting to the right side of the tablecloth along the outer edge, aligning the raw edges and *easing* the welting as you pin. Overlap, but don't cut, the ends.

10 Set the machine back to a straight stitch. Attach the zipper foot (page 11) and adjust it to the right of the needle. If your zipper foot is not adjustable, adjust the needle to the left of the foot. Slowly stitch the welting to the fabric, stitching over the existing stitches in the welting. Begin 2" (5 cm) from the end of the welting; remove pins as you come to them.

11 Stop stitching 2" (5 cm) from the point where the ends of the welting will meet. Cut off the end of the welting so it overlaps the beginning end by 1" (2.5 cm). Remove the stitching from the overlapping end of the welting, exposing the inner cording; trim the end of the cording so it just meets the other end.

TIP If you are using packaged welting and need to splice pieces together, use the technique in steps 11 and 12 to make a continuous welting while you are sewing it to the edge.

12 Fold under ½" (1.3 cm) of the fabric on the overlapping end of the welting. Wrap it around the beginning end and finish stitching it to the edge of the tablecloth.

13 Turn under the edges so the welting is at the outer edge of the tablecloth. Press lightly. Attach the general purpose presser foot, and reset the needle position to standard, if you changed it. With the right side up, stitch one more time around the outer edge, guiding the right edge of the presser foot along the welting edge and keeping the seam allowances turned under.

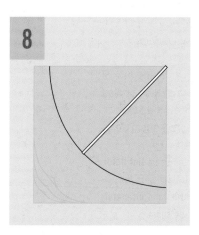

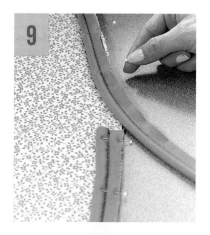

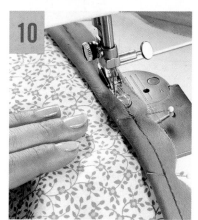

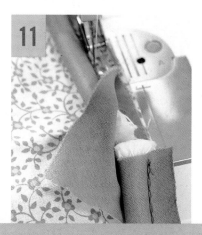

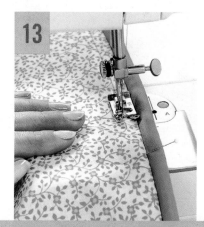

Alternate hemming method using BIAS TAPE

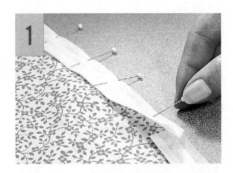

QUICK REFERENCE

Easing is a technique used when working with **BIAS** edges, such as the welting fabric. Avoid stretching the welting, keeping it relaxed as you pin or stitch it.

1 Follow steps 1 to 8, adding ½" (1.3 cm) to the tablecloth diameter before cutting. Open one fold of the bias tape. Pin the tape to the right side of the tablecloth along the outer edge, keeping the raw edges even and easing the tape as you pin. Overlap the ends about ½" (1.3 cm).

2 Straight-stitch around the edge, stitching in the crease of the tape fold. Remove pins as you come to them. Overlap the stitches ½" (1.3 cm).

3 Turn the tape to the underside so the seam is exactly on the edge. Press. Secure the tape temporarily with fabric glue stick. Stitch as close as possible to the inner fold of the tape.

WOW

Was it a long way around that edge? Give your round tablecloth a final pressing, center it over your table, and feel proud of yourself.

Rectangular TABLECLOTH

A simple rectangular tablecloth adds pattern or accents your color scheme and is easily changed for special holidays, the changing seasons, or your mood! The neatly **MITERED** corners look very professional, yet they are surprisingly easy to sew. This technique can be used for several other home decorating items, such as a square table topper to place over a floor-length round tablecloth, dinner napkins, placemats, or a dresser scarf.

WHAT YOU'LL LEARN

How to sew double-fold hems

How a glue stick will help to make perfect mitered corners

Even easy-to-sew items can make dramatic decorating statements

WHAT YOU'LL NEED

Fabric, amount determined in step 1

Thread

Fabric glue stick (page 34)

How to Sew a RECTANGULAR TABLECLOTH

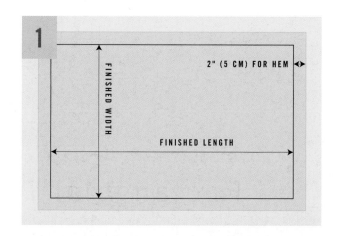

2" (5 CM) FOR HEM

FINISHED WIDTH

FINISHED LENGTH

LET'S BEGIN

1 Determine the desired finished size for your tablecloth; add 4" (10 cm) to both length and width for the **HEM**. Cut a rectangle of fabric equal to these measurements, following the cutting guidelines on pages 44 and 45.

TIP Select fabric that is wide enough for your tablecloth to be sewn in one piece: 48" (122 cm) fabric for a finished width up to 44" (112 cm), 54" (137 cm) fabric for a finished width up to 50" (127 cm), or 60" (152.5 cm) fabric for a finished width up to 56" (142 cm).

2 **PRESS** under 2" (5 cm) on all four edges of the cloth. Unfold the pressed edges and press each corner diagonally at the point where the creases intersect. Trim off the corner diagonally at the points where it crosses the fold-lines. Use a dot of fabric glue stick to hold the corner in place.

3 Turn each cut edge in, aligning it to the first fold line, and press the outer fold.

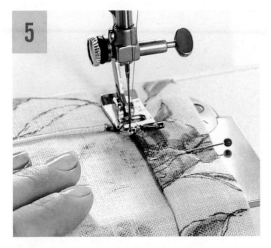

QUICK REFERENCE

Edgestitch. Stitch as close as possible to the inner edge of the hem. Align the presser foot so that the needle will enter the fabric just inside the inner edge. Note the point on the presser foot that aligns to the edge of the hem itself. As you sew, watch the fabric as it passes under that point on the foot rather than watching the needle. Stitch slowly for the best control.

4 Refold on the first fold line, encasing the raw edge to form a 1" (2.5 cm) *double-fold hem (p. 101)*. Pin the hem in place, *inserting pins perpendicular to the folds (p. 19)*. Use additional dots of glue stick to secure the mitered folds in the corners.

5 *Edgestitch* along the inner fold line. At the corners, stop with the needle down in the fabric and **PIVOT**. Overlap the stitches ½" (1.3 cm) where they meet. Press the tablecloth.

TIP Support the bulk of the fabric to your left with a card table or other surface, so the fabric feeds easily as you stitch. This will help you maintain a nice straight

VOILA

Smooth the tablecloth over the table, and step back to wait for the compliments!

Creative Tablecloth IDEAS

Layer a short round table topper over a floor-length tablecloth. Create a balloon effect in the short topper by gathering up the edge at evenly spaced intervals, using safety pins. Add bows for a feminine touch.

Sew pregathered lace to the edge of a round tablecloth on a bedside table. Subtract the width of the lace from the tablecloth radius before drawing the arc in step 8, page 160. Turn back the cut end of the lace ½" (1.3 cm) as you begin stitching, and overlap it with the opposite end as you finish the circle.

Stamp a design on the corners or along the border of a table topper. For best results, select a tightly woven natural fabric. Use acrylic fabric paints and neoprene stamps, following the manufacturer's directions.

Banded TABLECLOTH

Add a dash of decorating spice to your dining area with a custom banded tablecloth. A pleasing **DROP LENGTH** for dining tables is about 10" (25.5 cm). Decorator fabrics that are 54" (137 cm) wide are often not wide enough, especially after they have been hemmed. In this version, a 4" (10 cm) band of contrasting fabric is added around the lower edge, giving the tablecloth extra length and a designer touch. The **MITERED** corners of the band give it a professional look and are easier to sew than you might think. Careful measuring and cutting are the key ingredients to a perfect tablecloth.

How to Sew a BANDED TABLECLOTH

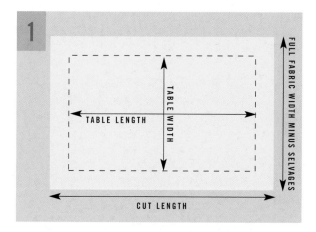

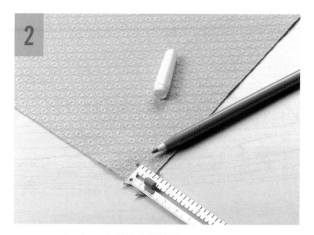

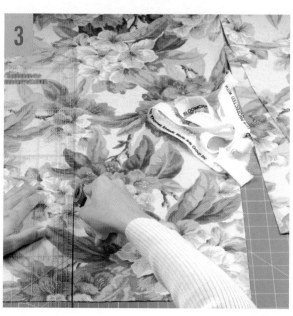

Figure 1 labels: TABLE LENGTH, TABLE WIDTH, FULL FABRIC WIDTH MINUS SELVAGES, CUT LENGTH

1 Preshrink the fabrics (page 31). Cut off the **SELVAGES** evenly, just beyond the tightly woven area. *Square off one end of the fabric,* following the cutting directions on page 44. Measure your tabletop width and subtract the measurement from the fabric width. Record the difference. Measure and mark the fabric length equal to the tabletop length plus the width difference you recorded. Cut the fabric squarely at the mark.

2 Mark a dot ½" (1.3 cm) from each corner on the center panel, using a fabric marker with disappearing ink (page 22). Measure the distance between dots on one long side and one short side. Record the measurements.

3 Cut the selvages from the band fabric. Cut the band fabric into four 9" (23 cm) strips running parallel to the **LENGTHWISE GRAIN.**

QUICK REFERENCE

Square off one end of the fabric. In order for the tablecloth to fit the table correctly and for the band to be sewn with accuracy, the fabric must be cut with perfect 90-degree corners.

4 Fold one end of one band strip in half lengthwise. Cut the end at a perfect 45-degree angle starting at the end of the fold. Unfold the strip. Mark short intersecting lines at the 45-degree corners on the 1/2" (1.3 cm) seamlines. Mark a dot 1/2" (1.3 cm) from the corner on the square point.

TIP If you don't have a ruler of other device with markings for cutting the 45-degree angle, fold a large square of paper in half diagonally, and use that as a pattern.

5 Place a pin on the opposite end of the strip a distance from the intersecting lines equal to the distance between dots on one long side of the center panel. Using the angled end as a guide and aligning the intersecting lines to the pin, angle-cut the other end. Cut a band for the other long side to match. Mark intersecting lines as in step 4.

CONTINUED

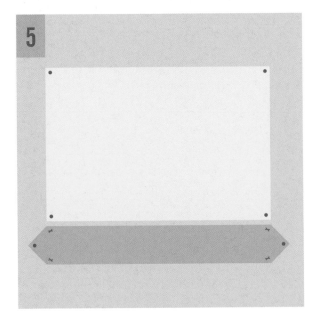

How to Sew a BANDED TABLECLOTH

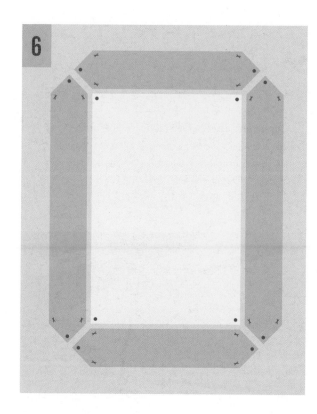

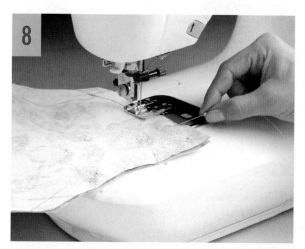

CONTINUED

6 Repeat steps 4 and 5 for the short bands, making the distance between intersecting lines equal to the distance between dots on the short sides of the center panel.

7 Pin the angled end of a short band to the angled end of a long band, right sides together, matching the dots and raw edges. *Insert the pins perpendicular to the edges (p. 19).*

8 Place the fabric under the presser foot so the angled edges align to the 1/2" (1.3 cm) *seam allowance guide (p. 19)* and the needle will enter the fabric just ahead of the intersection. *Backstitch (p. 19)* to the intersection. Then stitch forward guiding the raw edges along the 1/2" (1.3 cm) seam guide. *Remove pins as you come to them (p. 19).*

9 Stop with the needle down in the fabric at the marked dot on the square corner. Raise the presser foot; **PIVOT** the fabric. Lower the presser foot and continue stitching to the other marked intersection. Backstitch a few stitches. *Remove the fabric from the machine (p. 19).*

10 Repeat steps 7 to 9 to join the remaining ends of the band strips, alternating long and short, until you have sewn all of them into a large circle. Trim the seam allowances to 1/4" (6 mm). At the square corners, *trim the seam allowances diagonally (p. 193)* close to the pivot point. **PRESS** the seam allowances open.

11 *Press under (p. 185)* 1/2" (1.3 cm) on one continuous edge of the band.

CONTINUED

How to Sew a BANDED TABLECLOTH

CONTINUED

12 Pin the right side of the opposite (unpressed) band edge to the wrong side of the center panel, aligning the raw edges and matching the dots to the seam intersections. Stitch ½" (1.3 cm) seam on each side, pivoting at each corner dot, and removing pins as you come to them.

13 Press the seam allowances toward the band. Turn the band to the right side of the table-cloth so the inner fold just covers the stitching line. The band should be an even width without ripples. Pin it in place along the inner fold. Press a crease in the outer fold.

14 *Edgestitch* close to the inner fold, removing pins as you come to them and pivoting at the corners.

QUICK REFERENCE

Edgestitch. Align the presser foot so that the needle will enter the fabric as close as possible to the folded edge. Note the point on the presser foot that aligns to the fold. Then guide the fabric to pass under the foot at that point rather than watching the needle. Stitch slowly for best control.

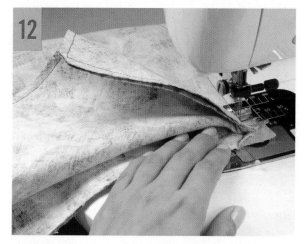

MORE IDEAS

Before pinning the band in place in step 12, page 318, center a length of jumbo rickrack over the stitching line to give your banded tablecloth a creative detail.

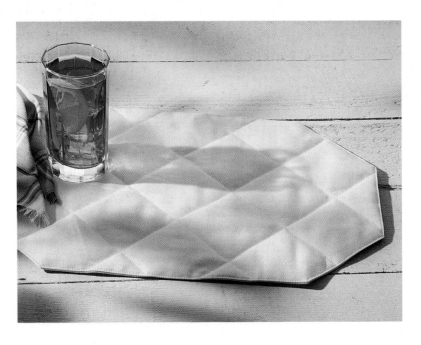

Make quilted placemats. Instead of welting, stitch a layer of thin polyester batting to the wrong side of the placemat top before stitching the top and bottom together. Trim the batting close to the seamline before turning the placemat right side out. Close the opening by machine and continue edgestitching, opposite, around the entire placemat. Then stitch diagonal lines across the placemat in both directions.

Make napkins with frayed edges. Set your machine for a narrow zigzag stitch, 2 mm long. Stitch 1/2" (1.3 cm) from the edge around the napkin, pivoting 1/2" (1.3 cm) from each corner. Then pull threads to fray the outer edges on each side, working from the cut edges up to the stitching line.

Lined TABLE RUNNER

Design and sew a nifty table runner to spark up your dining room table. Use a short runner as an accent in the center of the table or sew one that runs from end to end with an 8" to 10" (20.5 to 25.5 cm) **DROP LENGTH**. For a table runner that is used as placemats, make it 18" (46 cm) wide. You can adjust both width and length to whatever size you might desire.

This runner is **LINED TO THE EDGE** and can be made reversible by selecting two decorator fabrics. Welting (page 35), sewn into the outer edge of the runner, is available in many sizes and colors. For ease of application, choose welting no larger than ³⁄16" (4.5 mm).

WHAT YOU'LL LEARN

How to insert narrow welting into the seam of a lined project

Pointed ends are easy to create

Your sewing skills are increasing

WHAT YOU'LL NEED

Decorator fabric, amount depends on size of runner

Lining fabric, same amount as decorator fabric

Narrow welting, amount equal to slightly more than circumference of runner

Thread

How to Sew a LINED TABLE RUNNER

LET'S BEGIN

1 Determine the desired finished length and width of your table runner. Add 1" (2.5 cm) to both measurements to allow for ½" (1.3 cm) **SEAM ALLOWANCES** all around. **MARK** and cut a rectangle of decorator fabric for the front, following the cutting guidelines on pages 44 and 45. Cut the lining piece exactly the same size as the front.

TIP If you use the **CROSSWISE GRAIN** for the length, the maximum length of the runner is 1" (2.5 cm) shorter than the width of your fabric. Cutting the table runner on the **LENGTHWISE GRAIN** allows you to make it any length, but wastes more fabric. In that case, consider cutting both front and lining from the same fabric.

2 Fold the runner front in half lengthwise, aligning the cut edges; pin to keep the fabric from shifting. Mark a point 8½" (21.8 cm) from the end on the long cut edges. Draw a diagonal line from the mark on the side to the folded end. Carefully cut through both layers on the line, keeping the fabric edges aligned.

3 Repeat step 2 on the opposite end of the runner. Remove the pins and unfold the runner. Using the runner as a guide, cut points at the ends of the lining.

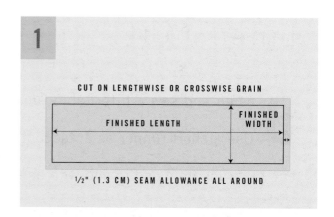

CUT ON LENGTHWISE OR CROSSWISE GRAIN

FINISHED LENGTH

FINISHED WIDTH

½" (1.3 CM) SEAM ALLOWANCE ALL AROUND

4 Pin the welting to the right side of the runner front along the outer edge, keeping the raw edges aligned and the welting relaxed. Plan for the ends to overlap along one long edge and leave tails unpinned. *Insert the pins perpendicular to the edges (p. 19).*

TIP **Keep the welting relaxed as you pin and actually "crowd"** the welting slightly at the corners so that it will lie flat when it is turned to its final position.

5 **CLIP** into the seam allowance of the welting at each corner of the runner at the exact point where the welting must bend. Clip *up to but not through* the stitching line, so that the welting seam allowances spread open and lie flat. Pin securely, keeping the raw edges of the welting and runner aligned.

QUICK REFERENCE

Up to but not through means exactly what it says. Any time you clip into a seam allowance, the clip should be right up to the stitching, but it must not cut the stitching threads, or you will create a hole in the seam.

CONTINUED

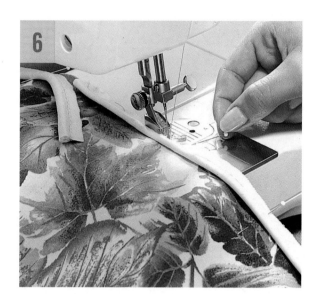

CONTINUED

6 Set the machine for a straight stitch of 10 stitches per inch, which equals 2.5 mm. Attach the zipper foot (page 11) and adjust it to the right of the needle. If your foot is not adjustable, adjust the needle to the left of the foot. Place the fabric under the presser foot 2" (5 cm) from the end of the welting. Slowly stitch the welting to the fabric, stitching over the existing stitches in the welting. *Remove pins as you come to them (p. 19).*

7 When you reach a corner, stop with the needle down in the fabric at the point of the clip. Lift the presser foot and **PIVOT** the fabric so the stitching line of the welting on the next side is in line with the needle. Lower the presser foot and continue stitching around the runner, pivoting at each corner.

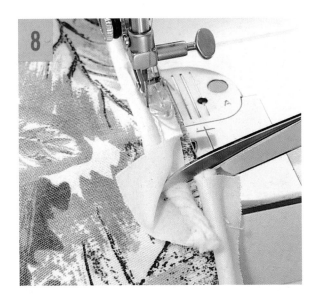

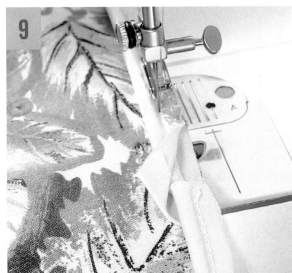

8 Stop stitching 2" (5 cm) from the point where the ends of the welting will meet. Cut off the end of the welting so it overlaps the beginning end by 1" (2.5 cm). Remove the stitching from the overlapping end of the welting, exposing the inner cording; trim the end of the cording so it just meets the other end.

9 Fold under ½" (1.3 cm) of the fabric on the overlapping end of the welting. Wrap it around the beginning and finish stitching it to the runner, overlapping the stitches ½" (1.3 cm) where they meet.

10 **PRESS** along the stitching line with the tip of your iron to relax the fabric and set the seam. Check that the fabric does not ripple or draw up where you have attached the welting.

CONTINUED

How to Sew a LINED TABLE RUNNER

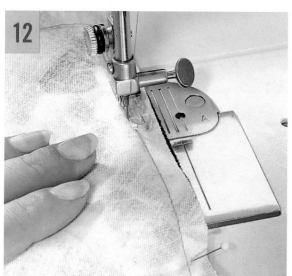

CONTINUED

11 Pin the front over the lining, right sides together, encasing the welting between the layers and aligning the outer edges. Leave a 7" (18 cm) opening unpinned along one side. Place the table runner under the presser foot, lining side down, just ahead of the unpinned area. Remove the pin marking the end of the opening before lowering the presser foot.

12 *Backstitch (p. 19)* three or four stitches; then stitch forward *over the previous stitches,* actually "crowding" the welting as you stitch. Pivot at each corner, and stop stitching at the opposite side of the opening. Backstitch three or four stitches, and *remove the fabric from the machine (p. 123).*

13 *Trim the seam allowances diagonally (p. 193)* at each corner. Turn back and press the lining seam allowance ½" (1.3 cm) from the edge in the unstitched area.

14 Reach in through the unstitched opening to grasp an end of the runner and pull it through the opening. Repeat for the other end, turning the runner right side out.

15 Use a point turner (page 33) to push out the corners, if necessary. Press the table runner up to the welting as you smooth and tug the welting out to the edge with your fingers. Slipstitch the opening closed, following the directions on page 22.

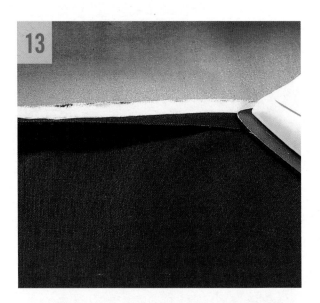

QUICK REFERENCE

Over the previous stitches. The second stitching line must be exactly over the first stitching line or slightly closer to the welting, so that the first stitching line does not show after the runner is turned right side out.

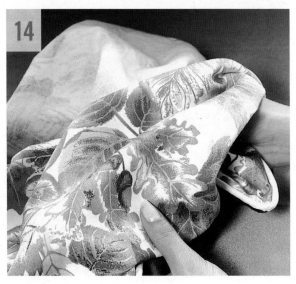

HURRAY

Smooth your new runner out on the table. Doesn't it add a fresh touch to your dining room décor?

PLACEMATS and NAPKINS

Spark up your dining room table or breakfast nook with reversible octagonal placemats. These placemats are **LINED TO THE EDGE** and can be made reversible by selecting two decorator fabrics. Welting (page 27), sewn into the outer edge of the placemat, is available in different sizes and colors. For ease of application, choose welting no larger than 3/16" (4.5 mm). Make napkins to match, simply by cutting, pressing, and hemming. If you want to be able to launder the placemats and napkins, choose fabrics that are washable and be sure to preshrink (page 33) the fabrics and the welting before you start cutting.

WHAT YOU'LL LEARN

How to cut fabric using a paper pattern

How to insert narrow welting into a seam

How to make neat corners and points

How to stitch a mitered double-fold hem

WHAT YOU'LL NEED

For four sets:

Craft paper for drawing a pattern

3/4 yd. (0.7 m) fabric for placemat fronts

3/4 yd. (0.7 m) fabric for placemat backs

7 yd. (6.4 m) welting

1 yd. (0.92 m) fabric for napkins

Thread to match fabrics

How to Sew a PLACEMAT

1 Draw a 13" × 19" (33 × 48.5 cm) rectangle on craft paper. Mark a point 3½" (9 cm) from each corner. Draw diagonal lines across each corner connecting marks; cut off the corners.

2 Preshrink the fabrics (page 31). To preshrink the welting, wrap it into large loops and tie it in the middle with a large loose knot. Soak the welting in warm water; squeeze out excess moisture. Place it in a net laundry bag or nylon stocking before tossing it in the dryer. This will keep it from getting too tangled.

3 Fold the fabric for the placemat front in half lengthwise, aligning the **SELVAGES**. Place the paper pattern with one short edge running parallel to and just beyond the selvages. This will ensure that the placemat is cut on-grain. Pin the pattern in place through both layers of fabric inserting pins about every 3" (7.5 cm) around the outer edge. Cut out the placemat. Remove the pins and cut two more fronts, following the same procedure. Then cut four placemat backs from the other fabric.

4 **PRESS** the flat edge of the welting if necessary. Pin the welting to the right side of the placemat front along the outer edge, keeping the raw edges aligned and the welting relaxed. Plan for the ends to overlap along one long edge and leave tails unpinned. *Insert the pins perpendicular to the edges (p. 19).*

TIP **Keep the welting relaxed as you pin and actually "crowd" the welting slightly at the corners so that it will lie flat when it is turned to its final position.**

5 Clip into the seam allowance of the welting at each corner of the placemat at the exact point where the welting must bend. *Clip to, but not through (p. 209)* the stitching line, so that the welting seam allowances spread open and lie flat. Pin securely, keeping the raw edges of the welting and placemat aligned.

6 Set the machine for a straight stitch of 10 stitches per inch, which equals 2.5 mm. Attach the zipper foot (page 11) and adjust it to the right of the needle. If your foot is not adjustable, adjust the needle to the left of the foot. Place the fabric under the presser foot 2" (5 cm) from the end of the welting. Slowly stitch the welting to the fabric, stitching over the existing stitches in the welting. *Remove pins as you come to them (p. 19).*

CONTINUED

How to Sew a PLACEMAT

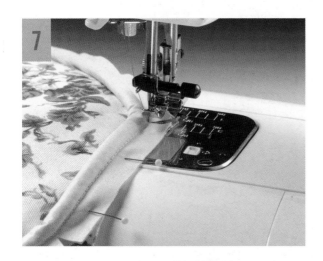

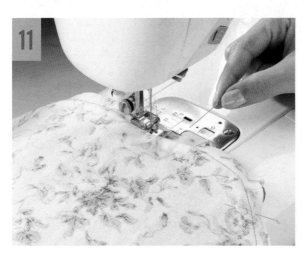

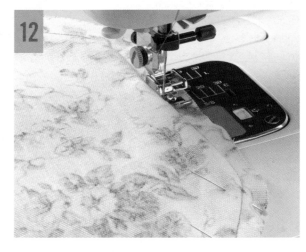

CONTINUED

7 When you reach a corner, stop with the needle down in the fabric at the point of the clip. Lift the presser foot and **PIVOT** the fabric so the stitching line of the welting on the next side is in line with the needle. Lower the presser foot and continue stitching around the placemat, pivoting at each corner.

8 Stop stitching 2" (5 cm) from the point where the ends of the welting will meet. Cut off the end of the welting so it overlaps the beginning end by 1" (2.5 cm). Remove the stitching from the overlapping end of the welting, exposing the inner cording; trim the end of the cording so it just meets the other end.

9 Fold under ½" (1.3 cm) of the fabric on the overlapping end of the welting. Wrap it around the beginning and finish stitching it to the placemat, overlapping the stitches ½" (1.3 cm) where they meet.

10 Press along the stitching line with the tip of your iron to relax the fabric and set the seam. Check that the fabric does not ripple or draw up where you have attached the welting.

11 Pin the placemat front over the back, right sides together, encasing the welting between the layers and aligning the outer edges. Leave a 7" (18 cm) opening unpinned along one side. Place the placemat under the presser foot, back side down, just ahead of the unpinned area. Remove the pin marking the end of the opening before lowering the presser foot.

12 *Backstitch (p. 19)* three or four stitches; then stitch forward *over the previous stitches,* actually "crowding" the welting with the zipper foot as you stitch. Pivot at each corner, and stop stitching at the opposite side of the opening. Backstitch three or four stitches, and *remove the fabric from the machine (p. 123).*

CONTINUED

QUICK REFERENCE

Over the previous stitches. The second stitching line must be exactly over the first stitching line or slightly closer to the welting, so that the first stitching line does not show after the placemat is turned right side out.

How to Sew a PLACEMAT

CONTINUED

---

13 *Trim the seam allowances diagonally (p. 193)* at each corner. Turn back and press the back seam allowance ½" (1.3 cm) from the edge in the unstitched area.

14 Reach in through the unstitched opening to grasp the opposite side of the placemat and pull it through the opening. Turn the placemat right side out.

15 Use a point turner to push out the corners, if necessary. Press the placemat up to the welting as you smooth and tug the welting out to the edge with your fingers. Slipstitch the opening closed, following the directions on page 22.

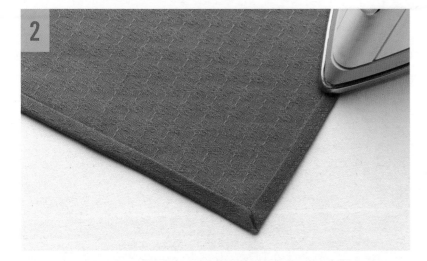

LET'S BEGIN

1 Cut squares for the napkins 1" (2.5 cm) larger than the desired finished size. Press under ½" (1.3 cm) on each side of the napkin. Unfold the corner, and refold it diagonally so that the pressed folds match. Press the diagonal fold, and trim the corner as shown. Repeat for each corner.

TIP For the most efficient use of your fabric, cut three 15" (38 cm) squares from 45" (115 cm) fabric or 18" (46 cm) squares from 54" (137 cm) fabric.

2 Fold the raw edges under to meet the pressed fold, forming a ¼" (6 mm) *double-fold hem (p. 101)*. The corners will form neat diagonal folds. Press the folds; pin only if necessary.

3 Stitch the hem close to the inner fold, using a short straight stitch and beginning along one side. At the corners, stop with the needle down in the fabric, between the diagonal folds, and pivot. Overlap the stitches about ½" (1.3 cm) where they meet.

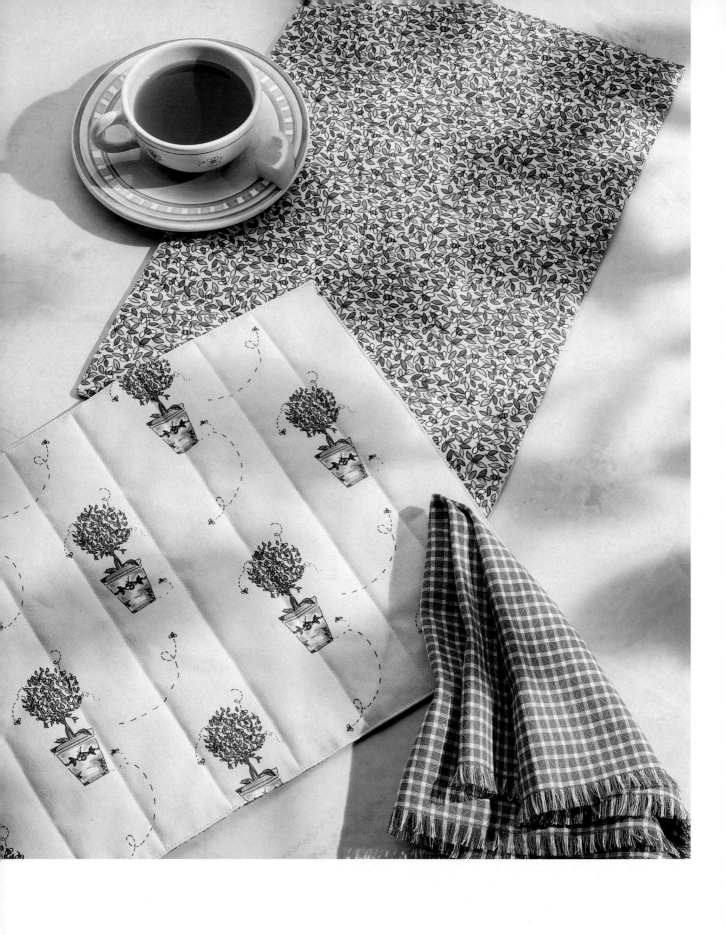

Quilted PLACEMATS

R eversible machine-quilted placemats add style to your dining room and, because they are easy to sew, help you gain confidence in your sewing skills. Placemats can be made in any size and shape. These rectangular placemats are a common finished size of 12" × 18" (30.5 × 46 cm).

Choose firmly woven, lightweight to mediumweight fabrics. Look for coordinating prints or solid color fabrics for the front and back, and purchase extra fabric to make matching napkins. Low-loft polyester or poly/cotton blend batting (page 35) is a good choice for placemats. It provides a subtle quilted look and holds up well through frequent laundering. The fabric and batting amounts suggested are enough for four placemats.

WHAT YOU'LL LEARN

How to LINE a project TO THE EDGE

How to use batting

Quilting by machine is really very simple

WHAT YOU'LL NEED

¾ yd. (0.7 m) fabric for placemat fronts

¾ yd. (0.7 m) fabric for placemat backs

¾ yd. (0.7 m) low-loft batting

Thread to match

Erasable marking pen or chalk (page 28)

6" × 24" (15 × 61 cm) quilting ruler or yardstick (meterstick)

Walking foot (page 11), optional

How to Sew a QUILTED PLACEMAT

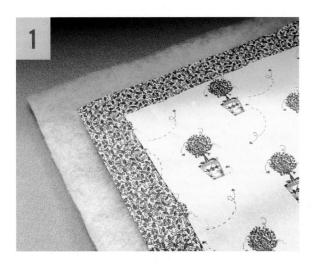

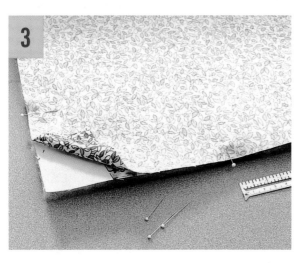

LET'S BEGIN

1 **PRESHRINK** your fabric (page 41). Cut one 13" × 19" (33 × 48.5 cm) rectangle of fabric for each placemat front and one 13" × 19" (33 × 48.5 cm) rectangle of fabric for each placemat back, following the cutting guidelines on pages 42 and 43. Remember to align the edges to the **LENGTHWISE** and **CROSSWISE GRAINLINES.** Also cut one 13" × 19" (33 × 48.5 cm) rectangle of batting for each placemat.

2 **MARK** a point 2½" (6.5 cm) from one side on the placemat front, near the upper edge, with chalk or an air-erasable pen. Make additional marks across the top every 2" (5 cm). The last mark should be 2½" (6.5 cm) from the opposite side. Repeat the marks along the lower edge. Draw parallel lines across the placemat front, connecting the marks. These are your *quilting lines.* Mark small dots ½" (1.3 cm) from the edges in each corner, on the wrong side of the placemat back.

3 Place the placemat front, right side up, on top of the batting, aligning the cut edges. Place the placemat back over the front, right sides together and align all four edges. Pin the layers together, along the outer edges, *inserting the pins perpendicular to the edges (p. 19).* In the center of one end, leave a 6" (15 cm) opening unpinned.

QUICK REFERENCE

Quilting lines. It is easier to mark these lines when the fabric is flat, before adding the batting and lining. Use a marker that can be easily removed; test to be sure. You'll find several markers to choose from in the notions department. Use air-erasable marker only if you are confident you will finish the project in one sewing session.

4 Set the machine for a straight stitch of 10 stitches per inch, which equals 2.5 mm. Place the fabrics under the presser foot, with the batting against the bed of the machine. Align the needle to enter the fabric just ahead of the opening with the cut edges of the fabrics aligned to the ½" (1.3 cm) *seam allowance guide (p. 19)* on the throat plate of your machine. Remove the pin that marks the opening before lowering the presser foot.

5 *Backstitch (p. 19)* three or four stitches; then stitch forward until you come to the dot in the first corner. Stop the machine with the needle completely down in the fabric at the dot.

6 Lift the presser foot and turn the fabric so the next side aligns to the ½" (1.3 cm) seam allowance guide. Lower the presser foot and continue stitching around all four sides, **PIVOTING** in this manner at each corner. Stop stitching at the opposite side of the opening; backstitch three or four stitches.

CONTINUED

How to Sew a QUILTED PLACEMAT

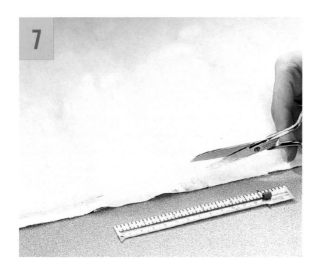

CONTINUED

7 *Remove the fabric from the machine (p. 123)* and trim the threads close to the fabric. Press the outer edges flat to set the stitches in the seam. Trim the batting seam allowance close to the stitching line and trim the batting away ½" (1.3 cm) from the edge in the opening area. *Trim the seam allowances diagonally (p. 193)* at each corner, cutting ⅛" (3 mm) from the stitches.

8 *Turn back the back seam allowance* and press, applying light pressure with the tip of the iron down the crease of the seam. In the area of the opening, turn back and press the seam allowance ½" (1.3 cm).

9 Turn the placemat over; turn back and press the remaining seam allowance of the opening. Turn the placemat right side out, reaching in through the opening to pull out each corner. Insert a point turner (page 33) or similar tool into the placemat, gently pushing the points out to form *perfect corners (p. 193)*.

10 Press the placemat flat, keeping the seam right on the edge of the placemat. Pin the opening closed, aligning the folded edges and placing the pins perpendicular to the edge. *Edgestitch (p. 309)* around the placemat, stitching the opening closed; pivot at each corner. Overlap the stitches where they meet.

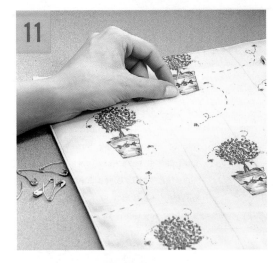

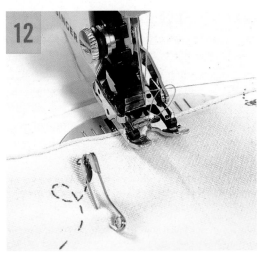

QUICK REFERENCE

Turn back the back seam allowance. It is difficult to fit a seam roll or hard cardboard tube into a placemat to press the seam allowances open. Turning back and pressing one seam allowance helps to separate them and make the seam look neater from the outside.

Pin-baste. Traditionally quilting projects are basted with a needle and thread, which, though more time-consuming, is certainly an alternative here. The basting is necessary to keep the fabrics and batting from shifting around while you quilt. Quilters often use safety pins that are angled for easier insertion. Pin-basting is a convenient method as long as you don't have to stop and remove the safety pins as you go along.

11 *Pin-baste* the layers together with small safety pins, working from the center to the sides. Place the pins about 4" (10 cm) apart and half-way between the marked lines so they won't get in the way of the presser foot while you are stitching on the quilting lines.

12 Attach a walking foot, if you have one, or use a general-purpose foot. Place the fabric under the presser foot, aligning the needle to the beginning of a marked quilting line near the center of the placemat. Lower the foot. Turn the handwheel by hand for one stitch, and stop with the needle at the highest position. Raise the foot and pull on the needle thread to bring the bobbin thread up through the fabric.

CONTINUED

How to Sew a QUILTED PLACEMAT

CONTINUED

13 Set your stitch length at almost 0. Draw both threads under the presser foot to one side. Lower the foot, with the needle aligned to enter the fabric at the edge of the placemat. Stitch several very short stitches to secure the threads at the beginning of the stitching line.

14 Increase the stitch length to 10 stitches per inch, which equals 2.5 mm. Stitch forward on the quilting line across the placemat. Slow your stitching as you approach the opposite side. Just before you reach the edge, decrease the stitch length to almost 0. Take several stitches to secure the threads. Remove the fabric from the machine.

TIP Keep both hands on the fabric as shown to ensure smooth, even stitching. However, don't pull or push; let the walking foot move the fabric. If you don't have a walking foot, it may be helpful to "flatten" the fabric in front of the foot with your fingers.

15 Follow steps 12 to 14 to machine-quilt on each marked line, working from the center out to the sides. Stitch in the same direction on each line to prevent diagonal ripples from forming between the quilting lines. When all the quilting is done, trim all the threads close to the fabric. Remove the safety pins.

TIP Steam the placemat lightly to "puff up" the quilting. Do not touch the iron to the fabric as you steam.

How to Sew Super Easy NAPKINS

LET'S BEGIN

1 Cut off the **SELVAGES** from the fabric. Cut out square napkins, following the grainlines (page 38) exactly. Pull threads out of the **CROSSWISE** and **LENGTHWISE** grains to mark the cutting lines, if possible (page 43). For the most efficient use of your fabric, divide the full width of 45", 48", or 54" (115, 122, or 137 cm) fabric into three equal squares. If your fabric is 60" (152.5 cm) wide, cut either four 15" (38 cm) or three 20" (51 cm) napkins.

2 Set your machine for a narrow zigzag stitch about 12 stitches per inch, which equals 2 mm. Stitch ½" (1.3 cm) from the edge around each napkin, **PIVOTING** ½" (1.3 cm) from the corners.

3 Pull threads to fray the outer edges on each side of the napkin, working from the cut edges up to the stitching.

!

DONE ALREADY

What could be easier? And think of the money you've saved!

1

EXAMPLE: CUT SIX 18" (46 CM) SQUARE
NAPKINS FROM 1 YD. (0.95 M) OF FABRIC

54" (137 CM)

18" (46 CM)

SELVAGE

2

3

More TABLE RUNNERS & PLACEMATS

Sew placemats from checked fabric and quilt them, following the lines of the check. Sew matching napkins, following the general directions for a rectangular tablecloth (page 162), but using ¼" (6 mm) *double-fold hems (p. 101)*.

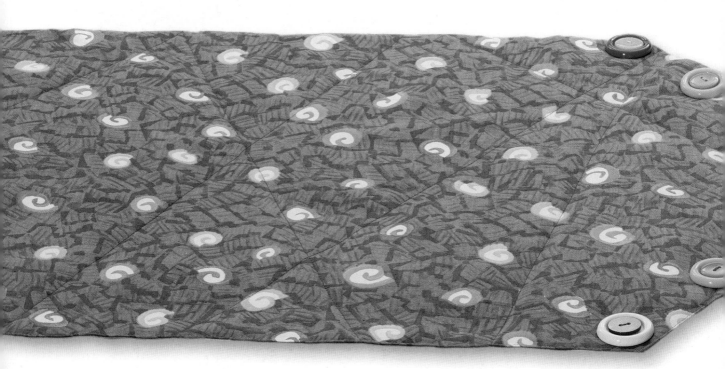

Use a dinner plate as a guide to round off the corners of a rectangle, creating an oval table runner or placemats. Omit batting in the placemats and add welting to the outer seam. Remember to ease (not stretch) the welting around the curves.

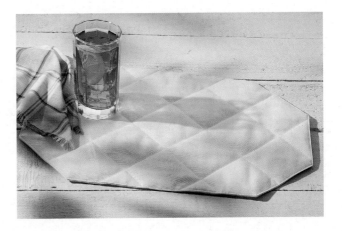

Make octagonal placemats. Prepare a paper pattern; cut off the corners diagonally, 3½" (9 cm) from the corners. Plan your quilting lines to echo the shape of the placemat.

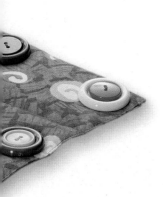

Omit the welting; add batting between the layers of a table runner, and quilt it in random diagonal lines. Sew colorful buttons along the angled ends of the table runner.

Sewing
OUTDOOR DÉCOR

Special Fabrics and Materials

Sewing for outdoor spaces has become more appealing and more practical because of the many advances in the performance and styling of indoor/outdoor decorator fabrics, trims, and cushions. Before you get started on a project, here's what you need to know about these incredible materials and products.

Indoor/Outdoor Fabrics

Fabric stores now carry water-repellant, fade-resistant fabrics that look and feel like regular decorator fabrics, such as upholstery brocades, printed plain weaves, and textured weaves. These performance fabrics are ideal for exposed areas like decks and patios and for sunrooms and screened porches where sunlight and dampness can damage regular fabrics.

Like other decorator fabrics, many of these special indoor/outdoor fabrics are available in color-coordinated collections that include fabric patterns of different scales, along with stripes, checks, and solids. These collections make it easy to plan coordinating pieces for your outdoor room and to mix and match fabrics for pillows or table linens. Also like indoor decorator fabrics, these new outdoor fabrics are available in light weights to upholstery weights, so you can find the perfect weight for any project from table coverings to durable cushion covers.

For a tablecloth or long cushion, you may need to stitch together lengths of fabrics. For a professional look, you should match the fabric design at the seams. To match prints, buy an extra repeat of fabric. The repeat is the distance from the beginning of a fabric motif to where it begins again along the selvage in the fabric design. Most fabrics have the pattern repeat listed on the identification label, but you can also measure it yourself.

While performance fabrics may look the same as indoor fabrics and are available in some of the same prints and colors, they are dyed, fabricated, and finished differently. The natural fibers, such as cotton, silk, and linen, used for many interior fabrics would weaken and rot when exposed to the elements over time. Many have applied color or designs that fade in direct sunlight, so they aren't recommended for outdoor use. Indoor/outdoor fabrics are made of weather-resistant acrylic or polyester fibers. They have been dyed in the fiber or yarn stage to make them colorfast and are treated to resist stains and mildew.

Sew these indoor/outdoor fabrics as you would any medium-weight decorator fabric, using a size 80 needle and all-purpose polyester sewing thread. If the fabric ravels easily, it's a good idea to finish the edges and seam allowances with zigzag stitching or serging.

Other fabrics, such as canvas and nylon, also are weather resistant and ideal for a number of outdoor projects. Plain canvas provides strong, invisible support for a hammock, for example. Striped canvas works great for a fanciful cabana top. Nylon is ideal for outdoor projects, such as flags and privacy screens. Because nylon is made with dyed filaments that are extruded to make fibers, it is naturally strong, durable, and weather resistant. It blocks wind, is colorfast, and dries quickly. The higher the denier count, the heavier the nylon. When sewing these fabrics, use a size 70 or 80 needle and avoid pinning or ripping seams where the holes will show.

Vinyl oilcloth is a waterproof fabric that is fade, stain, and soil resistant. It is available in a fun array of colors and prints and is practical and attractive for outdoor table coverings and accessories. As with nylon and canvas, holes from pins and needles will show in vinyl oilcoth, so pin only within seam allowances and avoid ripping seams. Use a size 80 needle to sew vinyl oilcloth.

Always ask about care requirements when purchasing these indoor/outdoor fabrics. Some are more weatherproof than others. All can be spot cleaned using mild soap and water, but not all can be machine washed or bleached. For extra protection against the elements, consider using UV protective sprays and water-repellant sprays.

Trims

The companies that produce indoor/outdoor fabrics also offer weather-resistant trims. These trims look the same as other decorator trims but are made of weather-resistant polyester fibers instead of the usual cotton or rayon. Options include twisted welting, brush fringe, and tassel fringe. Trims are available for two types of applications—sew-in or sew-on. Sew-in trims have a lip or extension designed to be sewn into a seam and not seen on the finished project. Sew-on trims have a finished or decorative header designed to show after application. The trims can be sewn on, glued on with fabric glue, or attached with paper-backed fusible adhesive.

Filler Materials

It is important to fill outdoor furniture cushions with drainable outdoor foam. Poly-fil®
NU-Foam®, for example, is a compressed
polyester upholstery foam alternative that
does not hold water or disintegrate and is
mildew resistant. It is available in thicknesses ranging from ½" to 4" (1.3 to 10
cm) and is sold by the yard and in precut
squares. Foam alternative is easily cut to
any shape with sewing shears or a rotary
cutter and mat. When cutting thick pieces
of NU-Foam, cut in thin layers rather than
trying to make a single cut.

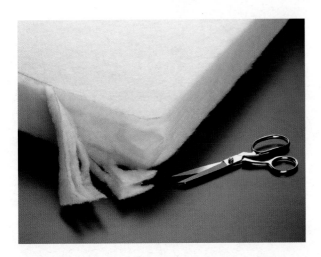

Polyester upholstery batting can be
used alone to stuff furniture cushions. It
can also be wrapped around foam or foam
alternative cushions for a thicker look and
to soften the edges. This synthetic batting
is resilient and naturally weather resistant.

Pillow forms come in several shapes
and sizes. Look for square, rectangular, and
round forms with a knife edge. Bolster pillow forms in several lengths and diameters
and square box-edge forms in several sizes
are also available. Select polyester fiber-
filled pillow forms; cover them with a plastic bag before inserting in the pillow cover
if they will be exposed to rain. You can also
look for inexpensive pillow forms with synthetic nonwoven covers that resist weather
better than woven cotton covers.

Notions

To complete your outdoor sewing projects,
you may also need hook-and-loop tape or
zippers for cushions or pillows. Choose
a regular or invisible polyester zipper rather
than one with metal teeth for best weather
resistance.

For wraps, straps, and ties, you will
need notions such as nylon strapping or
braid. When selecting ribbon for outdoor
use, choose polyester or other synthetic
fibers.

Sew your projects with all-purpose
polyester thread. Nylon monofilament
thread is also ideal for projects where you
don't want to see the thread.

Welted Cushions

You can renew your outdoor seating by sewing new deluxe cushions. The trend in outdoor chairs and benches is thick, really comfortable cushions. Often two different cushion styles are used on a piece of furniture, such as the firm, boxed seat cushion and softer, mock-box back cushion on this chair.

The same fabric was used for both cushions and all the welting on the chair shown here. However, you may want to mix and match coordinating fabrics, so yardage estimates are given separately for each cushion in the materials list. The amounts listed will make a 20" x 23" (51 x 58.5 cm) seat cushion and a 20" x 20" (51 x 51 cm) back cushion; adjust the yardage as necessary for your cushions.

Welting gives the seams more strength and better definition. Make the welting with polyester filler cord, which is more weather resistant than cotton filler cord. Choose a size that best suits your project and the look you want. Zippers at the back of the seat cushion and at the bottom of the back cushion make it easy to place and remove the inserts.

MATERIALS

- 1 yd. (0.92 m) indoor/outdoor decorator fabric, 54" (137 cm) wide for seat cushion cover

- ⅔ yd. (0.63 m) indoor/outdoor decorator fabric, 54" (137 cm) wide for back cushion cover

- ½ yd. (0.5 m) indoor/outdoor decorator fabric, 54" (137 cm) wide for seat cushion welting

- ½ yd. (0.5 m) indoor/outdoor decorator fabric, 54" (137 cm) wide for back cushion welting

- Nu-Foam upholstery foam alternative, 4" (10 cm) thick

- Medium-tip permanent marker

- Clear quilter's ruler or yardstick

- Polyester filler cord in desired diameter in amount equal to twice the circumference of seat cushion plus circumference of back cushion top and sides

- Seam sealant

- Two polyester zippers in closest length to cushion back width

- Basting tape

- Polyester upholstery batting

- Heavy-duty thread and hand-sewing needle

Cutting Directions

If you are replacing existing cushions that fit the furniture accurately, trace the cushions to make patterns. Otherwise, measure the seat dimensions for the box seat cushion. Draw the pattern on paper and add ½" (1.3 cm) to the outer edge for a seam allowance. Use the pattern to cut two fabric panels for the seat cushion cover. Center any large design motifs or stripe patterns on the panels, positioning the patterns to match the stripes at the seamlines.

For a seat cushion zipper strip with a finished width of 4" (10 cm), cut the strip 6¼" (15.7 cm) wide and 1" (2.5 cm) longer than the zipper length (measured from the top stop to the bottom stop); cut the strip in half lengthwise. Cut the seat cushion boxing strip 5" (12.7 cm) wide to fit the cushion circumference minus the zipper length plus 1" (2.5 cm) for seam allowances; piece as necessary. If working with striped fabric, plan the stripes of the boxing strip to align to the stripes of the cushion cover along the front.

Measure the back dimensions (with seat cushion in place) and trace the shape of the upper back. Draw the pattern on paper. This line will be the cutting line for the cushion insert. Draw the cutting line for the fabric 2½" (6.5 cm) from the cushion insert cutting line. Use the pattern to cut two fabric panels for the back cushion cover, centering any large design motifs or matching stripes.

Measure around the filler cord and add 1" (2.5 cm) to determine the width to cut the bias strips. To determine the length of welting strips needed for the seat cushion, measure the cushion circumference and add 6" (15 cm) for the overlap. For box cushions with two welted edges, multiply this measurement by two. To determine the length of welting strips needed for the back cushion, measure the top and sides of the cushion cover.

Making Welting

1 Cut the bias strips and seam them together as in steps 1 and 2 on page 362.

2 Wrap the bias strip around the cording with wrong sides together. Using a zipper or welting foot, machine-baste the layers together close to the cord.

3 Pin or use basting tape to apply the welting to the right side of the cushion cover panel, aligning the raw edges. Begin at the center of the least conspicuous edge. Clip the welting seam allowances up to the stitching at each corner to allow the welting to smoothly turn the corner. If your fabric frays easily, apply a drop of seam sealant to the end of the clip.

4 Begin stitching 1" (2.5 cm) from the welting end. Stitch just inside the basting line. Pivot at the corners. Stop stitching 2" (5 cm) from the point where the ends meet. Leave the needle down in the fabric.

5 Remove several basting stitches from the finishing end and open the fabric to expose the cording. Cut the cording even with the beginning end. Cut the excess fabric 2" (5 cm) beyond the beginning end. Fold under ½" (1.3 cm) of the overlapping bias strip. Lap it around the other end and finish stitching.

5

Box Seat Cushion

1 Trim the ½" (1.3 cm) seam allowance from the pattern. Place the pattern on the NU-Foam and trace the edges with a permanent marker. Repeat on the opposite side of the cushion, making sure the pattern position is identical on each side. Cut the foam alternative along the lines, using sharp shears and cutting in layers.

2 Wrap polyester upholstery batting over the cushion, and trim the edges so they just meet. Trim the batting corners diagonally, and fold them together so the edges just meet. Whipstitch the edges of the batting together, enclosing the cushion.

3 Follow the welting instructions (page 355) to make and apply welting to the edges of the top and bottom panels.

4 Pin the zipper strips right sides together. Stitch ⅝" (1.5 cm) seams ½" (1.3 cm) long at the ends. Baste the seam between the stitched ends. Press the seam open.

5 Apply basting tape to the right side of the zipper tapes along the outer edges. Remove the paper backing and center the zipper facedown over the basted part of the seam. Press with your fingers to firmly adhere the tapes to the seam allowances.

6 Using a zipper foot, stitch a continuous rectangle around the zipper ¼" (6 mm) from the teeth and across the ends just beyond the zipper stops.

7 Stitch the ends of the boxing strip to the ends of the zipper strip, right sides together, forming a ring. Press the seams away from the zipper. Remove the basting stitches from the zipper seam.

8 Pin the boxing strip to one panel of the cushion cover, right sides together, with the zipper at the back. Match any stripes at the cushion front. Clip the boxing strip at the corners to allow the seam allowance to open and turn the corner. Use a welting or zipper foot to stitch the layers together along the welting stitching line.

9 Open the zipper partway. Stitch the remaining panel to the other side of the boxing strip as in step 8.

10 Turn the cushion cover right side out through the zipper opening. Press the edges. Insert the cushion into the cover and zip it closed.

Mock-Box Back Cushion

1 Trim the pattern along the cushion insert cutting line. Cut the cushion and wrap it with batting as in steps 1 and 2, opposite. Make and apply welting to the side and top edges only of one cushion cover panel.

2 Fold one of the square bottom corners in half diagonally, right sides together and pin. Measure 2½" (6.5 cm) from the point along the fold and mark a line across the corner perpendicular to the fold. Stitch on the line. Trim the excess

fabric. Repeat for the other corner and for the corners of the other panel. Press the seams open.

3 Pin the lower edges of the panels right sides together, aligning the corner seams. Center the zipper on the bottom edge and mark the seam allowances just beyond the zipper stops. Stitch from 1" (2.5 cm) before the corner seam to the mark at each side of the cushion bottom. Baste the seam between the stitched ends. Press the seam open. Use basting tape to apply the zipper to the basted seam allowances and stitch in place as in steps 5 and 6, opposite. Remove the basting thread.

4 Open the zipper partway. Pin the side and top edges of the panels together. With the welted panel facing up, stitch the panels together just inside the welting basting line, using a welting or zipper foot.

5 Complete the cushion as in step 10, above.

Chair and Bench Pads

ads add color and style to basic wooden or resin chairs and benches. These lightly padded, reversible seat cushions are simple to sew and feature bias binding around the edges. The bias binding conforms easily to curved edges and rounded corners. Make your own bias binding for a customized look, using a bias tape maker. To speed up the project, you can use purchased bias binding.

Polyurethane foam is used for the inserts in these pads, so they should not be left out in the rain. For more weather resistance, substitute NU-Foam.

MATERIALS

- Decorator fabric

- ½" (1.3 cm) high-density firm polyurethane foam or Nu-Foam upholstery foam alternative

- ½" (1.3 cm) single-fold bias tape; or fabric and ¾" (2 cm) bias tape maker

- Marking pen

- Glue stick

Chair or Bench Pad

1 Make a paper pattern of the chair or bench seat, rounding any sharp corners. Cut the pattern; check the fit. This pattern is used for cutting the fabric.

2 Trace another pattern on a separate piece of paper; mark the cutting line ⅝" (1.5 cm) in from the traced line. Cut out the pattern on the inner marked line. This pattern is used for cutting the foam.

3 Cut the pad front and pad back from decorator fabric, using the pattern for fabric. Place the pattern for foam on the polyurethane foam; trace, using a marking pen. Cut the foam on the marked line, using a rotary cutter and mat or scissors.

4 Make bias tape (page 362) slightly longer than the pad circumference, or use purchased bias tape. Press the bias tape into a curved shape to match the shape of the pad. To prevent puckering, stretch the tape slightly as you press.

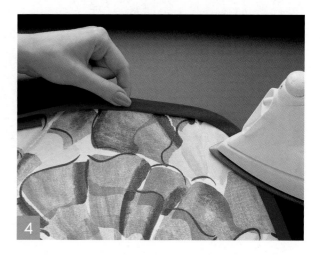

5 Center the foam on the wrong side of the pad back; place the pad front over the foam, right side up, matching the raw edges of the fabric. Pin the layers together.

6 Machine-baste a ¼" (6 mm) seam around the pad, using a zipper foot.

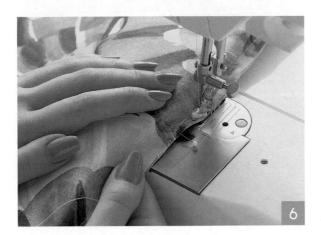

7 Apply a small amount of glue stick to the seam allowance of the pad back. Finger-press the wide side of the bias tape into position, with the raw edges of the pad fabric at the foldline of the tape; overlap the ends of the tape about 1" (2.5 cm).

8 Turn the pad over. Glue-baste the narrow side of the tape to the seam allowance of the pad front, using a small amount of glue stick. Join the ends of the tape by folding under ¼" (6 mm) on the overlapped end; glue-baste.

9 Stitch along the inner edge of the tape, using a zipper foot, with the narrow edge of the tape facing up.

Making Bias Tape

1 Fold the fabric in half diagonally on the bias grain; cut along the fold. Cut bias strips 1¾" (4.5 cm) wide.

2 Join the strips, right sides together, by placing them at right angles, offset ¼" (6 mm); the strips will form a "V." Stitch a ¼" (6 mm) seam across the ends. Press the seam open; trim off the seam allowance points even with the edges. The raw edges match on the long edges after the seam is stitched.

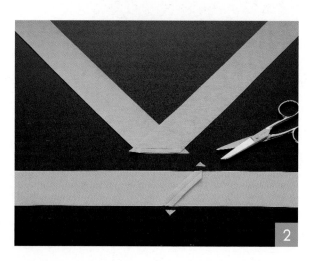

3 Thread the pointed end of the bias strip through the channel at the wide end of the tape maker, bringing the point out at the narrow end. Using a pin, pull the fabric through the slot opening; pin the point of the strip to a pressing surface.

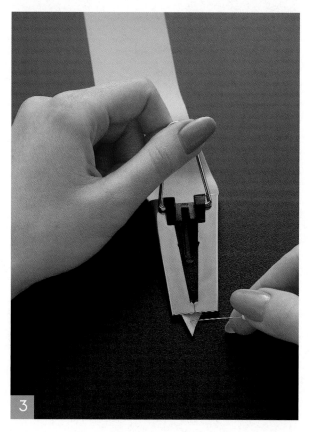

4 Press the folded bias strip as you pull the tape maker the length of the strip. The tape maker automatically folds the raw edges to the center of the strip.

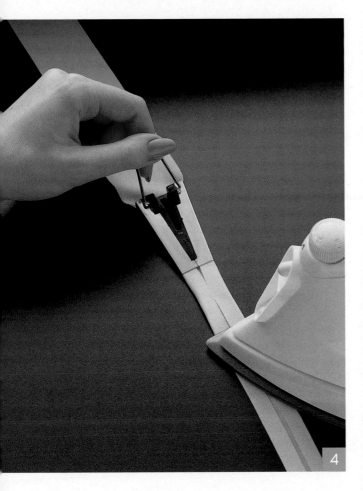

5 Fold the bias tape lengthwise, with the folded edge on the bottom extending a scant ⅛" (3 mm) beyond the folded edge of the upper layer; press.

Decorator Pillows

illows add a wonderful finishing touch to any décor, indoors or out. The fabric and trims shown here are designed for the outdoors, but the inserts are regular pillow forms. If they will be left outdoors during long periods of rain, cover the pillow form with a plastic bag before inserting it in the cover.

Part of the fun of sewing for your home is mixing and matching fabrics and trims, and pillows give you the chance to experiment without making a big investment. Choose coordinating prints in different sizes to combine with stripes, plaids, or checks.

While you're having fun selecting fabrics, don't forget the trims; they give any pillow a polished look. Trims can be stitched in place or adhered with permanent fabric adhesive or fusible web tape.

There are several ways to close the pillows. The square pillow has an overlapped closure held in place with hook-and-loop tape. The bolster pillow closes with an invisible zipper. Both closures make it

easy to remove the cover for cleaning or to replace the insert. If you don't want to remove the cover, you can slip-stitch it closed.

MATERIALS FOR SQUARE PILLOW

- ⅝ yd. (0.6 m) indoor/outdoor decorator fabric, 54" (137 cm) wide

- ½ yd. (0.5 m) sew-on hook-and-loop tape

- 2¼ yd. (2.1 m) indoor/outdoor twisted cording with lip

- Masking or clear tape, ½" (1.3 cm) wide

- 18" (46 cm) pillow form

MATERIALS FOR BOLSTER

- ½ yd. (0.5 m) indoor/outdoor decorator fabric for center panel

- ¼ yd. (0.25 m) contrasting indoor/outdoor decorator fabric for ends

- 12" (30.5 cm) invisible zipper

- Invisible zipper presser foot

- 14" x 6" (35.5 x 15 cm) bolster pillow form

- 1¼ yd. (1.15 m) indoor/outdoor tassel fringe with decorative header

- Permanent fabric adhesive

Cutting Directions

For the square pillow, cut a 19" (48.5 cm) square for the front; for the back, cut two 19" x 11" (48.5 x 28 cm) rectangles. For the bolster, cut a 16" x 21" (40.5 x 53.5) rectangle for the center panel; from the contrasting fabric, cut two 7" (18 cm) circles for the ends.

Square Pillow with Twisted Cord Welting

1 Finish one long edge of each pillow back piece with serging or zigzag stitches. Center the hook side of the tape on the right side of one piece, ¼" (6 mm) from the finished edge. Stitch in place along both sides. Repeat with the loop side of the tape for the remaining pillow back.

2 Turn under the edge with the hook tape 1½" (3.8 cm) and stitch in place ¼" (6 mm) from the finished edge. Overlap the back pieces and press the tapes together. Baste across the ends of the overlap to form a 19" (48.5 cm) square.

3 Pin the twisted welting to the pillow back with the right sides of the fabric and welting facing up and the outer edge of the welting lip aligned to the raw edge of the fabric. Plan for the ends to overlap in the center of one side. Avoid extra bulk by not overlapping them at the closure. Clip into the welting lip at the corners. Using a zipper foot, stitch ½" (1.3 cm) from the edge. Leave 1½" (3.8 cm) unstitched between the ends; leave 3" (7.5 cm) tails.

4 Remove the stitches holding the welting to the lip on the tails. Trim the lip ends so they overlap 1" (2.5 cm). Separate the cord plies, and wrap the end of each ply with tape to prevent raveling. Arrange the plies so those on the right turn up and those on the left turn down.

(continued)

5 Insert the plies on the right under the crossed lip ends, twisting and pulling them down until the welting is returned to its original shape. Secure in place with tape.

6 Twist and pull the plies on the left over the plies on the right until the join looks like continuous twisted welting from both sides. Tape in place.

7 Position the zipper foot on the left of the needle, if possible. Place the pillow back to the right of the needle; this will allow you to stitch in the direction of the cord twists. Machine-baste through all layers to secure the welting. If you are unable to adjust your machine to stitch in this position, remove the presser foot and stitch manually over the thick cords. Be sure the presser foot lever is down so the thread tension is engaged.

8 Pin the pillow front to the pillow back, right sides together. With the pillow back facing up, stitch ½" (1.3 cm) from the edge, stitching just inside the basting stitches, crowding the welting.

9 Separate the hook-and-loop tapes and turn the pillow cover right side out. Insert the pillow form and close the cover.

Bolster Pillow

1 Open the zipper. Center the zipper along one long edge, right sides together, with the zipper coil aligned to the seamline. Pin in place. Finish the seam allowance, catching the zipper tape in the stitches.

2 Attach the invisible zipper foot to the machine; position the zipper coil under the appropriate groove of the foot. Stitch, starting at the top of the zipper until the zipper foot touches the pull tab at the bottom.

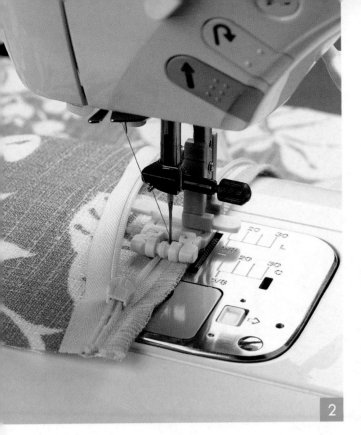

2

6 Pin a circle to one end, right sides together, aligning the raw edges. The cylinder ends will fan out at the clips. Stitch a ½" (1.3 cm) seam, keeping the outer edges even. Repeat at the opposite end.

6

3 Secure the other side of the zipper to the other long edge, as in step 1. Position the coil under the appropriate groove of the zipper foot. The bulk of the fabric will be on the opposite side of the needle. Stitch, starting at the top of the zipper until the zipper foot touches the pull tab at the bottom.

4 Close the zipper. Adjust the zipper foot to get as close as possible to the zipper. Stitch the rest of the seam above and below the zipper. Open the zipper partway.

5 Staystitch a scant ½" (1.3 cm) from the edge at each open end of the cylinder. Clip up to the stitching line every ½" (1.3 cm).

7 Open the zipper and turn the bolster cover right side out. Insert the pillow form and close the zipper.

8 Apply permanent fabric adhesive to the tassel fringe heading, and glue the trim, with fringe turned outward, to the ends of the bolster. Overlap the ends at the seamline.

Tablecloths
for Umbrella Tables

Round and oval tables with a center umbrella are found on lots of patios and decks. Here is a tablecloth that is constructed with a center hole for the umbrella's pole. A hook-and-loop tape closure extends from the center hole so you don't have to remove the umbrella when positioning the tablecloth. To keep the breeze from blowing the tablecloth up onto the table, drapery weights are stitched along the lower edge of the tablecloth.

For tablecloths with body, select firmly woven, medium-weight fabrics, such as poplin or denim. It is often necessary to seam two or more lengths of fabric together for the desired width. If the fabric width being added to the full fabric width is 10" (25.5 cm) or narrower, stitch the additional fabric width to one side of the full fabric width; the seam falls within the drop length of the tablecloth and is not noticeable. If the additional width needed is more than 10" (25.5 cm), use a full fabric width in the center and stitch equal narrow panels to the sides.

MATERIALS

- Indoor/outdoor decorator fabric

- Pencil

- Yardstick

- Scrap of nonwoven interfacing

- Hook-and-loop tape, ¾" (2 cm) wide

- Plastic-covered drapery weights

Cutting Directions

For a round table, measure the diameter of the table; add 20" (51 cm) to determine the measurement for the finished tablecloth. This allows for a 10" (25.5 cm) drop length or overhang. Cut a square of fabric 1" (2.5 cm) larger than this size; piece two fabric widths together, if necessary, and press the seams open.

For an oval table, measure the center length and width of the table; add 20" (51 cm) to each measurement to determine the dimensions for the finished tablecloth; this allows for a 10" (25.5 cm) drop length or overhang. Cut a rectangle of fabric 1" (2.5 cm) larger than this size; piece two fabric widths together, if necessary, and press the seams open.

Round Tablecloth

1 Fold the square of fabric in half lengthwise, then crosswise. Pin the layers together. Divide the measurement for the finished tablecloth by two and add ¼" (6 mm) to determine the radius of the cut circle. Using a pencil, mark an arc, measuring from the folded center of the fabric, a distance equal to the radius.

2 Mark another arc 1" (2.5 cm) from the folded center of the fabric.

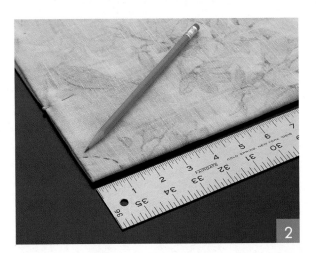

3 Cut on the marked lines through all the layers. Cut along one folded edge; this will be the opening of the tablecloth.

4 Cut two 3" (7.5 cm) strips of fabric for the placket opening, with the length of each strip equal to the cut length of the tablecloth opening plus 1" (2.5 cm).

5 Cut an 8" (20.5 cm) fabric square for the facing; fold the square in half lengthwise, then crosswise. Mark an arc, measuring 3" (7.5 cm) from the folded center of the fabric. Mark a second arc 1" (2.5 cm) from the folded center.

(continued)

6 Cut the fabric on the marked lines; cut along one folded edge.

7 Use serging or zigzag stitching to finish the outer curved edge of the facing. Pin the facing to the tablecloth, right sides together and raw edges even. Stitch a ¼" (6 mm) seam around the center of the facing. Clip the seam allowances.

8 Press the seam allowances toward the facing. Understitch by stitching on the right side of the facing, close to the seamline. Press the facing to the underside of the tablecloth.

9 Press under a scant ½" (1.3 cm) on one long edge of the placket. Pin the placket to the opening edge of the tablecloth, with the right sides together and raw edges even; extend the placket ends ½" (1.3 cm) beyond the edges of the tablecloth. Stitch a ½" (1.3 cm) seam.

10 Press the seam allowances toward the placket. Fold the placket right sides together, with the folded edge of the placket extending a scant ⅛" (3 mm) beyond the seamline; pin. Using a piece of paper folded in quarters, mark an arc 1 ¼" (3.2 cm) from the folded center; cut on the marked line. Unfold the paper pattern to make a circle. Using the circle pattern, mark a curved seamline on the placket. Stitch on the marked line; trim the seam.

11 Turn the placket right side out, with the pressed edge of the placket just covering the seam on the back of the tablecloth; pin. Stitch in the ditch on the tablecloth top by stitching over the seamline in the well of the seam; catch the placket on the back of the tablecloth in the stitching.

12 Trim the ends of the placket even with the outer edge of the tablecloth. Apply the second placket to the remaining opening edge, following steps 9 to 11.

(continued)

13 Finish the raw edge of the tablecloth with serging or zigzag stitches. Press under the fabric ¼" (6 mm) from the edge. Machine-stitch the hem in place.

14 Cut the hook-and-loop tape into 1" (2.5 cm) strips. Pin the hook side of the tape to the overlap, centering the tape on the placket; stitch around the tape. Pin the loop side of the tape to the placket underlap, directly under the hook side of the tape; stitch. Repeat to position the hook-and-loop tape at about 6" (15 cm) intervals.

15 Secure drapery weights along the lower edge of the tablecloth at about 24" (61 cm) intervals; reinforce the fabric at the stitching lines with small pieces of firm, nonwoven interfacing.

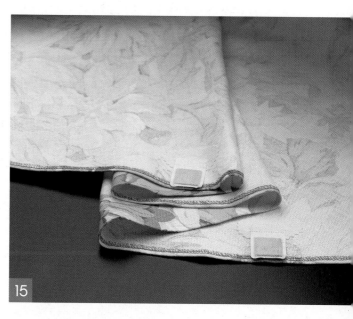

Oval Tablecloth

1 Fold the fabric square in half lengthwise, then crosswise. Pin the layers together. Follow steps 2 to 12 on pages 373 to 375; in step 3, cut along one of the short folded edges.

2 Place the tablecloth on the table; weight the fabric down. Measure and mark around the tablecloth an amount equal to the desired drop length plus ¼" (6 mm). Cut on the marked line.

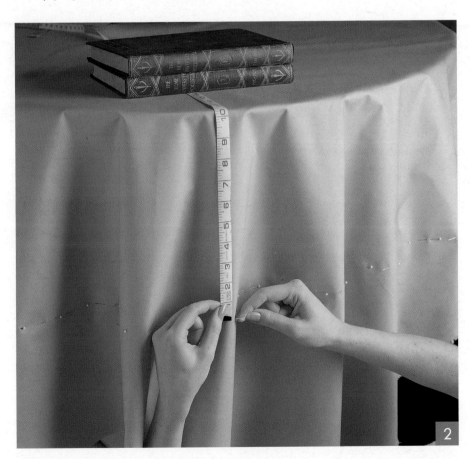

3 Complete the tablecloth as in steps 13 to 15, opposite.

Retro
Oilcloth Placemats

reate a fun retro look in your outdoor dining with oilcloth placemats edged in giant rickrack. Colorful and easy to make, these placemats can be easily cleaned with a wipe of a damp cloth.

Oilcloth was once made by soaking fabric in linseed oil and varnish to make it waterproof. Modern oilcloth is actually vinyl-coated fabric or printed vinyl sealed to a woven base to give it more stability. A popular and practical fabric, vinyl oilcloth is now available in many bold, colorful prints and solids. The materials listed make two placemats.

Cutting Directions

Cut two 14" x 19" (35.5 x 48.5 cm) rectangles from the oilcloth.

Oilcloth Placemat

1 Cut two 19" (48.5 cm) lengths and two 14" (35.5 cm) lengths of rickrack. Begin and end each length at the same point on the rickrack curve. Apply seam sealant to the cut ends to prevent raveling.

2 Apply basting tape along one long edge on the right side of the placemat. Peel back the paper backing from one end. Position the rickrack along the edge of the placemat with the peaks extending ½" (1.3 cm) beyond the edge.

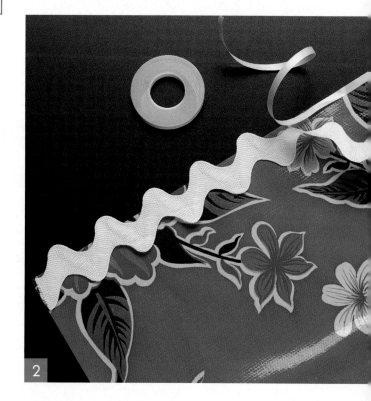

3 Baste the rickrack in place ⅜" (1 cm) from the edge of the placemat.

4 Fold the rickrack to the back along the basting line. Topstitch ⅜" (1 cm) from the edge of the placemat. Stitch again halfway between the topstitching line and the edge.

5 Repeat steps 2 through 4 to finish the remaining long edge; then repeat to finish the short edges.

6 On the wrong side of the placemat, use fabric adhesive to glue the overlapping corners in place as needed to lie flat.

Colorful Hammock

Where better to spend your relaxation time than in a hammock in your own backyard? This style is not only comfortable but decorative, made from a bold decorator print fabric with an inner layer of sturdy canvas. If you want to be able to leave your hammock outdoors, be sure to use indoor/outdoor decorator fabric and canvas. Closet-pole rods and nylon rope support the hammock. The instructions make a hammock bed 49" x 77" (125 x 195.6 cm).

Metal rings are secured to each end, so the hammock can be easily hung on a purchased hammock frame. You can also tie the hammock between the trunks of two trees with additional lengths of rope secured to the metal rings.

MATERIALS

- 2¾ yd. (2.55 m) outer fabric, 54" (137 cm) wide

- 2¾ yd. (2.55 m) heavy-duty canvas, 54" (137 cm) wide, for lining

- Two 50" (127 cm) lengths of hardwood closet pole, 1¼" (3.2 cm) in diameter

- Pencil

- Clamp

- Scrap lumber

- Drill and ½" spade bit

- Exterior primer; exterior paint

- 40 ft. (12.2 m) braided nylon rope, ⅜" (1 cm) in diameter; bodkin

- Bodkin

- Masking tape

- Two #2 x 2" (5 cm) steel rings

Cutting Directions

Cut one 53" x 78" (134.5 x 198 cm) rectangle from the outer fabric, trimming the selvages. Cut one 52" x 78" (132 x 198 cm) rectangle from the canvas lining, trimming the selvages. For the pole sleeves, cut two 8" x 45" (20.5 x 115 cm) rectangles from both the outer fabric and the lining.

Hammock

1 Pin the outer fabric and lining for one pole sleeve, right sides together, matching the raw edges. Stitch ½" (1.3 cm) seams at the short ends. Repeat for the remaining pole sleeve.

2 Press the seam allowances open. Turn the sleeve right side out; press. Fold one pole sleeve in half lengthwise, wrong sides together; pin along the raw edges. Repeat for the remaining pole sleeve.

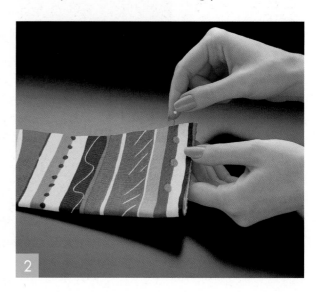

3 Pin-mark the center of each pole sleeve; pin-mark the center of the hammock outer fabric at the upper and lower edges. Pin one sleeve to the right side of the hammock outer fabric at each end, matching pin marks and raw edges; the outer fabric extends beyond the sleeves at the sides. Machine-baste a scant ½" (1.3 cm) from the raw edges.

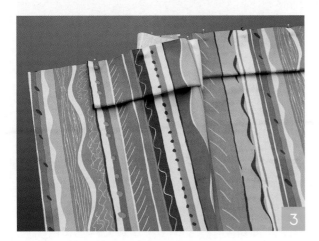

4 Pin the hammock lining and outer fabric, right sides together, along the upper and lower edges; center the lining so the outer fabric extends ½" (1.3 cm) beyond the lining at the sides. Stitch ½" (1.3 cm) seams.

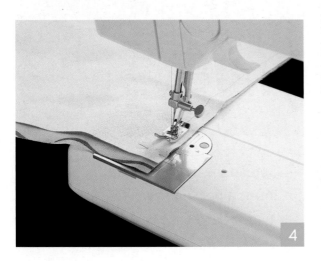

5 Turn the hammock right side out; press. Topstitch ⅛" and ⅜" (3 mm and 1 cm) from the seam.

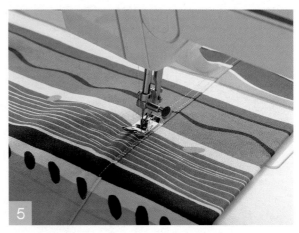

6 Place the hammock on a flat surface, lining side up. Pin the fabric and lining together at the sides, 5" (12.7 cm) from the raw edges of the outer fabric.

7 Press up ½" (1.3 cm) on the long edges of the outer fabric, encasing the edges of the lining. Then press the outer fabric and lining up 1½" (3.8 cm); pin.

(continued)

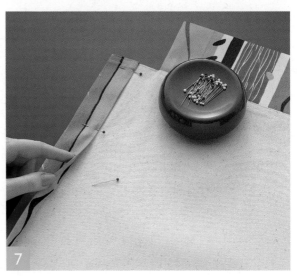

8 Stitch close to the folded edge to make the casing; stitch again ¼" (6 mm) from the first row of stitching.

9 Hold the pole firmly against the table; using a pencil placed flat on the table, draw a line on the pole.

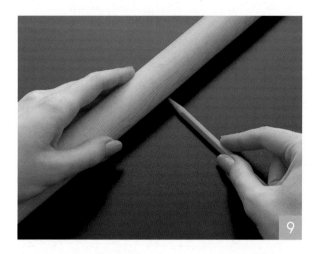

10 Mark a point on the line 1" (2.5 cm) from each end. Clamp the pole to the work surface, placing a scrap of lumber under the pole at the marking. Using a ½" (1.3 cm) spade bit and placing the point of the bit at the mark, drill a hole; repeat at the opposite end. Drill holes at the ends of the remaining pole.

11 Apply primer to the poles, applying two coats at the ends. Paint the poles as desired.

12 Cut the rope in half; wrap the ends with masking tape to prevent raveling. Using a bodkin, thread the rope through the side casing, with the ends extending evenly. Repeat to thread the rope through the opposite casing.

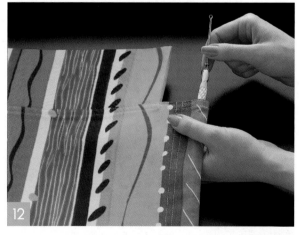

13 Spread the hammock on a flat surface. Insert a pole into each rod sleeve. Tie an overhand knot 1½" (3.8 cm) beyond the end of the casing. Thread the rope through the hole in the pole, and push the pole firmly against the knot. Tie a second overhand knot to secure the pole. Repeat at each corner of the hammock, making sure there is no slack in the rope.

14 Secure the ropes to metal rings for hanging the hammock; the length of the ropes depends on the distance between the hammock frame ends or trees. Mark dots on the ropes at the desired length. Secure one rope at one end of the hammock to a ring, using a fisherman's bend knot as shown in the following two photos.

15 Secure the free end of the rope with two half hitches as shown. Secure the remaining rope at this end of the hammock; then secure the ropes to the ring at the opposite end of the hammock.

16 Hang the hammock on the hammock frame or secure it to trees, using an additional length of rope.

Deluxe Picnic Quilt

This tufted and padded quilt is perfect for a picnic or lounging on your lawn. The colorful indoor/outdoor decorator fabric on the face of the quilt resists stains and fading. The wipe-clean vinyl backing is waterproof, making it ideal for dry or damp ground. Polyester batting gives the quilt comfortable loft.

Spread out your quilt for an instant backyard dining space or a place for the kids to stretch out and read a book.

A fabric wrap with handles makes it easy to store the quilt or take it along to a park or the beach.

MATERIALS

- Medium-loft polyester batting for full-size quilt

- 2½ yd. (2.3 m) indoor/outdoor decorator fabric

- 2 yd. (1.85 m) lightweight vinyl

- Permanent fabric adhesive

- Disappearing fabric marker

- Coordinating yarn

- Sharp, large-eye needle

- ⅓ yd (0.32 m) hook-and-loop tape, ¾" (2 cm) wide

- 2½ yd. (2.3 m) nylon strapping, 1" (2.5 cm) wide

- Candle and match

Cutting Directions

Cut one 54" x 72" (137 x 183 cm) rectangle each from the decorator fabric and vinyl; trim off the selvages. Cut one 54" x 72" (137 x 183 cm) rectangle from the batting. For the quilt wrap, cut two 11" x 28" (28 x 71 cm) rectangles from decorator fabric and one from the batting.

Picnic Quilt

1 Place the batting on the wrong side of the fabric and trim it even with the fabric edges. Machine-baste the edges of the batting and fabric together.

2 Pin the decorator fabric and vinyl right sides together, pinning ¼" (6 mm) from the edges. Sew together, using a ½" (1.3 cm) seam allowance and leaving a 12" (30.5 cm) opening for turning on one short edge.

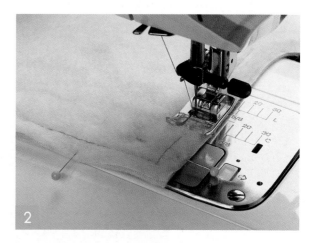

3 Trim the corners diagonally. Turn the quilt right side out. Turn the opening seam allowances under and use fabric adhesive to glue the edges together.

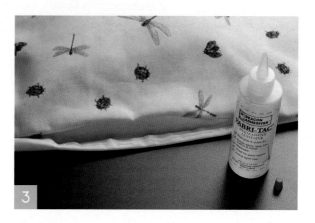

4 Use your fingers to press the edges to crease; do not press with an iron. Topstitch ¼" (6 mm) from the edges.

5 Mark the quilt top for tufting in four evenly spaced rows of three marks each, using a fabric marker.

6 Thread the needle with a double strand of yarn. Working from the right side of the quilt, make a ¼" (6 mm) stitch through all the layers at a mark. Leave a 1½" (3.8 cm) tail of yarn. Knot the yarn tight against the quilt surface and trim the tails evenly. Repeat at each mark, rethreading the needle when the yarn gets too short.

7 Place the fabric layers for the quilt wrap right sides together and place the batting on top. Stitch with the batting on top, leaving an opening in one short end for turning. Trim the corners diagonally. Turn the wrap right side out and press. Press the opening seam allowances under and pin closed. Topstitch ¼" (6 mm) from the edges all around the wrap.

8 Cut a 9½" (24.3 cm) length of the hook-and-loop tape and separate the strips. Sew the loop strip across one short end of the wrap, ¼" (6 mm) from the end. Turn the wrap over and sew the hook strip 2" (5 cm) from the other end.

9 Seal the cut ends of the nylon strapping by holding them close to a candle flame. Allow them to cool. Overlap the ends 1" (2.5 cm) and stitch along both edges with a zigzag stitch, forming the strap into a circle.

10 Center the strap circle on the wrap 1" (2.5 cm) from each side of the wrap; the loop ends should extend evenly beyond the ends of the wrap. Pin the strap in place, placing the first and last pins on each side 3½" (9 cm) from the short ends of the wrap. Sew the strap to the wrap, sewing along both edges between the first and last pins. Zigzag back and forth across the strap at the ends of the stitching lines to secure.

Decorative Flags

Decorative flags add a splash of color to your landscape. They add a festive touch to celebrations such as birthdays or barbeques and serve as easy-to-spot markers for guests. These flags are made using a reversible appliqué technique, so the design of the flag is visible from both sides. Select simple designs like those shown here. Patterns for these flag appliqués are on pages 406 and 407. You can also create your own appliqués by drawing the shapes or enlarging copyright-free illustrations.

For a flag that hangs well and can withstand several seasons of outdoor use, select a heavyweight nylon fabric, such as 200-denier nylon. This heavier fabric is especially easy to handle when applying appliqués using the reversible technique.

If you will be hanging the flag from a flagpole, select a pole that has a screw or clip at the end of the staff. This allows you to fasten a

small tab on the flag to the pole, which prevents the flag from shifting downward. Flags can be made in any size. A popular size for flags displayed on flagpoles is 28" x 40" (71 x 102 cm).

MATERIALS

- 200-denier nylon fabric for flag and appliqué pieces

- Appliqué pattern

- Liquid fray preventer

- Monofilament nylon thread; machine embroidery thread

- Chalk or water-soluble marking pen

- Appliqué scissors

- Water-soluble stabilizer

- Paper towels

- ¼" (6 mm) grosgrain ribbon, for streamers, optional

- Flagpole and mounting bracket for flagpole, or wood pole set

Decorative Flag

1 Cut the flag from the background fabric, adding 2" (5 cm) to the desired finished width and 5" (12.7 cm) to the desired finished length; this allows for hems and the upper casing. Cut appliqués in the desired shapes and colors.

2 Cut one 1" x 4" (2.5 x 10 cm) rectangle for the tab from the background fabric, if the flag will be hung from a flagpole; apply liquid fray preventer to the raw edges. Fold the fabric in half crosswise; stitch a ½" (1.3 cm) buttonhole about ¼" (6 mm) from the folded edge as shown. Set aside.

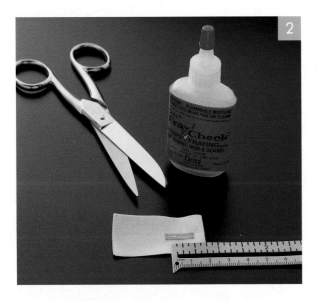

3 Press under ½" (1.3 cm) twice on one long edge of the flag. Straight-stitch close to the first fold, using monofilament thread. Repeat to hem the opposite long edge.

4 Press under ½" (1.3 cm) on the upper edge of the flag; then press under 3" (7.5 cm), for the casing. For a flag with a tab, center the tab on the foldline of the casing, on the wrong side of fabric, with the folded edge of the tab about ⅛" (3 mm) from the hemmed edge. Stitch in place as shown.

5 Fold the casing in place; pin. Stitch close to the first fold; then stitch ¼" (6 mm) above the first row of stitching.

6 Press under ½" (1.3 cm) at the lower edge of the flag; then press under 1" (2.5 cm). Pin in place. Stitch close to both folded edges; then stitch another row, centered between the previous stitching.

(continued)

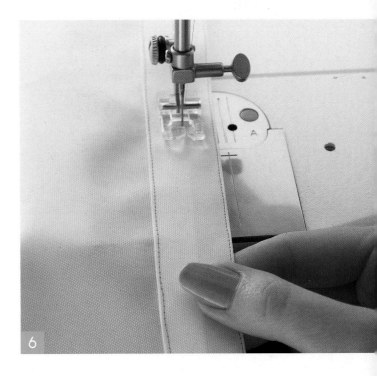

7 Position the appliqué pieces on the flag, and pin in place. For a layered design, pin the first layer only and mark the placement of the foreground layers, using a water-soluble marking pen or chalk.

8 Straight-stitch around the appliqué piece, about ⅛" (3 mm) from the raw edges, using monofilament thread.

9 Separate the fabric layers, working from the back of the flag; trim away the background fabric, close to the stitching.

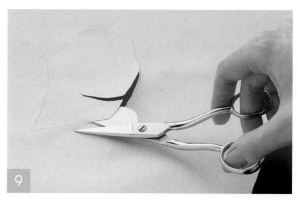

10 Repeat steps 8 and 9 for each background appliqué piece, then for any foreground appliqué pieces.

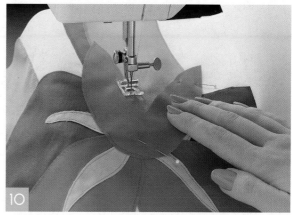

11 Cut water-soluble stabilizer about 2" (5 cm) larger than the area to be appliquéd. With the back of the flag facing up, position the stabilizer over the appliqué area; pin in place.

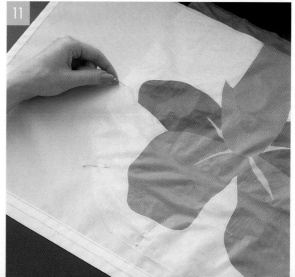

12 Set the machine for a short, wide zigzag stitch; use machine embroidery thread in the needle and bobbin. Satin-stitch around the appliqués, covering the raw edges of the fabric on the front and back of the flag; stitch the background appliqués first, then the foreground appliqués.

13 Mark any detail lines, such as veins of leaves or flowers, using chalk or water-soluble marking pen. Stitch, tapering the zigzag stitching at the ends by using narrower stitches.

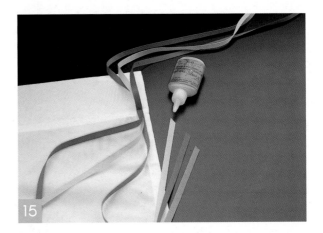

14 Trim excess stablizer from the back of the flag. Mist any remaining stabilizer with water to dissolve it; wipe the flag with an absorbent paper towel.

15 Stitch ribbon streamers to the upper corner of the flag, if desired, stitching over the previous stitching of the casing. Apply liquid fray preventer to the ribbon ends to prevent fraying. Hang the flag.

Design Extending off the Edge

1 Follow step 1, cutting the appliqué pieces so they extend to the raw edge of the background fabric. Continue as in steps 2 to 7, except do not stitch the hems and casing in place.

2 Stitch the appliqués as in steps 8 to 10, unpinning the hems and casing as necessary. Complete the flag as in steps 11 to 14. Stitch the hems and casing in place.

Windsocks

indsocks with bright appliqués are decorative accents for yards or decks. Make a windsock that can be used year-round, or make several for the seasons.

Sewn from nylon fabric, a windsock can withstand sunlight, rain, and other weather conditions without fading or deteriorating. Lightweight nylons, such as ripstop and nylon broadcloth, are used because they catch the wind easily. To allow the windsock to turn freely in the breeze without tangling, it is hung with sturdy nylon cording or fishline attached to a swivel.

A fusible appliqué technique is used for sewing windsocks, making it easy to stitch the appliqués on lightweight nylon without puckering. Use the appliqué patterns on pages 404 and 405 to sew the windsocks shown here, or enlarge designs from coloring books or gift-wrapping paper to use as patterns for the appliqués.

MATERIALS

- ½ yd. (0.5 m) nylon fabric, for body of windsock and tails

- ¼ yd. (0.25 m) nylon fabric in one or two colors, for appliqués and tails

- Paper-backed fusible web

- Fabric marker or chalk

- 19" (48.5 cm) length of heavy-weight covered wire

- Waterproof vinyl tape

- Large-eye needle

- 1 yd. (0.92 m) nylon cording or monofilament nylon fishline for hanging windsock

- Windsock swivel or #5 or #6 ball-bearing fishing swivel to be used as hanger

Cutting Directions

Cut one 16½" x 18½" (41.8 x 47.3 cm) rectangle from the ½ yd. (0.5 m) piece of fabric for the body of the windsock. Cut a total of six tails, 3¼" x 22" (8.2 x 56 cm) each, on the crosswise grain, cutting two or three tails from each color of fabric as desired.

As in steps 1 and 2, opposite, cut the appliqués in the desired shapes and colors, using the remaining fabric.

Windsock

1. Trace the desired appliqué shapes onto the paper side of fusible web; for asymmetrical designs, trace the mirror image. Apply fusible web to the wrong side of the fabric, following the manufacturer's instructions.

2. Cut the appliqué pieces, following the marked lines on the fusible web; remove the paper backing.

3. Arrange the appliqué pieces on the body of the windsock, allowing for ¼" (6 mm) seams at the side and lower edges and a 1" (2.5 cm) casing at the top. Fuse the appliqués in place.

4. Mark any lines for design details. Stitch around the appliqués and along the marked lines, using short zigzag stitches of medium width.

5. Turn the long edges of the tails ¼" (6 mm) to the wrong side; stitch close to the fold. Trim the excess fabric close to the stitching.

(continued)

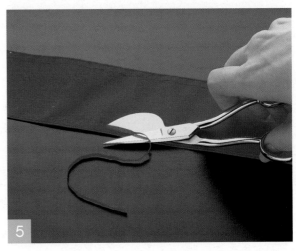

6 Turn the long edges to the wrong side again, enclosing the raw edge. Stitch over the previous stitches.

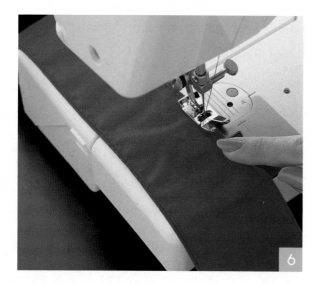

7 Fold the lower end of the tail in half, right sides together. Stitch a ¼" (6 mm) seam across the end. Press the seam open. Turn the end of the tail right side out, to form a point; press. Stitch and turn the remaining tail ends.

8 Pin the tails evenly along the lower edge of the windsock, with right sides together and raw edges even; leave ¼" (6 mm) seam allowance on the sides of the body. Stitch a ¼" (6 mm) seam along the lower edge; finish the seam, using serging or a zigzag stitches.

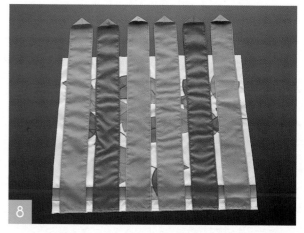

9 Turn the seam toward the windsock body, with the tails extending down. Topstitch the seam in place.

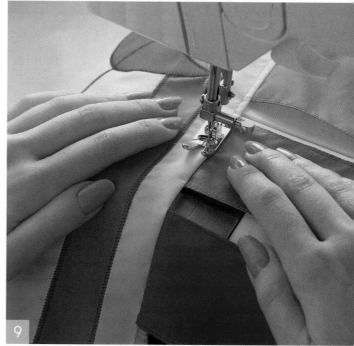

10 Fold the windsock body in half, matching raw edges at the side; stitch a ¼" (6 mm) seam. Finish the seam with serging or zigzag stitches. Turn the windsock right side out.

11 Press under ¼" (6 mm) on the upper edge of the windsock. Then press under ¾" (2 cm); pin in place to form a casing. Stitch close to the first fold; leave a 2" (5 cm) opening for inserting the wire.

12 Insert a 19" (48.5 cm) length of covered wire into the casing. Wrap the overlapped ends of wire together with waterproof tape to secure. Stitch the opening in the casing closed.

13 Divide the top of the windsock into thirds; mark. At each mark, take a single stitch through the casing, just below the wire, using a large-eye needle and a 12" (30.5 cm) length of nylon cording or fishline.

14 Tie the end of the nylon cording or fishline securely to the windsock.

15 Hold the ends of the cords together, keeping the lengths equal. Thread the ends through the eye of the ball-bearing swivel; tie securely. Hang the windsock.

Patterns

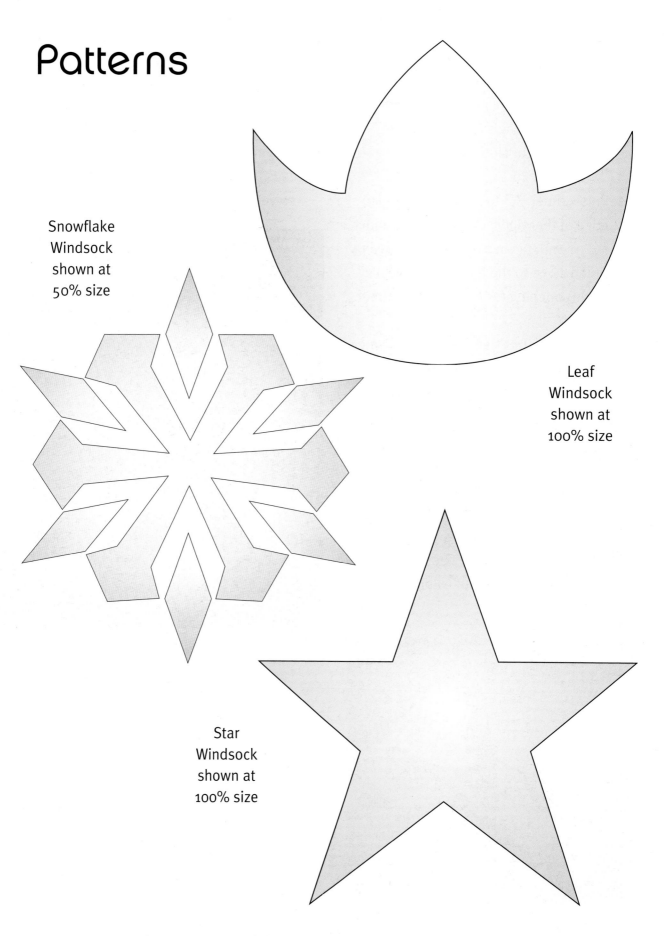

Snowflake
Windsock
shown at
50% size

Leaf
Windsock
shown at
100% size

Star
Windsock
shown at
100% size

Tulips
Windsock
shown at
50% size

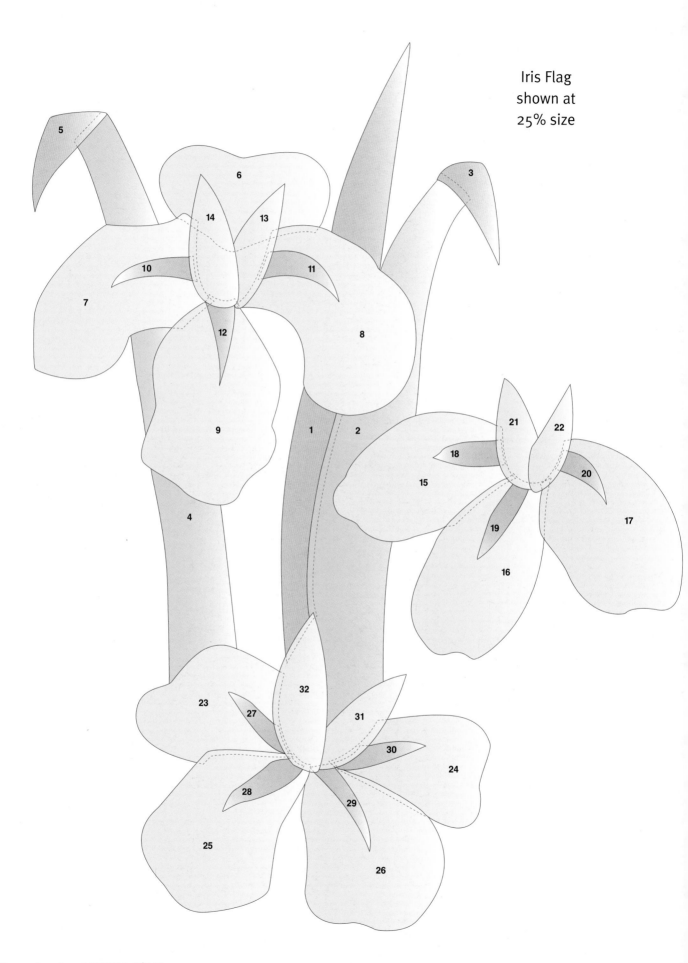

Iris Flag
shown at
25% size

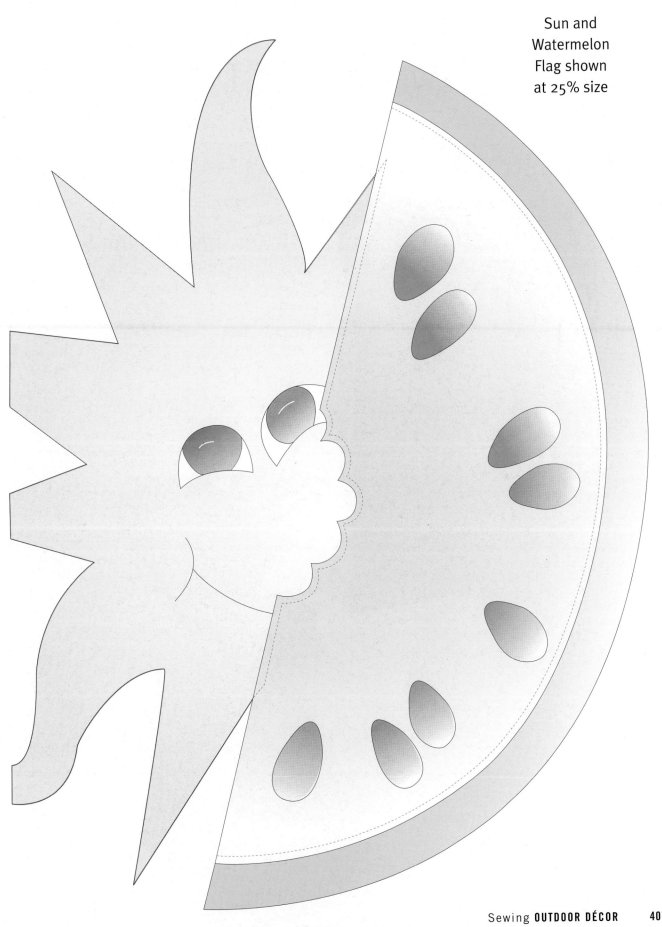

Sun and
Watermelon
Flag shown
at 25% size

Sewing GIFTS

SILK BEAUTY BAG

MATERIALS

Copy machine or graph paper for enlarging pattern

Paper and pencil for drawing pattern

Carpenter's square or T-square ruler

⅝ yd. (0.6 m) print fabric, 44" (112 cm) wide

½ yd. (0.5 m) solid fabric, 44" (112 cm) wide

⅝ yd. (0.6 m) lightweight transparent vinyl

Lightweight quilt batting, 15" × 17" (38 × 43 cm)

Fabric marking pen or pencil

¾ yd. (0.7 m) double-fold bias tape

Thread

18" (46 cm) zipper

Hand-sewing needle

Seam ripper

¼ yd. (0.25 m) lightweight fusible interfacing

Bodkin or tube turner

Pretty on the outside but practical on the inside, this makeup bag will please a woman who loves to travel. The easy-clean vinyl lining has six pockets to hold cosmetics (or jewelry). The full-length zipper closure allows the bag to open wide, and the bag is lightly padded to protect what's inside. You can dress up the bag with an embroidered silk, or choose a washable fabric for durability.

FINISHED SIZE: 11½" WIDE × 6" TALL × 2" DEEP (29.3 × 15 × 5 CM)

1 Enlarge the patterns for the outer bag/lining and pockets on page 82, and cut them out. Draw three patterns using paper, pencil, and a carpenter's square or T-square ruler:

Boxing strip: 3" × 21" (7.5 × 53.5 cm)

Handle: 2" × 10" (5 × 25.5 cm)

Handle interfacing: 9½" × 1" (24.3 × 2.5 cm).

These patterns and dimensions include ½" (1.3 cm) seam allowances.

2 Cut one outer bag and two boxing strips from the print fabric. Cut one bag lining and four handles from the solid fabric. Cut one bag lining and one pocket piece from the vinyl. Cut one bag body from the batting. Cut two handle interfacing pieces. Transfer the pocket stitching lines and bottom stitching lines to the solid lining piece. Transfer the handle placement marks to the outer bag.

3 Wrap double-fold bias tape over each of the two straight edges of the vinyl pocket piece and stitch in place. Place the vinyl pocket piece over the vinyl lining piece, using the pattern as a guide. Place the vinyl pieces over the right side of the solid lining piece. Stitch through all three layers along the pocket stitching lines.

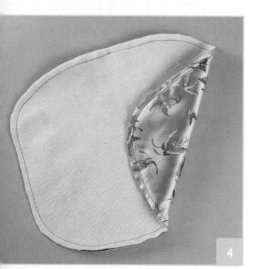

4 Place the batting over the wrong side of the outer bag. Baste the two layers together ¼" (6 mm) from the edge.

5 Press one boxing strip in half to mark the center; unfold. Mark a point on the fold 1½" (3.8 cm) from each end. Pin the boxing strips right sides together. Stitch from the ends to the marks, backstitching at the marks. Machine-baste down the center between marks. Fold each boxing strip wrong sides together so the right sides face out on both sides and the basted seam is down the center. Press.

6 Center the zipper, right side down, over the basted part of the boxing strip seam. Hand-baste the zipper in place.

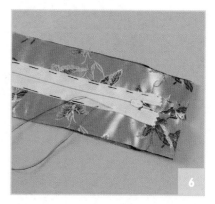

7 Attach the zipper foot to the machine and stitch the zipper to the boxing strip, stitching about ⅜" (1 cm) from the teeth on both sides. Using a seam ripper, pick open the basted part of the seam to expose the zipper.

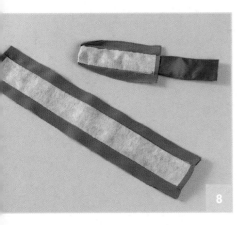

10 Pin a handle to each side of the bag on the right sides, aligning the ends to the marks.

11 Pin one long edge of the boxing strip to one curved edge of the bag, right sides together. Clip the seam allowance of the boxing strip as necessary to fit the curved edge of the bag; pin often. Stitch the strip to the bag, beginning and ending with backstitches exactly at the bottom stitching line of the bag.

8 Center an interfacing piece on the wrong side of two of the handle pieces. Fuse them in place. Pin the plain handles to the interfaced handles, right sides together. Stitch ½" (1.3 cm) seams on the long sides. Using a bodkin or tube turner, turn the handles right side out. Topstitch each long edge.

9 Pin the outer body/batting piece to the lining/pocket piece, wrong sides together. Baste through all layers ¼" (6 mm) from the edge. Through all layers, stitch on the bottom stitching lines (marked on the lining), crossing the pocket stitching lines.

12 Unzip the zipper. Repeat step 11 for the opposite side.

13 Clip the seam allowance of the bag at the bottom stitching lines up to the end of the stitching from steps 11 and 12 . Stitch the ends of the boxing strip to the bag bottom, beginning and ending at the ends of the other stitching lines. Trim and clean-finish the seam allowances. Turn the bag right side out.

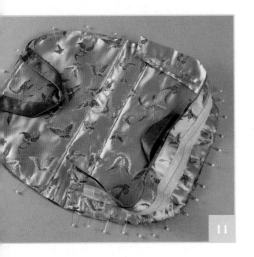

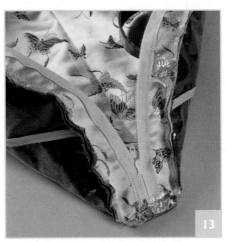

KNITTER'S ROLL

MATERIALS

Yardstick (meterstick) or tape measure

Fabric marking pen or pencil

⅝ yd. (0.6 m) each of two coordinating print fabrics

⅝ yd. (0.6 m) lightweight quilt batting

Thread

Paper and pencil for drawing pattern

Small plate

2½ yd. (2.3 m) extra-wide double-fold bias tape

Hand-sewing needle

Two D-rings, ¾" (2 cm) wide

1¼ yd. (1.15 m) grosgrain ribbon or webbing trim, ¾" (2 cm) wide

This quilted tool wrap makes a great gift for someone who loves to knit. It has lots of slender pockets for holding knitting needles, stitch holders, scissors, and yarn needles. When it's folded up or rolled closed, a strap with D-ring closure keeps the tools snug inside. Adjust the size of the roll and the width of the pockets to make a roll-up for sewing supplies, artist paintbrushes, or other craft supplies.

FINISHED SIZE: 17" WIDE × 13½" TALL (43 × 34.3 CM)

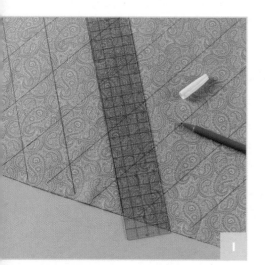

1 Cut a 21" (53.5 cm) square of each of the two fabrics. Using a fabric marking pen or pencil, mark a diagonal line (30 to 45 degrees) on the right side of one fabric square. Parallel to the first line, mark lines evenly spaced 1" to 2" (2.5 to 5 cm) apart across the entire piece. Repeat in the opposite direction.

2 Cut a 21" (53.5 cm) square of batting. Layer the batting between the fabric pieces, with the right sides of the fabric facing out. Pin the layers together around the edge and several places toward the center. Stitch through all layers along all the lines, working first in one direction and then the other, to make quilted fabric.

3 To make the pattern, draw an 18" × 19" (46 × 48.5 cm) rectangle on paper. Using a small plate as a guide, round off the corners of the pattern. Mark a fold line 5" (12.7 cm) from one short end. Cut out the pattern. Use the pattern to cut a piece from the quilted fabric.

4 Unfold the bias tape. Pin one edge of the tape to the edge of the quilted fabric, on either side. Stitch the tape to the fabric along the crease of the outer fold. Begin about 2" (5 cm) from the end of the tape and stop before you reach the beginning end again.

5 To join ends of tape, cut one end diagonally following the fabric grain. Mark a dotted line on the opposite end of the tape even with the diagonally cut edge. Mark a solid line ½" (1.3 cm) from the dotted line and cut the tape on the solid line.

6 Place the diagonally cut ends of the tape right sides together so the folds will align when you stitch the seam. Stitch ¼" (6 mm) seam. Press the seam allowances open. Finish sewing the tape to the quilted fabric.

7 Refold the bias tape, wrap it over the edge of the quilted fabric to the other side, and pin in place. Hand-stitch the free side of the bias tape in place.

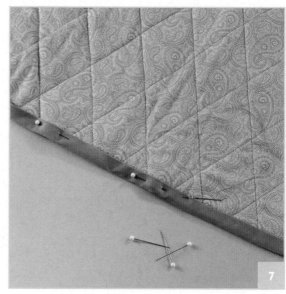

8 Turn up 5" (12.7 cm) on one long edge and pin. Flip the roll over, with the fold at the bottom. Turn back the right side 1½" (3.8 cm), and pin. Stitch through all layers along the inner edge of the bias tape to secure the narrow fold in place.

9 Slip both ends of the ribbon through both D-rings. Turn under the raw edges of the ribbon at the base of the D-rings and stitch the strap to roll at the center of the narrow flap.

10 With the bottom flap facing up, mark parallel stitching lines the desired distance apart on the flap. Stitch through all layers to form the pockets.

DESIGNER'S TIP

Speed up the assembly by starting with pre-quilted, reversible fabric.

BEACH BABE TOTE

MATERIALS

Copy machine or graph paper for enlarging pattern

Paper and pencil for drawing pattern

Carpenter's square or T-square ruler

Pencil-and-string compass

½ yd. (0.5 m) print canvas

¼ yd. (0.25 m) first coordinating solid color of canvas

2 yd. (1.85 m) second coordinating solid color of canvas

Contrasting thread

1¼ yd. (1.15 m) filler cord, ³⁄₁₆" (4.5 mm) diameter

Welting foot or zipper foot

Hand-sewing needle

Eight silver grommets, ³⁄₈" (1 cm) diameter, and application tool

Medium-weight fusible interfacing

2 yd. (1.85 m) cotton twisted cord, ³⁄₈" (1 cm) diameter

Make a sunny gift for someone who loves going to the beach or hanging by the pool. This drawstring bag is large enough to hold everything for the day. The wide, sturdy handle makes carrying comfortable, and the grommeted tie holds it all inside. Tuck in a towel, hat, or sunscreen to enhance the gift.

FINISHED SIZE: 11" WIDE × 18" TALL (28 × 46 CM)

1 Enlarge the handle pattern on page 83, and cut it out. Draw these patterns using paper, pencil, a carpenter's square or T-square ruler, and a string-and-pencil compass:

Bag body: rectangle 35½" wide × 14" tall (90.3 × 35.5 cm)

Top border: rectangle 35½" wide × 3" tall (90.3 × 7.5 cm)

Bottom border: rectangle 35½" wide × 4" tall (90.3 × 10 cm)

Base: circle with 12" (30.5 cm) diameter

Lining: rectangle 35½" wide × 17" tall (90.3 × 43 cm)

These patterns and dimensions include ½" (1.3 cm) seam allowances.

2 Cut one bag body from the print fabric. Cut two top borders from the first solid-color fabric. Cut one bottom border, two bases, one lining, and two handles from the second solid-color fabric. Also cut two 1⅞" × 20" (4.7 × 51 cm) bias strips for welting from the second solid-color fabric.

3 Pin the bottom border to the bottom of the bag body, right sides together. Stitch. Pin and stitch one top border to the top of the bag body. Press the seam allowances apart. Topstitch on both sides of each seam using contrasting thread. Pin the sides of the bag body, right sides together, matching border seams. Stitch, creating a cylinder. Set aside.

4 Stitch the bias welting strips together end-to-end and press the seam open. Encase the cotton filler cord inside the bias strip with wrong sides together and long raw edges of fabric even. Attach the zipper foot or welting foot to your sewing machine, and machine-baste close to the cord.

5 Pin the welting to the right side edge of one base piece, aligning the raw edges. Stitch, beginning a few inches from one end and stopping before you reach the beginning end again. The ends will overlap.

6 Cut one end of the welting straight across. Cut the other end so that it overlaps the first by about 2" (5 cm). Remove 2½" (6.5 cm) of the basting in the long end, exposing the filler cord. Trim the exposed cord so that it butts up against the trimmed and covered end of the cord. Wrap the fabric over both cord ends, turning under the raw edge to finish. Pin in place and finish basting the welting to the base. Set the welted base aside.

7 Pin the remaining top border to the upper edge of the lining, right sides together. Stitch. Press the seam open. Pin the sides of the lining, right sides together, matching border seams. Stitch, leaving a 12" (30.5 cm) opening in the center of the seam.

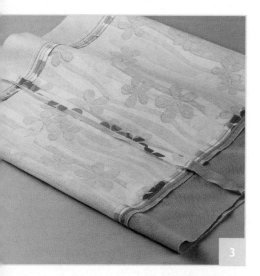

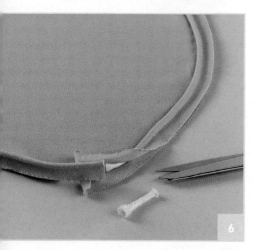

8 Stitch a line a scant ½" (1.3 cm) from the lower edge of the lining. Clip to the stitching line at ¾" (2 cm) intervals. Using plenty of pins, pin the lower edge of the lining to the remaining base piece, right sides together. The lining edge will spread at the clips to conform to the curved edge of the base. Stitch ½" (1.3 cm) seam. Set aside.

9 Repeat step 8 to attach the outer bag to the welted base.

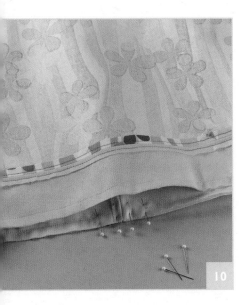

10 With the outer bag right side out and the lining inside out, slip the outer bag into the lining and pin them together at the upper edge. Stitch, leaving a 2" (5 cm) opening centered over the back seam for inserting the handle later.

11 Turn the bag right side out through the large opening in the lining seam. Slipstitch the opening closed.

12 Pin the handle pieces right sides together and stitch the long, shaped seams. Trim the seam allowances, turn the handle right side out, and press. Insert the handle ends between the outer bag and lining through the opening in the upper edge at the back seam. The handle ends should extend slightly below the top border. Topstitch the upper edge, catching the handle in the stitching and closing the opening. Stitch over the topstitching on both sides of the border seam, stitching through the handle ends to secure.

13 Following the manufacturer's instructions, attach a grommet in the center of the top border, 2¼" (6 cm) on each side of the back seam. Attach six more grommets evenly spaced around the border.

14 Lace the decorative cotton cord through the grommets as in the photo on page 419.

TWO-STORY TOTE

MATERIALS

Paper and pencil for drawing pattern

Carpenter's square or T-square ruler

½ yd. (0.5 m) polka-dot fabric

½ yd. (0.5 m) lining fabric

¾ yd. (0.7 m) striped fabric

1 ½ yd. (1.4 m) medium-weight fusible interfacing, optional

Thread

Two separating, nylon sport zippers, 12" (30.5 cm) long

Seam ripper

Hand-sewing needle

1 ½ yd. (1.4 m) webbing, 1" (2.5 cm) wide

Four buttons, 1" (2.5 cm) diameter

Stiff cardboard or foam core board

This tote has a "downstairs" to keep a pair of shoes separate from everything else. Everyone needs a fun tote—and this one is a particularly good gift for a woman who commutes or is always on the go.

FINISHED SIZE: 11" WIDE × 14" TALL × 6½" DEEP (28 × 35.5 × 16.3 CM)

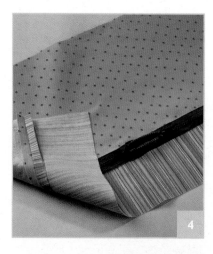

1 Draw these patterns using paper, pencil, and a carpenter's square or T-square ruler:

> *Top front:* rectangle 25" wide × 11" tall (63.5 × 28 cm)
>
> *Top back:* rectangle 12" wide × 11" tall (30.5 × 28 cm)
>
> *Bottom front:* rectangle 25" wide × 5" tall (63.5 × 12.7 cm)
>
> *Bottom back:* rectangle 12" wide × 5" tall (30.5 × 12.7 cm)
>
> *Base:* rectangle 12" wide × 7½" deep (30.5 × 19.3 cm)

Dimensions include ½" (1.3 cm) seam allowances.

2 Cut one top front, one top back, and one base from polka-dot fabric. Cut one top front, one top back, and one base from lining fabric. Cut two bottom fronts, two bottom backs, and two bases from striped fabric. To reinforce lightweight fabrics and strengthen the bases, cut one each of the top front, top back, bottom front, and bottom back and two bases from interfacing. Fuse the interfacing to the wrong sides of all the pieces.

3 Pin one long edge of the top front to the bottom front, right sides together. Machine-baste, using ½" (1.3 cm) seam allowances. Press the seam open.

4 Pin the two zippers, right side up, on the right side of the assembled piece, with the zipper teeth centered over the seam and the pull tabs centered in front. Overlap the tops of the zipper tapes so the ends of the tapes are ½" (1.3 cm) from sides of the fabric. Stitch the zippers in place close to the outer edges, taking care not to catch the seam allowances underneath.

5 Unzip the zippers. Using a seam ripper, pick open the basted seam to separate the top from the bottom. Set the bottom aside. Fold up the zipper tape on the front, and pin it away from the seam allowance.

6 Pin the top front to the top back, right sides together, along the short sides. Stitch, stopping and backstitching ½" (1.3 cm) from the lower edge on each seam. Press the seams open.

7 Pin the top to the polka-dot base, right sides together, aligning the center fronts and center backs. The seams of the top section should align to the back corners of the base. Clip into the seam allowance of the top to allow it to spread at the front corners of the base. Stitch the front and side edges only, leaving the back edge open.

8 Repeat steps 6 and 7 for the lining of the top front, back, and base.

9 Pin the upper edge of the assembled top to the upper edge of the assembled lining, right sides together, matching seams. Stitch the upper edge.

10 Turn the top right side out through one of the back openings. Press. Top-stitch the upper edge. Set the top aside.

11 Pin the bottom front to the bottom back, right sides together, along the short sides. Stitch, starting and stopping by backstitching ½" (1.3 cm) from the upper and lower edges on each seam. Press the seams open.

12 Place the two striped bases, wrong sides together, and pin-baste the edges. Pin the assembled bottom to the pin-basted base, right sides together, aligning the center fronts and center backs. The seams of the bottom section should align to the back corners of the base. Clip into the seam allowance of the bottom to allow it to spread at the front corners of the base. Stitch the front and side edges only, leaving the back edge open.

13 Assemble the remaining striped bottom front and back pieces, as in step 11, for the bottom lining. Pin the lining

to the base on the opposite side of the assembled bottom, clipping the seam allowances at the front corners. Stitch.

14 Turn the bottom right side out. Pin the back edges of the top (including the lining and base) to the back edge of the bottom (not including the lining), right sides together. Stitch. Turn under the upper seam allowances of the bottom lining, and slipstitch in place to cover the raw edges.

15 Zip the top and bottom together. Cut the webbing in half to make two handles. Turn under the ends and stitch one handle to the center front and one to the center back, with the ends about 6" (15 cm) apart. Stitch a button at each end of the handles.

16 To help support the base of the tote and the base of the shoe section, cut two 6½" × 11" (16.3 × 28 cm) rectangles from stiff cardboard or foam core board and place into position on each floor.

DESIGNER'S TIP

Since zipper colors are limited, choose your zipper color first and then have fun selecting three colorful, coordinating fabrics.

13

14

LUXURY SHOE BAGS

MATERIALS

(For one pair)

Paper and pencil for drawing pattern

Carpenter's square or T-square ruler

⅝ yd. (0.6 m) faux suede, 60" (152.5 cm) wide

Fabric marking pen or pencil

3" (7.5 cm) Velcro, ¾" (2 cm) wide

Thread

Fusible letter appliqués, 1" (2.5 cm) tall

When the frequent travelers in your life are on the road, remind them that you're thinking of them with these luxurious shoe bags. The generously sized shoe bags will also be a hit with someone who cultivates a well-organized closet. The bags are made of light, washable faux suede and feature Velcro closures and press-on monograms.

FINISHED SIZE: 5" × 5" × 13" (12.7 × 12.7 × 33 CM)

I Draw two patterns using paper, pencil, and a carpenter's square or T-square ruler:

Bag body: rectangle 21" tall × 17" wide (53.5 × 43 cm). Draw vertical fold lines on the pattern 3" (7.5 cm) from the long cut edges. Draw two more fold lines dividing the center into three 5" (12.7 cm) spaces.

Flap: rectangle 10" tall × 6" wide (25.5 × 15 cm). Angle the corners by drawing diagonal lines 2" (5 cm) up and over from each corner.

These dimensions include ½" (1.3 cm) seam allowances.

2 Cut one bag body and two flaps for each shoe bag. Transfer fold lines to the right side of the bag body, using a fabric marking pen or pencil. Mark placement for Velcro in the center of the body, 3½" (9 cm) from the top and in the center of the flap, 1¼" (3.2 cm) from the bottom.

3 Cut a 1½" (3.8 cm) piece of Velcro. Stitch the hook side to the right side of the bag body at the mark. Stitch the loop side to the right side of one flap section at the mark.

4 Fold the bag body in half lengthwise, right sides together. Stitch the back seam; pivot at the corner and stitch the bottom seam. Trim the seam allowances to ¼" (6 mm).

5 To create a paper-bag bottom for the shoe bag, fold the lower corner, aligning the bottom seam over the back seam. Measure along the bottom seam 2½" (6.5 cm) from the point, and draw a line perpendicular to the seams. The line should be 5" (12.7 cm) long. Stitch on the marked line through all layers, keeping the seam allowances on both sides turned open. Trim away the triangle ¼" (6 mm) from the stitching line. Repeat for the other corner, centering the bottom seam in the 5" (12.7 cm) stitching line.

6 Pin two flap pieces right sides together. Stitch the sides and angled bottom, leaving the other end open. Trim the seam allowances.

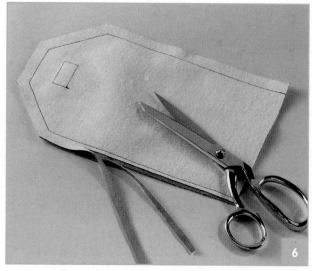

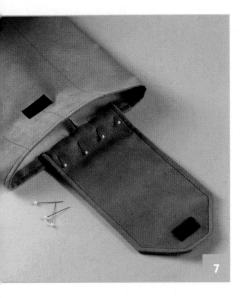

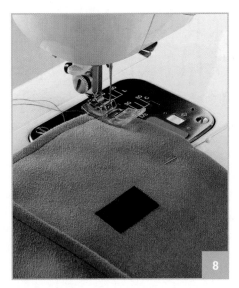

7 Turn the bag body and flap right side out. Turn under ½" (1.3 cm) on the upper edge of the bag body. Topstitch ¼" (6 mm) from the fold. Topstitch ¼" (6 mm) from the outer seamed edges of the flap. Center the open end of the flap over the back seam of the body, aligning the raw edges. Topstitch the flap to the body over the previous stitching line.

8 Fold the body along the marked lines, and pin. Topstitch ¼" (6 mm) from the folds, stopping and back-stitching ¼" (6 mm) from the bottom corners. Fold, pin, and stitch a crease in each edge at the base of the bag, start-ing and stopping with backstitches at the ends of the previous stitching lines.

9 Fuse the monogram letters to the flaps.

DESIGNER'S TIP

The bag is sized for a man's shoe up to size 12. Simply shorten or lengthen the body to fit smaller or larger shoes.

FIRST-PLACE STADIUM CUSHION

Paper and pencil for drawing pattern

Carpenter's square or T-square ruler

Pencil-and-string compass

½ yd. (0.5 m) light color fabric

1¼ yd. (1.15 m) dark color fabric

Matching and contrasting thread

15" (38 cm) square of fabric in each of two ball colors:

(black and white = soccer)

(red and white = baseball)

(brown and white = football)

(brown and black = basketball)

½ yd. (0.5 m) paper-backed fusible web

Fabric marking pen or pencil

4 yd. (3.7 m) filler cord, ⅜" (1 cm) diameter

Welting foot, optional

8" (20.5 cm) webbing, 1" (2.5 cm) wide

Hand-sewing needle

15" × 17" × 3" (38 × 43 × 7.5 cm) foam

1 yd. (0.92 m) lightweight upholstery batting, optional

No more hard, cold bleacher seats for some lucky sports fan! Easy to carry and full of team spirit, this stadium cushion will provide hours of comfort at sporting events.

Make the cushion in the fan's team colors and add a soccer, baseball, basketball, or football theme using one of the appliqué patterns provided on pages 480 and 481.

Parents who go to lots of youth games would love one, too!

FINISHED SIZE: 15" × 17" × 3" (38 × 43 × 7.5 CM)

1 Trace the soccer ball appliqué pattern(s) on page 84 or enlarge desired patterns on page 85, and cut them out. Draw these patterns using paper, pencil, a carpenter's square or T-square ruler, and a string-and-pencil compass:

> *Front:* rectangle 9½" wide × 8½" tall (24.3 × 21.8 cm)
>
> *Back:* rectangle 18" wide × 16" tall (46 × 40.5 cm)
>
> *Boxing strip:* rectangle 4" wide × 33" long (10 × 84 cm)
>
> *Ball:* circle with 10" (25.5 cm) diameter

Dimensions include ½" (1.3 cm) seam allowances.

2 Cut two front pieces and two boxing strips from light fabric. Cut two fronts and one back from dark fabric. Also cut four 1⅞" × 35" (4.7 × 89 cm) bias strips for welting from the dark fabric.

3 Stitch a light front to a dark front, right sides together, along the shorter sides. Repeat for the second set. Press the seams open. Stitch the two sets right sides together, matching the seams and alternating color placement.

4 Fuse paper-backed web to the wrong side of the ball fabrics, following the manufacturer's instructions. Trace the appliqué patterns on the paper backing of the appropriate fabrics. Cut out the shapes. Peel away the paper backing from the shapes. Fuse the ball to the center of the assembled front. Fuse other appliqué pieces in place. For the soccer ball, fuse the pentagons in place, spacing the edge pieces evenly. Use a fabric marker to draw lines connecting the points of the pentagons, as in the photo on page 431.

5 Set the sewing machine for a zigzag or appliqué stitch with a medium width and very short length. Using contrasting thread, satin stitch all the raw edges and design lines.

6 Stitch two bias welting strips together end-to-end and press the seam open. Encase the cotton filler cord inside the bias strip with wrong sides together and long raw edges of fabric even. Attach the zipper foot or welting foot to your sewing machine, and machine-baste close to the cord.

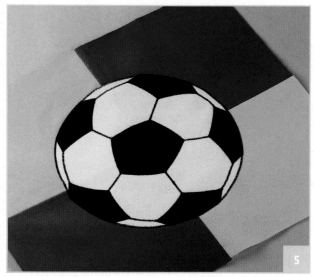

7 Pin the welting to the right side edge of the cushion front, beginning in the center on one side and aligning the raw edges. Clip into the welting seam allowance at the corners to allow it to spread and turn the corner smoothly. Stitch, beginning a few inches from one end and stopping before you reach the beginning end again. The ends will overlap.

8 Cut one end of the welting straight across. Cut the other end so that it overlaps the first by about 2" (5 cm). Remove 2½" (6.5 cm) of the basting in the long end exposing the filler cord. Trim the exposed cord so that it butts up against the trimmed and covered end of the cord. Wrap the fabric over both cord ends, turning under the raw edge to finish. Pin in place and finish basting the welting to the front. (see the photo on page 420, step 6).

9 Repeat steps 6 to 8 for the cushion back.

10 Locate the center of one boxing strip, and mark points 2½" (6.5 cm) to each side of center for the handle placement. Turn under ½" (1.3 cm) on each end of the webbing handle and stitch securely to the boxing strip at the marks.

11 Stitch the boxing strips together end-to-end to make a ring. Press the seams open. Pin the boxing strip to the cushion front, centering the seams at the sides and the handle at the top, and sandwiching the welting between the fabrics. Clip into the boxing strip seam allowance at the corners to allow it to spread and turn the corner smoothly. Stitch.

12 Repeat step 11 to attach the other side of the boxing strip to the cushion back. Leave an opening in one side at least 15" (38 cm) long.

13 Turn the cushion cover right side out through the opening.

14 For a softer cushion, wrap the foam in batting, cutting the edges to just meet. Hand-stitch the edges together.

15 Insert the foam into the cushion cover and slipstitch the opening closed.

DESIGNER'S TIP

To speed up the project, buy fabric-covered decorator's welting in a color that coordinates with your fabrics.

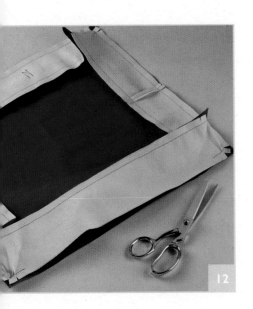

CUSTOM NECKTIE

MATERIALS

Copy machine or graph paper for enlarging pattern

Paper and pencil for drawing pattern

⅞ yd. (0.8 m) lightweight silk or synthetic fabric

¼ yd. (0.25 m) lining fabric

⅞ yd. (0.8 m) non-fusible woven interfacing or wool underlining

Thread

Fabric marking pen or pencil

Hand-sewing needle

2½" (6.5 cm) satin ribbon, ¾" (2 cm) wide

Next Father's Day, don't buy him a tie—make him one. Choose silk in a traditional pattern or a novelty print about something he loves, like fishing, golf, or wine. For a finishing touch, embroider his name or initials on the ribbon that holds the tail.

FINISHED SIZE: 3½" AT THE WIDEST END × 58" LONG (9 × 147 CM)

1 Enlarge the four tie patterns on pages 482 and 483, and cut them out. Draw a long line on paper and place the center line of the two tie front patterns on the line, with the inner edges of the patterns 20" (51 cm) apart. Connect the lines to complete the pattern. Repeat for the tie back patterns, spacing them 16" (40.5 cm) apart. Trace the interfacing patterns from the centers of the tie patterns. Enlarge the lining patterns on page 484. All patterns include 1/4" (6 mm) seam allowances.

2 Placing all patterns on the bias, cut one tie front and one tie back from the outer fabric, one front lining and one back lining from the lining fabric, and one front interfacing and one back interfacing.

3 Stitch the narrow ends of the front and back outer tie, right sides together. Trim the seam allowances and press them open.

4 Transfer the two pairs of dots to the wrong side of fabric at the front and back points, using a fabric marking pen or pencil. Fold the pointed end of the tie front in half lengthwise, right sides together, matching the dots. Stitch the short distance from the dots to the fold, backstitching at both ends. Repeat for the tie back.

5 Open the fold and pin the front lining to the front tie, right sides together, matching the angled edges. Stitch the two angled edges, breaking the stitches at the point and beginning again on the other side of the small stitched pleat. Trim the seam. Repeat for the pointed end of the tie back.

6 Roll the seams of the front point inward 1/4" (6 mm) and pin them in place. Do not press. Stitch the sides of the lining piece to the sides of the tie with 1/4" (6 mm) seams. Repeat for the other point.

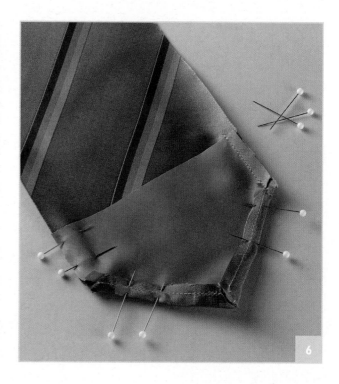

7 Turn the points to the right side and press very lightly, pushing the seam allowances toward the lining.

8 Stitch the interfacing together by overlapping the ends and zigzagging. Slip the interfacing under the linings and pin it to the tie, centering it along the entire length.

9 Fold one long edge of the tie over the interfacing and hand-stitch the edge to the interfacing. Turn the other edge under ½" (1.3 cm) and pin. Fold the pinned edge over the interfacing and hand-stitch the fold to the center of the tie, catching the interfacing underneath but not the tie front.

10 Turn under the ends of the ribbon, and hand-stitch them to the back of the tie front 8" (20.5 cm) from the point.

DESIGNER'S TIP

Choose a lightweight luxury fabric like silk. Select a solid color or a small print, keeping in mind the fabric will be cut diagonally.

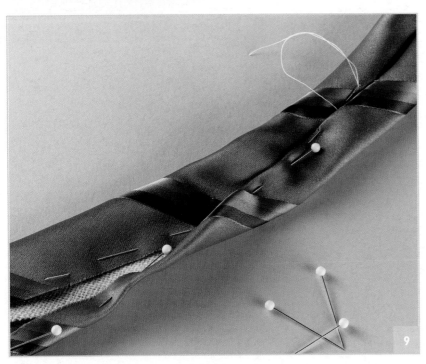

FRIENDLY ELEPHANT BIB

MATERIALS

Copy machine or graph paper for enlarging pattern

Paper and pencil for drawing pattern

½ yd. (0.5 m) lightweight terry cloth

⅜ yd. (0.35 m) solid or subtle print fabric, 44" (112 cm) wide

Pink felt, 2" (5 cm) square

Lightweight quilt batting, 8" × 12" (20.5 × 30.5 cm)

Thread

6" (15 cm) grosgrain ribbon, ⅞" (2.2 cm) wide

Hand-sewing needle

⅝" (1.5 cm) Velcro, 1" (2.5 cm) wide

Black embroidery floss and needle

2½ yd. (2.3. m) double-fold bias tape

Pacifier with loop handle

Here's a unique and thoughtful baby gift. While the bib protects clothing, the elephant keeps track of a pacifier— no more searching everywhere for it. Choose a fabric in pink, blue, or unisex pastels like green or yellow.

FINISHED SIZE: 11" × 12" (28 × 30.5 CM)

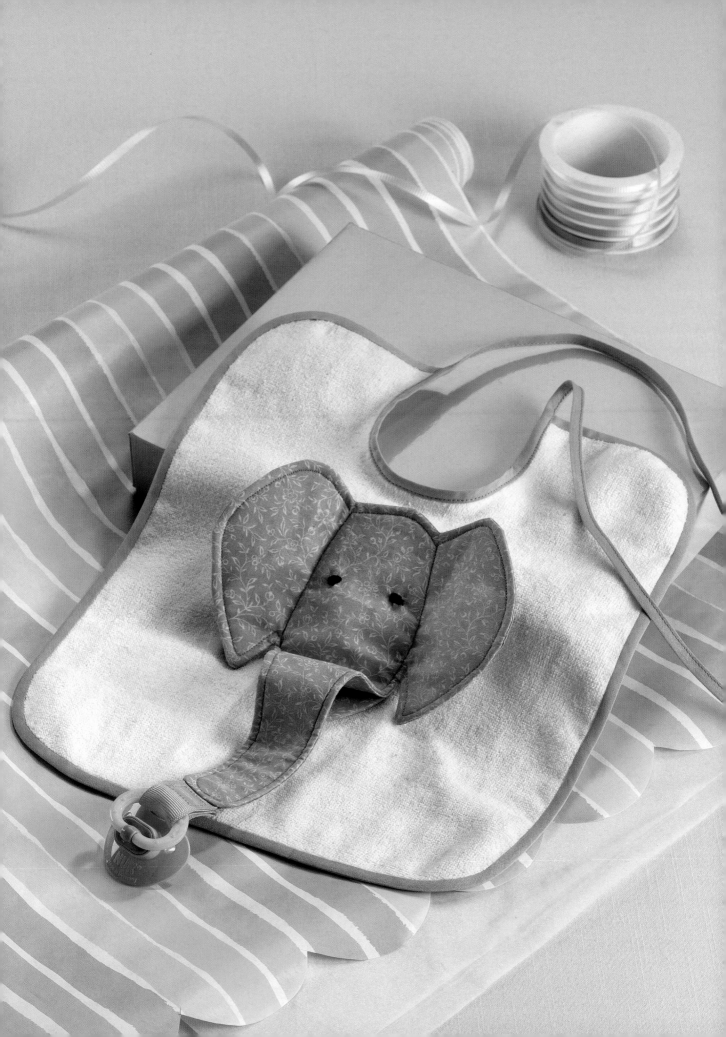

1 Enlarge the bib, elephant, mouth, and tongue patterns found on pages 485, 486, and 487, and cut them out. Patterns include 1/4" (6 mm) seam allowances.

2 Cut one bib from terry cloth. Cut two elephants and two mouths from fabric. Cut one tongue from pink felt. Cut one elephant from batting.

3 Pin or baste quilt batting to the wrong side of one elephant piece along the edges.

4 Fold ribbon in half crosswise. Aligning cut edges, pin the ribbon to the right side of the end of the elephant's trunk.

5 Pin the elephants right sides together, sandwiching the ribbon between them. Stitch 1/4" (6 mm) from all edges, leaving a 3" (7.5 cm) opening along the straight section of an ear. Clip up to the seam at corners.

6 Pin the two mouth pieces right sides together. Stitch the long curved edge.

7 Turn the elephant and mouth pieces right side out. Slipstitch the openings closed and press flat.

8 Topstitch the elephant 1/4" (6 mm) from the outer edge. Stitch one side of the Velcro to the underside of the ribbon, through both layers, just below the trunk. Stitch the other side to the underside of the ribbon just above the fold. Embroider the eyes.

9 Unfold the bias tape and pin the edge with the narrower fold to the right side of the bib edge, beginning and ending at the neck edges. Stitch in the crease of the fold.

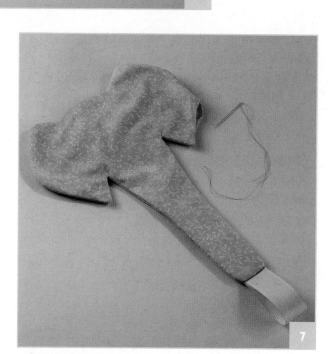

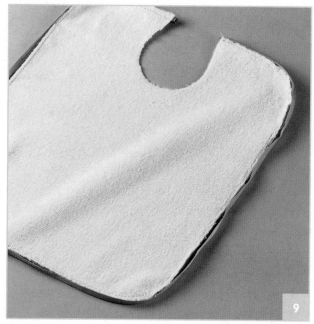

10 Wrap the bias tape to the back of the bib, encasing the raw edge. Pin the tape, with the fold just covering the stitching line. Slipstitch the fold in place.

11 Cut a 1-yd. (0.92 m) length of bias tape. Repeat steps 9 and 10 at the neck edge, centering the tape to the neck to finish the raw edge and create bib ties. Beginning at the end of one tie, topstitch close to the folds of the tape, continuing the stitching around the neck edge to the end of the other tie.

12 Stitch the mouth to the center of the bib, 4" (10 cm) below the neck edge. Pin the tongue to the upper straight edge of the mouth, and stitch in place.

13 Pin the elephant head on the bib, over the mouth, and stitch through all layers between the head and ears. Wrap the ribbon around the pacifier, and press the Velcro pieces together to secure.

CURLY SOFT BEAR

MATERIALS

Copy machine or graph paper for enlarging pattern

Paper and pencil for drawing pattern

⅛ yd. (0.15 m) soft faux fur

¾ yd. (0.7 m) curly faux fur, 60" (152.5 cm) wide

Fabric marking pen or pencil

Thread

Two domed, shank-style buttons, ¼" (6 mm) diameter or safety eyes, if bear is for a small child

Hand-sewing needle

Scrap of felt

Embroidery thread

Four sew-through buttons, flat, ½" (1.3 cm) diameter

Polyester fiberfill

1 yd. (0.92 m) wide ribbon

A teddy bear is a gift of love and comfort for anyone, from newborn to ninety. Faux fur is available in a wide variety of fun colors and textures and is a forgiving fabric for a beginning sewer. Making and giving this teddy will be as much fun as receiving one.

This teddy has button eyes. Use safety eyes if your gift is for a baby or small child.

FINISHED SIZE: 17" (43 CM) TALL

1 Enlarge the nine bear patterns on pages 487 and 485, and cut them out. Trace the arm pattern a second time and cut it off where indicated for the underarm. Patterns include ¼" (6 mm) seam allowances.

2 Cut two ears, two paws, and two soles from soft fur. Cut four legs, one nose, and two each of the remaining pieces (including two ears) from curly fur. Be sure to cut mirror-image pieces of those that are multiples. (Either cut the pieces with the fabric folded right sides together or flip the pattern over when cutting a single layer of fabric.) Transfer all marks.

3 Pin a paw to the straight lower edge of the underarm, right sides together; stitch. Stitch the upper arm to the lower arm, leaving a 4" (10 cm) opening on the long edge. Repeat for the other arm. Turn the arms right side out.

4 Stitch the front pieces together along the center front. Stitch the darts in the back pieces; turn them upward. Stitch the back pieces together along the center back. Pin the front to the back on the sides and stitch.

5 Pin two leg pieces together on the curved edge, and stitch. Pin the straight edges together and stitch, leaving a 4" (10 cm) opening in the center of the seam. Pin the sole to the lower edge of the leg, and stitch. Repeat for the other leg. Turn the legs right side out.

6 Match up the front and back seams of one leg and pin flat. Pin the leg to the lower edge of the assembled body, sandwiched between the front and back. Make sure the toes are pointing forward. Pin the other leg into position. Stitch across the bottom of the body through all layers. Turn the body right side out.

7 Pin a curly fur ear to a soft fur ear along the curved edge, and stitch. Repeat for second ear. Turn the ears right side out.

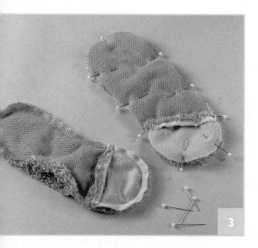

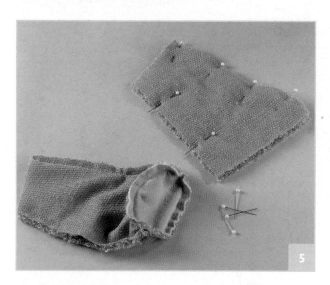

10 Stitch button eyes to the face. If the bear is for a small child, attach safety eyes instead. Cut a small triangle of felt for the nose tip. Stitch it to the point of the nose, using embroidery thread.

11 Using two buttons as washers, stitch the underarm to the shoulder of the body at the side seam. Work through the neck opening to get inside the body and through the opening in the back seam of the arm. Stitch back and forth through the button holes several times to attach the arm securely. Repeat for the other arm.

8 Stitch the head side pieces together at the center front. Pin the top of the center front seam to the point of the nose, and finish pinning the nose edges to the upper edges of the head sides. Stitch. Stitch the head back pieces together at the center back.

9 Pin the ears to the upper edge of the head front assembly, leaving 1 1/2" (3.8 cm) between them and making sure the soft fur faces forward. Stitch the head back to the head front assembly, catching the ears in the seam.

12 Stuff the legs and arms with fiberfill and slipstitch the openings closed.

13 Machine-stitch the front of the body to the front of the head at the neck edge, stitching just beyond the side seams. Stuff the body and head. Slipstitch the back neck opening closed.

14 Wrap the ribbon around the bear's neck and tie a big bow in the front.

PUPPY-DOG
HAT AND SCARF

MATERIALS

Copy machine or graph paper for enlarging pattern

Paper and pencil for drawing pattern

Carpenter's square or T-square ruler

⅝ yd. (0.6 m) colored fleece

Thread

Two stuffed or bean animals, about 6" (15 cm) long

Hand-sewing needle

3 yd. (2.75 m) narrow ribbon or trim

¼ yd. (0.25 m) white fleece

Make a child giggle with this fun set. All you need is fleece and a pair of little stuffed animals.

1 Enlarge the hat crown pattern on page 93, and cut it out. Draw two patterns using paper, pencil, and a carpenter's square or T-square ruler:

Scarf: rectangle 6" × 50" (15 × 127 cm)

Hat brim: rectangle 6" × 23" (15 × 58.5 cm)

Dimensions include ½" (1.3 cm) seam allowances.

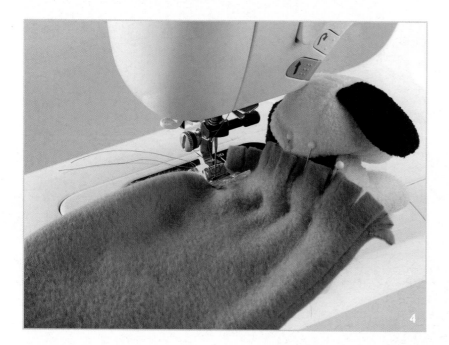

SCARF

1 Cut two scarf pieces from the colored fleece.

2 Pin the two scarf pieces right sides together, along the long edges. Stitch, starting and stopping ¾" (2 cm) from the short ends. Knot the thread tails securely at the ends of the seams.

3 Fringe the short ends of the scarf by making cuts ¾" (2 cm) deep and ½" (1.3 cm) apart. Turn the scarf right side out.

4 Coax the stuffing away from the center of the animal and cut the animal in half. Baste each side closed. Pin one end of the animal between the fringed layers at one end of the scarf, just beyond the fringe. Stitch through all layers by hand or machine. Repeat at the other end.

5 Cut ribbon into four lengths, each 27" (68.5 cm) long. Tie one length of ribbon into a bow around each end of the scarf over the stitching.

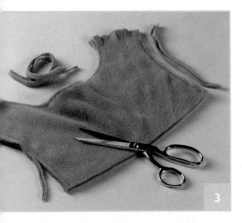

crown. Knot the thread tails securely at the ends of the seams.

3 Fringe the short ends of the crown by making cuts ¾" (2 cm) deep and ½" (1.3 cm) apart. Trim seams and turn the crown right side out.

4 Pin the short ends of the brim together and stitch, forming a circle. Pin one edge of the brim to the lower edge of the crown, right sides together. Stitch.

5 Turn the hat inside out. Fold the brim in half lengthwise. Turn under ½" (1.3 cm) on the cut edge of the brim and pin it over the seam line. Slipstitch the fold in place.

6 Attach animal halves to the short ends of the crown, as in step 4 for the scarf. Tie the two remaining lengths of ribbon over the stitches.

HAT

1 Cut two crowns from the colored fleece. Cut one brim from the white fleece.

2 Pin the crown pieces, right sides together, on the curved sides and top seams. Stitch, starting and stopping ¾" (2 cm) from the short ends of the

DESIGNER'S TIP

The brim of this hat is 22" (56 cm) around. For a perfect fit, measure the circumference of the child's head and alter the length of the brim and width of the crown by pinching or splitting each pattern in the center.

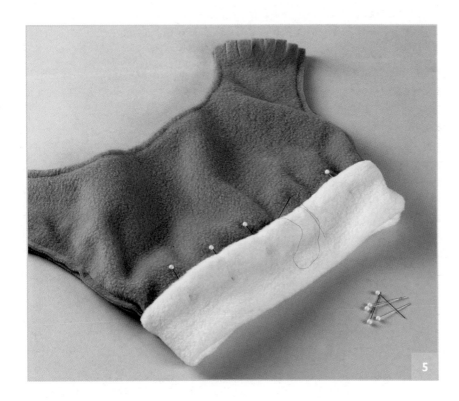

CHARMED SOCKS

Charm a little girl by decorating socks with dangling beads and personalized charms. You start with plain socks—choose ones with stretchy rib knit cuffs. The "lettuce edging" is done with a simple zigzag stitch while you stretch the socks as much as possible.

MATERIALS

(For one pair)

Pair of colored socks

Fabric marking pen or pencil

Ruler

Contrasting thread

28-gauge craft wire

Wire cutter

20 charms, ½" (1.3 cm)

30 colored glass beads, 6 to 8 mm

50 metal beads, 6 to 8 mm

20 metal double rings, 7 mm

Hand-sewing needle, optional

1 Mark three lines on the ribbed cuff about 1½" (3.8 cm) apart, beginning at least ¾" (2 cm) from the top, using a fabric marking pen or pencil. Turn the sock inside out.

2 Set the sewing machine for a zigzag stitch with medium width and short length. Fold the cuff down along the top marked line. Place the fold under the presser foot and, with one hand in front and one in back, stretch the folded edge. Zigzag along the fold, allowing the left swing of the needle to go into the sock and the right swing of the needle to go over the edge. Stop as necessary to reposition your hands. Repeat at each marked line.

3 To make the beaded dangles, cut 10 pieces of wire, each 12" (30.5 cm) long and 10 pieces of wire each 8" (20.5 cm) long. String a charm onto the center of each wire and twist the wire ends together. String three metal beads and two glass beads on each of the longer twisted wires, alternating metal and glass; string two metal beads and one glass bead on the shorter wires. Add a wire ring at the top of each dangle and twist the wire ends tightly to secure. Cut off the excess wire.

4 Stitch the dangles randomly to the lettuce-edged folds, either by hand or by machine.

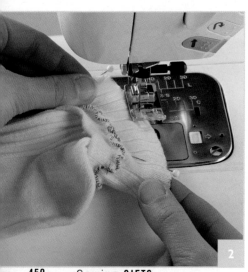

BALLERINA TUTU

MATERIALS

3 yd. (2.75 m) sheer fabric

Yardstick (meterstick) or tape measure

Thread

4 yd. (3.7 m) heavy-duty thread or lightweight string

1 package extra-wide double-fold bias tape

3 yd. (2.75 m) feather boa trim

Hand-sewing needle

1⅛ yd. (1.05 m) strung imitation pearls, ⅛" (3 mm) diameter

1¼ yd. (1.15 m) satin ribbon, ⅜" (9 mm) wide

1¼ yd. (1.15 m) sheer ribbon, ⅞" (23 mm) wide

15 assorted buttons, bows, and ribbon-rose novelties

Glue, optional

The first thing a little girl will do in this skirt is twirl and twirl! Select a sheer fabric with embroidery and ornamentation or choose inexpensive netting, then embellish with ribbons and pearls. She'll feel so special!

FINISHED SIZE: 24" WAIST, 10" LENGTH
(61 × 25.5 CM)

I Straighten the cut ends of the sheer fabric, if necessary. Cut two rectangles 11" (28 cm) wide the full length of the sheer fabric.

2 Turn under 1" (2.5 cm) on one long edge of one piece, and press. Tuck in the cut edge to meet the crease and press again, creating a ½" (1.3 cm) double-fold hem. Stitch along the inner fold. Repeat for one long edge of the other piece. Then stitch double-fold hems in the short ends of both pieces.

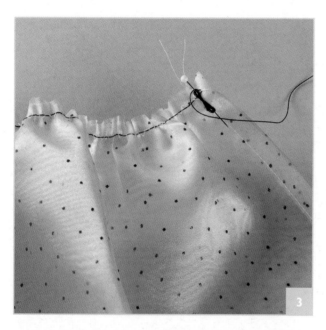

3 Layer the two long pieces right side up, aligning the upper raw edges. Pin. Set the sewing machine for a wide, long zigzag stitch. Working from the right side, stitch the layers together along the entire long edge, ¼" (6 mm) from the cut edges, zigzagging over a heavy thread or thin cord. Pull the cord to gather the skirt edge to a length of 24" (61 cm). Secure each end of the gathering cord by wrapping the thread in figure-eight fashion around a pin.

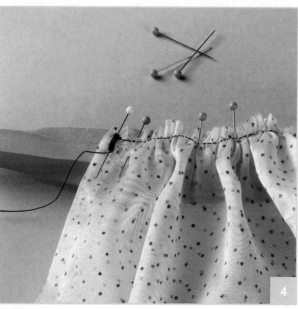

4 Cut 2½ yd. (2.3 m) of the bias tape and mark off the center 24" (61 cm). Unfold the tape. Pin the wrong side of the gathered skirt edge to one edge of the tape between the marks, distributing the fullness evenly.

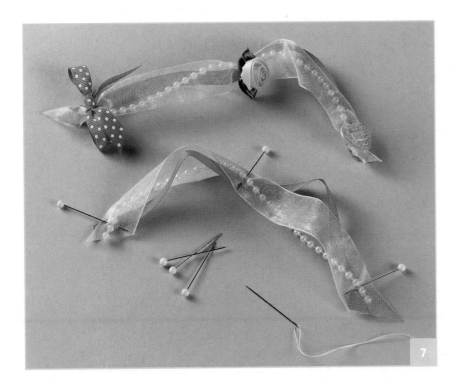

DESIGNER'S TIP

The anticipation of the completed project will become even greater if you allow the child to select her own buttons and ribbons for a surprise gift yet to come.

5 Stitch the tape to the skirt, stitching in the crease of the first fold. Wrap the tape to the wrong side, encasing the raw edges. Pin the tape, with the fold just covering the stitching line. Slipstitch the fold in place. Beginning at the end of one tie, topstitch close to the folds of the tape, continuing the stitching above the skirt to the end of the other tie.

6 Hand-stitch boa feathers to the hem of the top skirt, catching the boa at the beginning and end and every few inches.

7 Cut the pearls into five 8" (20.5 cm) lengths. Cut the ribbons into five 9" (23 cm) lengths. Group a sheer ribbon, a satin ribbon, and a pearl string, and hand-tack them together at both ends and at the center. Stitch or glue a novelty button or bow at each stitched location. Repeat to make four more ribbon embellishments.

8 Hand-tack the ribbon embellishments, evenly spaced, to the waistline of the skirt.

MY OWN LUNCH BAG

A bright, insulated lunch bag is a perfect gift for a kid. When it's time for lunch, there will be no mistaking this personalized lunch bag from the others. It's roomy and wipes clean. An outside pocket holds milk money or a note from Mom or Dad.

FINISHED SIZE: 7½" WIDE × 10" TALL × 3½" DEEP (19.3 × 25.5 × 9 CM)

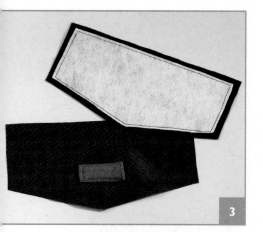

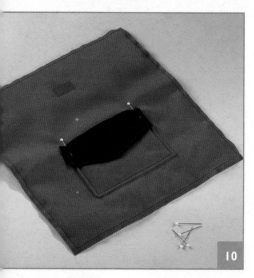

1 Draw two patterns using paper, pencil, and a carpenter's square or T-square ruler:

Bag body: rectangle 2¾" tall × 12" wide (32.4 × 30.5 cm)

Pocket: rectangle 9" tall × 6½" wide (23 × 16.3 cm)

Enlarge the pocket flap and lid on page 94, and cut them out. Dimensions include ½" (1.3 cm) seam allowances.

2 Using the patterns, cut four bag bodies and one pocket from the colored fabric. Cut two pocket flaps and two lids from the contrasting fabric. Cut two bodies and one lid from batting. Cut one pocket and one pocket flap from interfacing. Cut two lengths of Velcro, each 1½" (3.8 cm) long.

3 Machine-baste interfacing to the wrong side of one pocket flap, ¼" (6 mm) from the edges. Trim the interfacing close to the stitches. Center the loop tape on the right side of the other pocket flap, 1¾" (4.5 cm) below the upper edge. Stitch the tape to the flap along the edges.

4 Pin the flaps right sides together. Stitch along the edges, leaving a 4" (10 cm) opening in the center of the upper edge. Trim the seam allowances and clip the corners diagonally. Turn the flap right side out and press. Topstitch the sides and angled lower edge.

5 Machine-baste the batting to the wrong side of one lid flap, ¼" (6 mm) from the edges. Trim the batting close to the stitches. Center the loop tape on the right side of the other lid flap, 5¼" (13.2 cm) below the long straight edge. Stitch the tape to the lid around all edges.

6 Pin the lids right sides together. Stitch along the edges, leaving a 4" (10 cm) opening in the center of the upper edge. Trim the seam allowances and clip the corners diagonally. Turn the lid right side out and press. Topstitch the sides and angled lower edge.

7 Machine-baste interfacing to the wrong side of one pocket, ¼" (6 mm) from all edges. Trim the interfacing close to the stitches. Fold the pocket in half crosswise, right sides together, and stitch all edges, leaving a small opening centered along one edge. Trim the seam allowances and clip the corners diagonally. Turn the pocket right side out and press.

8 Center the hook tape on the right side of the pocket, ¾" (2 cm) below the folded edge. Stitch the tape to the pocket along the edges.

9 Machine-baste the batting to the wrong side of each bag body, ¼" (6 mm) from the edges. Trim the batting close to the stitches.

10 Pin the pocket to the right side of one body, centering it with the open (lower) edge 2½" (6.5 cm) from the lower edge of the body. Topstitch the pocket in place on the sides and lower edge. Pin the pocket flap above the pocket and topstitch in place along the upper edge, taking care not to catch the pocket in the stitches. Center the hook tape 2" (5 cm) below the upper edge of the body and stitch in place.

12

DESIGNER'S TIP

Interline your lunch bag with a standard quilt batting or choose a batting that contains a hot/cold reflecting layer for added insulation.

11 Pin the two body pieces right sides together along the sides and lower edge. Stitch. Trim the corners diagonally and press the seams open.

12 To create a paper-bag bottom for the lunch bag, fold the lower corner, aligning the bottom seam over the side seam. Measure along the bottom seam 1¾" (4.5 cm) from the point, and draw a line perpendicular to the seams. The line should be 3½" (9 cm) long. Stitch on the marked line through all layers, keeping the seam allowances on both sides turned open. Trim away

the triangle ¼" (6 mm) from the stitching line. Repeat for the other corner.

13 To make the lining, repeat steps 11 and 12 with the other two body pieces, leaving an 8" (20.5 cm) opening along one side.

14 Turn the outer bag right side out. Pin the lid to the center back upper edge of the outer bag, right sides together. Pin the ends of the webbing handle to the right side upper edge of the outer bag over the side seams.

15 With the outer bag right side out and the lining inside out, slip the outer bag into the lining and pin the two together along the upper edge, sandwiching the lid and handle between them. Stitch.

16 Turn the bag right side out through the opening in the lining. Stitch the opening closed. Topstitch the upper edge of the bag. Adhere the monogram to the bag front.

15

DRESSY GUEST TOWELS

This is a great hostess gift. Plain hand towels are quickly transformed with crisply pleated sheer fabric and tasseled trim.

MATERIALS

(For one towel)

Terry cloth hand towel with plain transition stripe

Yardstick (meterstick) or tape measure

⅓ yd. (0.32 m) sheer, washable organdy or organza fabric, 60" (152.5 cm) wide

Thread

Fabric marking pen or pencil

Washable tassel trim

Long, thin silk-type straight pins, optional

1 Measure the length of the towel from the top of the transition stripe to the hem. Add 1" (2.5 cm) to this measurement to find the cut length of the sheer fabric. Measure the width of the towel, multiply by 3, and add 4" (10 cm) to determine the width to cut the sheer fabric.

2 Cut a sheer fabric strip, using the measurements found in step 1. Turn under 1" (2.5 cm) along one long edge of the fabric and press. Tuck the cut edge in to meet the crease and press again, creating a ½" (1.3 cm) double-fold hem. Stitch close to the inner fold.

3 Turn under 2" (5 cm) along one short end and press. Tuck the cut edge in to meet the crease and press again, creating a 1" (2.5 cm) double-fold hem. Stitch close to the inner fold. Repeat for the other short end.

4 With the strip right side up, beginning on the right end, mark the strip at top and bottom 2" (5 cm) from the end. Then mark the rest of the strip at 3" (7.5 cm) intervals.

5 Beginning on the right end, fold the fabric at the first marks and align the fold to the hemmed edge; pin, using silk pins. Fold the fabric at the next marks and form a 1" (2.5 cm) knife pleat just behind the first one. Continue pleating the strip into consecutive 1" (2.5 cm) knife pleats to the other end. Adjust spacing as necessary to fit the towel. Press the pleats. Baste pleats in place along the cut edge.

6 Pin the pleated strip to the towel, aligning the lower edges. Pin the tassel trim over the pleated strip, hiding the raw edge. Tuck under the ends of the trim. Stitch along the top and bottom of the trim heading.

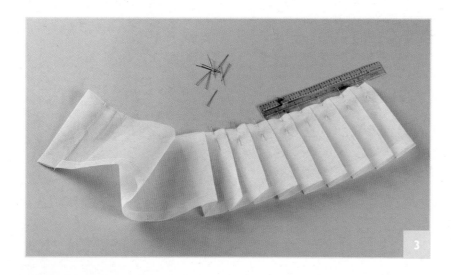

3

DELUXE
LINEN NAPKINS

MATERIALS

(For one napkin)

Paper and pencil for drawing pattern

Carpenter's square or T-square ruler

⅝ yd (0.6 m) linen, natural color

⅜ yd (0.35 m) linen, bright color

Fabric marking pen or pencil

Thread

Hand-sewing needle, optional

Why match when you can mix? Each dinner napkin in this set has a different colored border. Choose natural-colored linen for the napkin and coordinating jewel tones for the generous borders. You can, of course, make a matched set instead, or supersize the instructions and make a bordered tablecloth. Give a set to your host, to a bride and groom, or to anyone who loves to set a beautiful table.

FINISHED SIZE: 18" (46 CM) SQUARE.

1 Draw two patterns using paper, pencil, and a carpenter's square or T-square ruler:

> *Napkin base:* square 18½" (47.3 cm)
>
> *Napkin border:* rectangle 2½" × 22" (6.5 × 56 cm)

These dimensions include ¼" (6 mm) seam allowances.

2 Cut one napkin base from natural fabric. From colored fabric, cut four napkin borders. Using a fabric marking pen or pencil, mark a dot at each corner of the napkin ¼" (6 mm) from the cut edges.

3 Center a border, right side down, on the wrong side of the napkin, matching raw edges; pin. Stitch a ¼" (6 mm) seam, beginning and ending with backstitching at the marked dots. Repeat for the remaining three sides. Press the seam allowances open.

4 Lay the napkin flat with the border ends overlapping. Draw diagonal lines on the overlapped borders from the corner dots to the points where the inner edges of the borders intersect. Mark a point on each line ⅜" (1 cm) from the inner edge. Pin the borders together and stitch along the marked line, beginning and ending with backstitching at the dots. Take care not to catch the napkin in the stitching. Repeat for the remaining three corners.

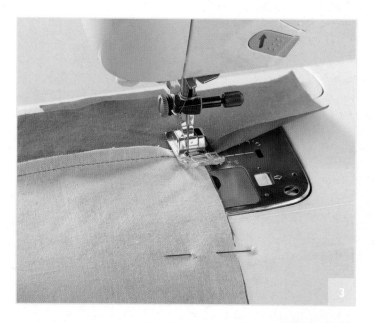

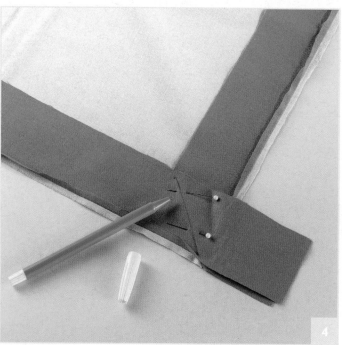

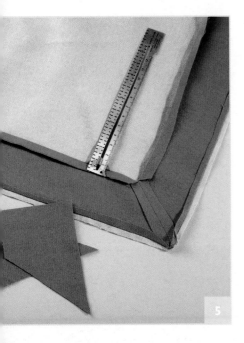

5 At each corner, trim away the border ends ¼" (6 mm) from the stitched lines. Press the seam allowances open. Turn back the inner edges ¼" (6 mm) and press.

6 Turn the borders to the right side of the napkin and press the edges and corners flat. Hand-baste or pin in place. Stitch the border in place using a decorative or zigzag stitch.

DESIGNER'S TIP

Accurate measuring and marking will ensure perfectly mitered corners every time.

AUTUMN LEAVES RUNNER

The leaves are falling on this luxurious faux suede table runner. Give it in autumn when someone is decorating for the season. It would be a perfect present for the host of Thanksgiving dinner. Imitation suede is not only fabulous, but easy for sewers since the edges can be left raw. The material is washable, too.

MATERIALS

½ yd. (0.5 m) imitation suede for runner

Carpenter's square or T-square ruler

Fabric marking pen or pencil

Paper and pencil for drawing pattern

¼ yd. (0.25 m) imitation suede in each of three colors for leaves

All-purpose thread in three colors to contrast with leaves

1 Mark a rectangle 15" × 50" (38 × 127 cm) on the imitation suede, using a carpenter's square or T-square ruler and a fabric marking pen or pencil. Cut out the rectangle. Mark the center of one short end; mark points 7½" (19.3 cm) from the end on the long edges. Using a straightedge, draw diagonal lines between the center mark and the side marks. Cut along the marked lines to shape the pointed end. Use the first end to cut the same shape at the other end.

2 Trace the leaf patterns on page 491, and cut them out. Assign a leaf type for each color of contrasting fabric. Trace each leaf eight times on the fabric, some the mirror image of others. Cut them out.

3 Using a fabric marking pen or pencil, draw vein lines on each leaf. Arrange the leaves randomly along the outer edges of the runner, keeping them at least ½" (1.3 cm) from the runner's edge and overlapping them only slightly if necessary.

4 Set the sewing machine for a zigzag stitch of medium width and short length. Satin stitch along the vein lines of each leaf, extending the center vein below the leaf to make a stem.

DESIGNER'S TIP

It is important to choose an imitation suede, such as Ultrasuede, that won't ravel on the cut edges.

FINISHED SIZE: 15" × 50" (38 × 127 CM)

BEADED TABLE SCARF

A table scarf is an elegant gift for someone who loves to decorate and entertain. The style today is to curve and scrunch up a table runner down the middle of a table or buffet, then add candlesticks or other table decorations along the sides. The reverse is a different color, and the contrast is lovely. Select a beautifully embroidered, beaded, or lace fabric and a coordinating plain silk. Add posh bead fringe trim to the scarf ends, and in minutes you've created a masterpiece.

MATERIALS

2 yd. (1.85 m) embellished fabric
Carpenter's square or T-square ruler
Fabric marking pen or pencil
2 yd. (1.85 m) plain silk fabric
7/8 yd. (0.8 m) bead fringe trim
Thread
Hand-sewing needle

1 Mark a rectangle 16" × 71" (40.5 × 180.5 cm) on the wrong side of the embellished fabric, using a carpenter's square or T-square ruler and a fabric marking pen or pencil. Cut out the rectangle. Use this piece to cut a matching piece of the plain silk. Dimensions include 1/2" (1.3 cm) seam allowances.

2 Examine the fabric carefully for beads or sequins that may be along the seam lines. Snip away these embellishments without compromising the fabric to avoid breaking a needle while sewing.

3 Cut two lengths of bead fringe trim, each 15" (38 cm) long. Pin the heading of one trim piece to one short end of the scarf on the right side with the beads facing inward. The inner edge of the heading should be 1/2" (1.3 cm)

from the edge. Baste the heading to the seam line. Repeat for the other end of the scarf.

4 Pin the plain fabric to the embellished fabric, right sides together, sandwiching the trim between them. Attach a zipper foot to the sewing machine. Stitch 1/2" (1.3 cm) seam around the entire scarf, leaving a 10" (25.5 cm) opening on one side. On the short ends, stitch slowly and carefully, taking care not to stitch into a bead.

5 Trim the seam allowances at the corners diagonally. Turn the scarf right side out and press carefully. Slipstitch the opening closed.

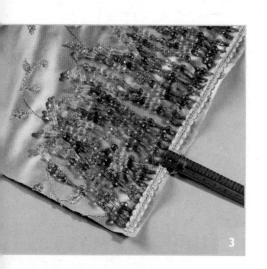

FINISHED SIZE: 15" × 70" (38 × 178 CM)

SPECIAL YEAR ORNAMENT

MATERIALS

Paper and pencil for drawing pattern

Small amounts of lightweight cotton fabrics with small or tiny-grained prints: five colors for new home, three colors for marriage, three colors for new baby

8" (20.5 cm) square lightweight fusible interfacing

10" (25.5 cm) square paper-backed fusible web

Contrasting thread

Hand-sewing needle

Embellishments: gold stud, 1/8" (3 mm) diameter, for new home ornament; 10 pearl beads, 1/8" (3 mm) diameter and 15" (38 cm) rattail braid, for marriage ornament; 4" (10 cm) each satin ribbon and narrow lace trim, for new baby ornament

1/2 yd. (0.5 m) fabric-covered piping, 1/8" (3 mm) diameter

1/2 yd. (0.5 m) each satin ribbon in two colors, 1/8"(3 mm) wide

Paper tag

Will someone on your holiday gift list be celebrating the first Christmas after marriage, a new home, or a baby's birth? Celebrate with them by making a special ornament that will bring back memories for years to come. Apply simple appliqués by machine using the patterns provided on page 492 and then embellish them by hand. Add a paper tag so they can write the name, year, or other identifiers.

FINISHED SIZE: 4 1/2" × 6" (11.5 × 15 CM) EXCLUDING HANDLE AND TAG

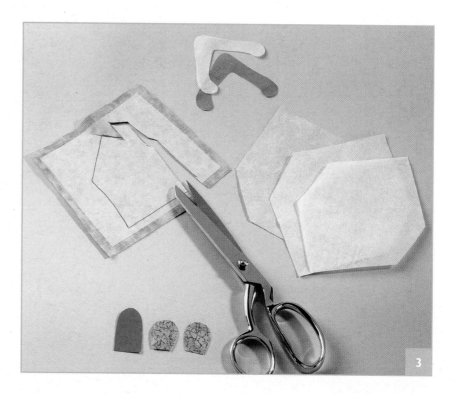

1 Trace the ornament and desired appliqué patterns on page 492. The ornament pattern includes ¼" (6 mm) seam allowances.

2 Cut two ornaments from fabric and one from interfacing. Trim the seam allowances from the interfacing and fuse it to the wrong side of one ornament piece.

3 Cut pieces of paper-backed fusible web a little larger than each of the appliqué pieces. Fuse them to the wrong side of each appliqué fabric. Trace the appliqué patterns onto the paper backing. Cut out the appliqués, and remove the paper backing.

4 Arrange the appliqués on the right side of the interfaced ornament piece, following the numbered sequence. Fuse them into place.

5 Set the sewing machine for a zigzag stitch with a medium width and very short length. Satin stitch along all cut edges of the appliqué pieces, following the numbered sequence.

6 Hand-stitch embellishments, following the photograph on page 471.

7 Pin the piping around the edge of the ornament, aligning the cut edges, beginning and ending along one straight edge. Clip into the piping seam allowance at the corners to allow it to spread and turn the corner smoothly. Attach a zipper foot to the sewing machine. Baste, beginning a short distance from one end and stopping before you reach the beginning end again. The ends will overlap.

8 Cut one end of the piping straight across. Cut the other end so that it overlaps the first by about 2" (5 cm). Remove 2½" (6.5 cm) of the basting in the long end, exposing the filler cord. Trim the exposed cord so that it butts up against the trimmed and covered end of the cord. Wrap the fabric over both cord ends, turning under

the raw edge to finish. Pin in place and finish basting the piping to the ornament.

9 Cut two lengths of each of the narrow ribbons, each 9" (23 cm) long, and stitch the cut ends to the right side of the ornament.

10 Pin the ornament front to the back, right sides together. Using a zipper foot, stitch just inside the basting line. Leave a short opening along one straight edge.

11 Turn the ornament right side out and slipstitch the opening closed.

12 Cut a 4" (10 cm) length of narrow ribbon and slip it through the hole in a paper tag. Stitch the ribbon ends to the back of the ornament at the bottom point. Write the date and greeting on the tag.

DESIGNER'S TIP

Fat quarters purchased at a quilt shop are great for the ornaments and appliqués. These pre-cut pieces measure 18" × 22" (46 × 56 cm), so there is less waste and they are often arranged in coordinating groups.

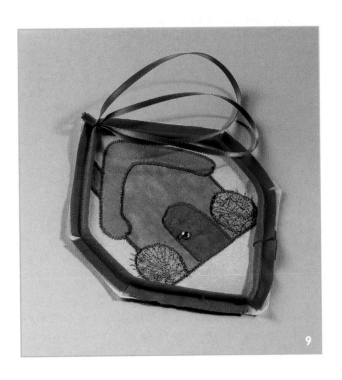

9

SHEER GIFT BAGS

MATERIALS

Paper and pencil for drawing pattern

Carpenter's square or T-square ruler

Sheer organdy or organza fabric, amount determined in step 1

Thread

Fabric marking pen or pencil

1 yd. (0.92 m) sheer ribbon

Gift tag

Present a gift in a sheer bag you made yourself. Sheer fabric that is crisp and firmly woven, such as organdy, works best because it will hold its shape. Directions are given for three different sizes: a tall bag, which is especially useful for a bottle of wine; a medium size bag, perfect for a pillar candle; and a small bag that might hold a gift of jewelry.

FINISHED SIZES:

TALL BAG 4" WIDE × 14" TALL (10 × 35.5 CM)

MEDIUM BAG 6" WIDE × 11" TALL (15 × 28 CM)

SMALL BAG 3" WIDE × 5" TALL (7.5 × 12.7 CM)

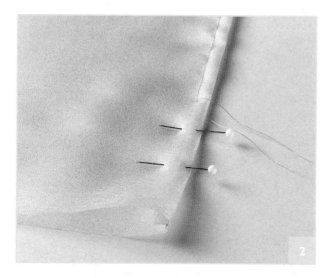

1 Using paper, pencil, and a carpenter's square or T-square ruler, draw a pattern for the size bag you want to make:

Tall bag: 17" wide × 18" tall (43 × 46 cm)

Medium bag: 25" wide × 15" tall (63.5 × 38 cm)

Small bag: 13" wide × 10" tall (33 × 25.5 cm)

2 Cut one piece of sheer fabric, using the pattern. Sew the sides in a French seam as follows: Fold the fabric in half lengthwise, wrong sides together. Stitch a scant 1/4" (6 mm) from the edges. Press the seam open; then turn the bag wrong side out and fold it on the stitching line. Stitch again 1/4" (6 mm) from the stitched edge, encasing the raw edges.

3 Stitch the bottom edges together in a plain 1/4" (6 mm) seam. Turn under the upper edge 1" (2.5 cm) and press. Tuck the cut edge in to meet the crease and pin a 1/2" (1.3 cm) double-fold hem. Stitch along the inner fold.

4 To create a paper-bag bottom for the bag, fold the lower corner, aligning the bottom seam over the side seam. Measure along the bottom seam 2" 5 cm) from the point, for the tall bag; 3" (7.5 cm) from the point for the medium bag; or 1 1/2" (3.8 cm) from the point for the small bag, and draw a line perpendicular to the seams. The line should be 4" (10 cm) long for the tall bag, 6" (15 cm) long for the medium bag, or 3" (7.5 cm) long for the small bag. Stitch on the marked line through all layers. Trim away the triangle 1/4" (6 mm) from the stitching line. Repeat for other corner, centering the bottom seam in the stitching line.

5 Turn the bag right side out. Divide the upper edge into four equal sections, with the seam in the center of one section. Fold the bag from one mark to the bottom corner, and pin. Topstitch ¼" (6 mm) from the fold, stopping and backstitching ¼" (6 mm) from the bottom corner. Repeat for the other three sides of the bag.

6 Fold, pin, and stitch a crease in each edge at the base of the bag, starting and stopping with backstitches at the ends of the previous stitching lines.

7 Insert your gift. Tie the top closed with a ribbon and add a gift tag.

DESIGNER'S TIP

No ribbon handy? Just cut a narrow strip of the fabric itself.

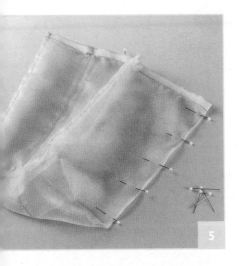

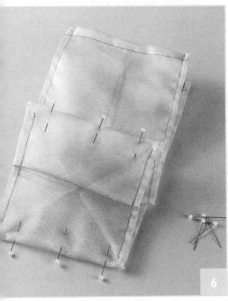

PATTERNS

Silk Beauty Bag
(enlarge 200%)

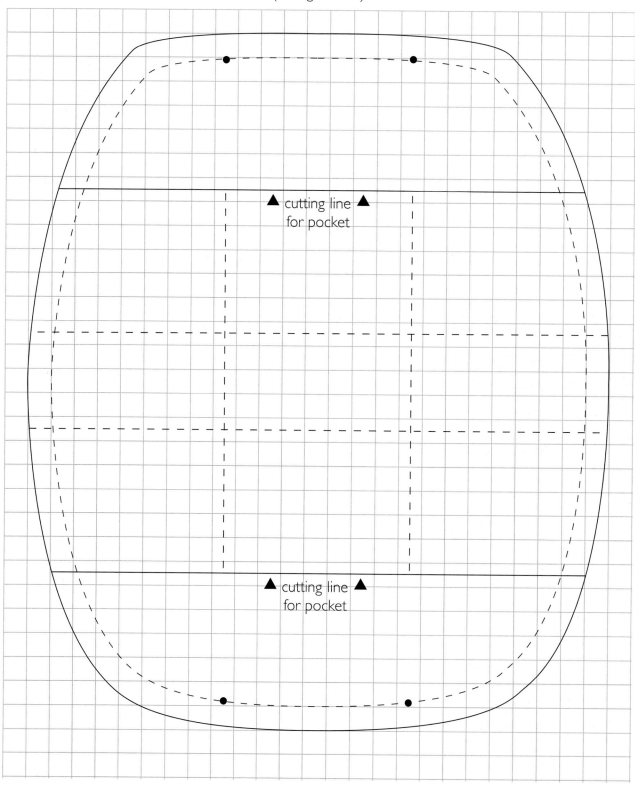

▲ cutting line ▲
for pocket

▲ cutting line ▲
for pocket

1 square = ½" (1.3 cm)

Beach Babe Tote
(enlarge 200%)

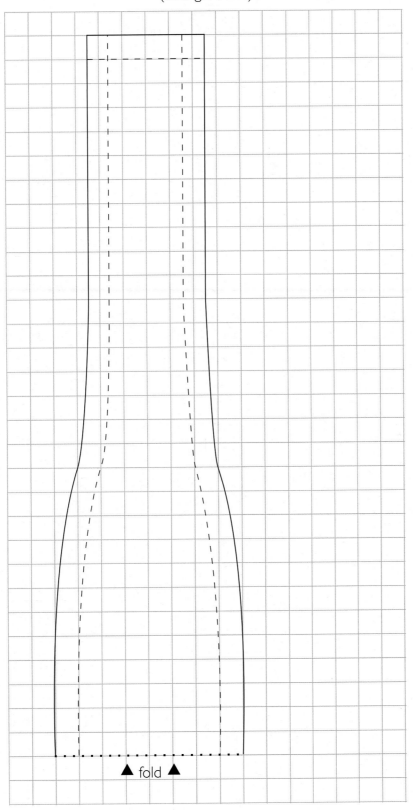

▲ fold ▲

1 square = ½" (1.3 cm)

Stadium Cushion Soccer Ball (full size)

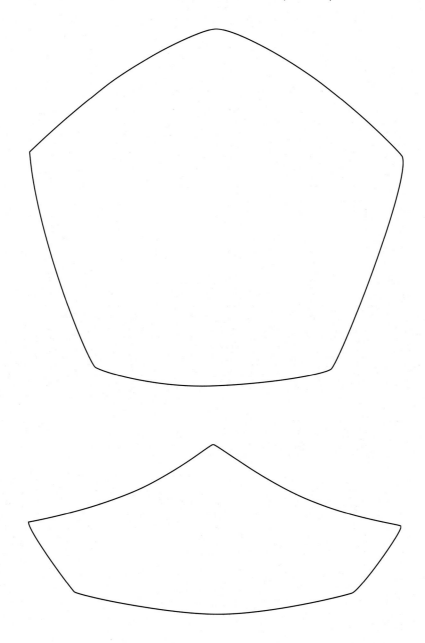

Stadium Cushion Baseball
(enlarge 200%)

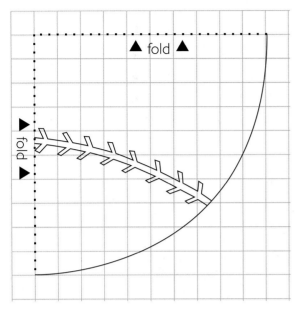

I square = ½" (1.3 cm)

Stadium Cushion Basketball
(enlarge 200%)

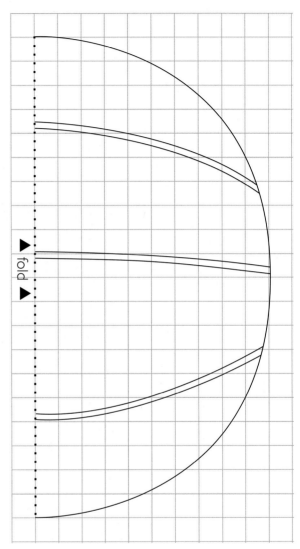

I square = ½" (1.3 cm)

Stadium Cushion Football
(enlarge 200%)

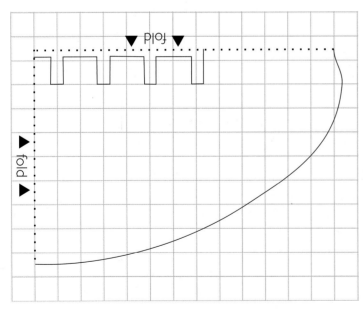

I square = ½" (1.3 cm)

Custom Necktie Front
(enlarge 200%)

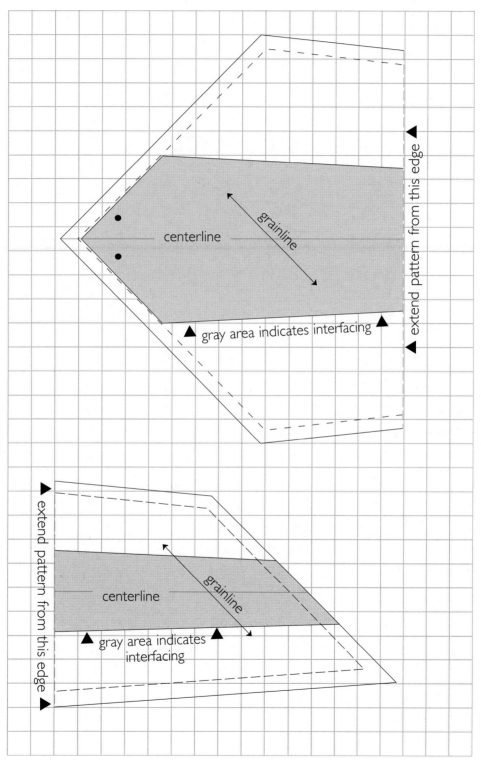

extend pattern from this edge

centerline

grainline

gray area indicates interfacing

extend pattern from this edge

centerline

grainline

gray area indicates
interfacing

1 square = ½" (1.3 cm)

Custom Necktie Back
(enlarge 200%)

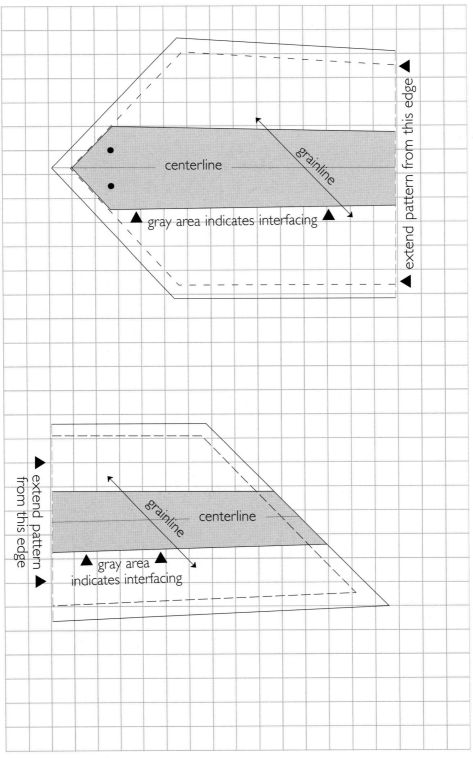

- centerline
- grainline
- gray area indicates interfacing
- extend pattern from this edge

- extend pattern from this edge
- grainline
- centerline
- gray area indicates interfacing

I square = ½" (1.3 cm)

Custom Necktie Lining
(enlarge 200%)

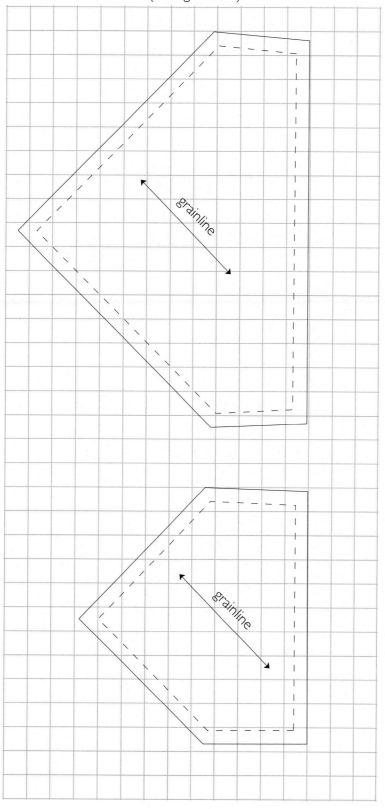

grainline

grainline

1 square = 1/2" (1.3 cm)

Friendly Elephant Bib Head
(enlarge 133%)

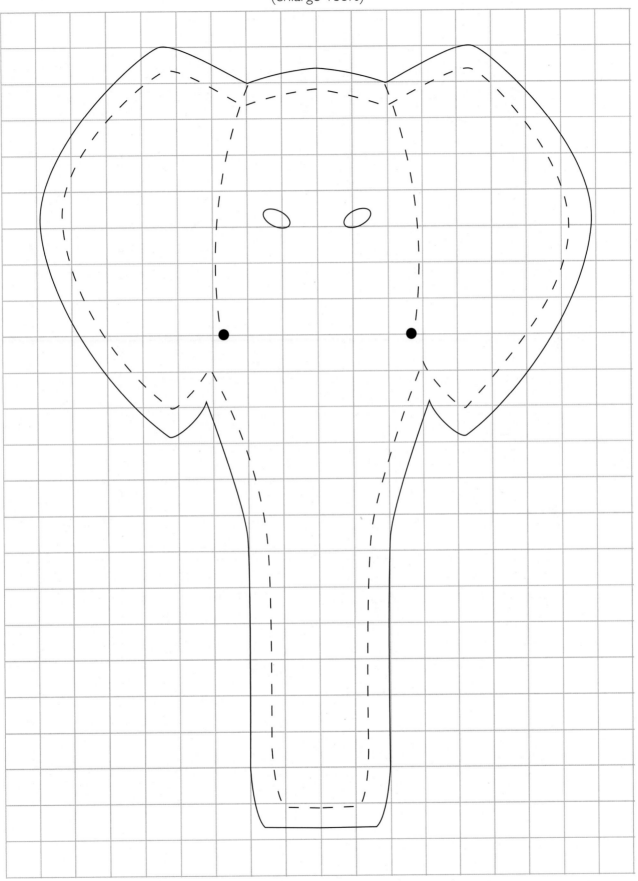

1 square = 1/2" (1.3 cm)

Friendly Elephant Bib (enlarge 133%)

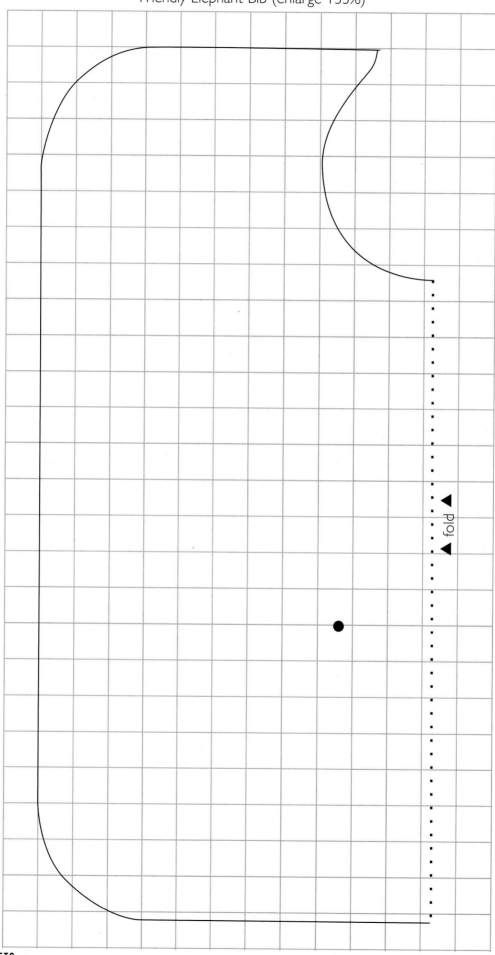

fold ◀ ◀

1 square = 1/2" (1.3 cm)

Friendly Elephant Mouth & Tongue (enlarge 133%)

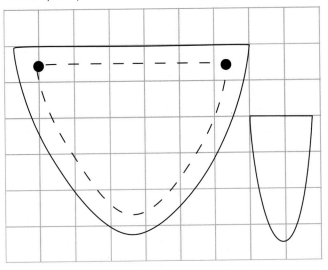

Curly Soft Bear (enlarge 200%)

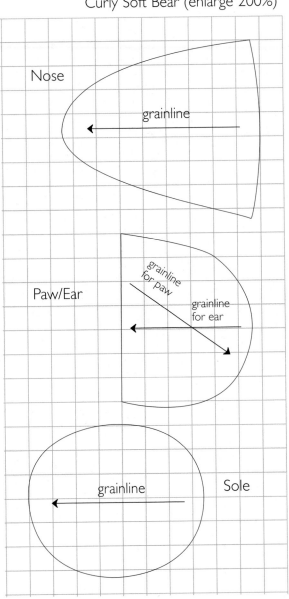

Nose

grainline

Paw/Ear

grainline for paw

grainline for ear

grainline

Sole

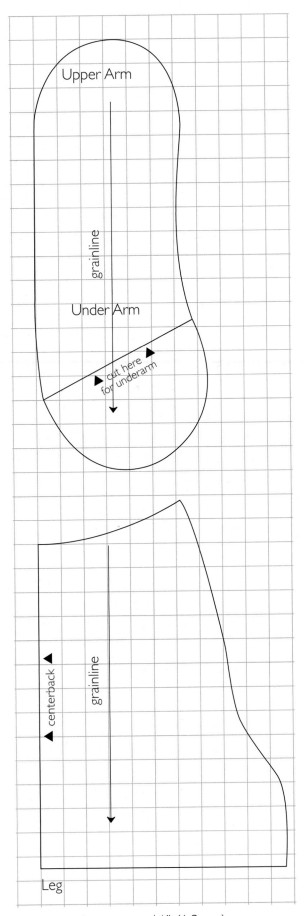

Upper Arm

grainline

Under Arm

cut here for underarm

centerback

grainline

Leg

1 square = 1/2" (1.3 cm)

Curly Soft Bear (continued)
(enlarge 200%)

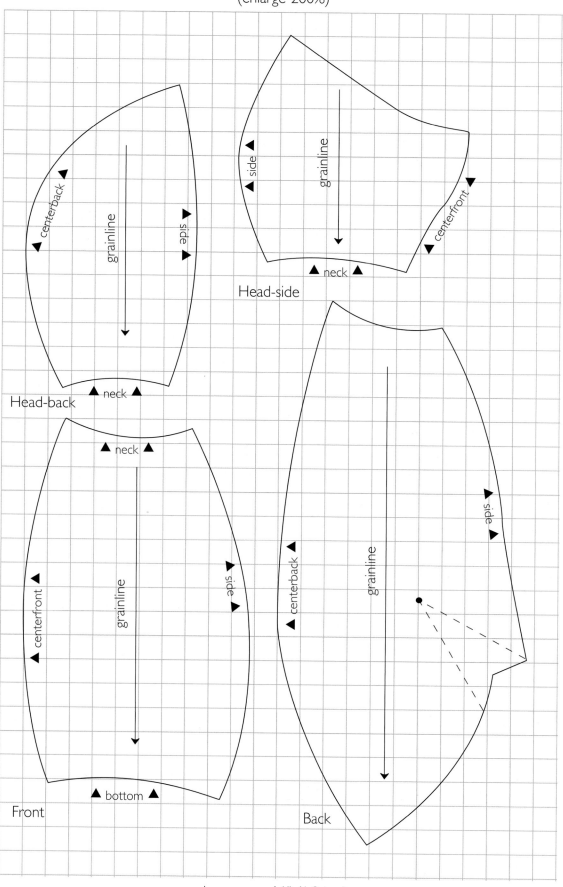

Head-back

Head-side

Front

Back

1 square = 1/2" (1.3 cm)

Puppy-Dog Hat
(enlarge 133%)

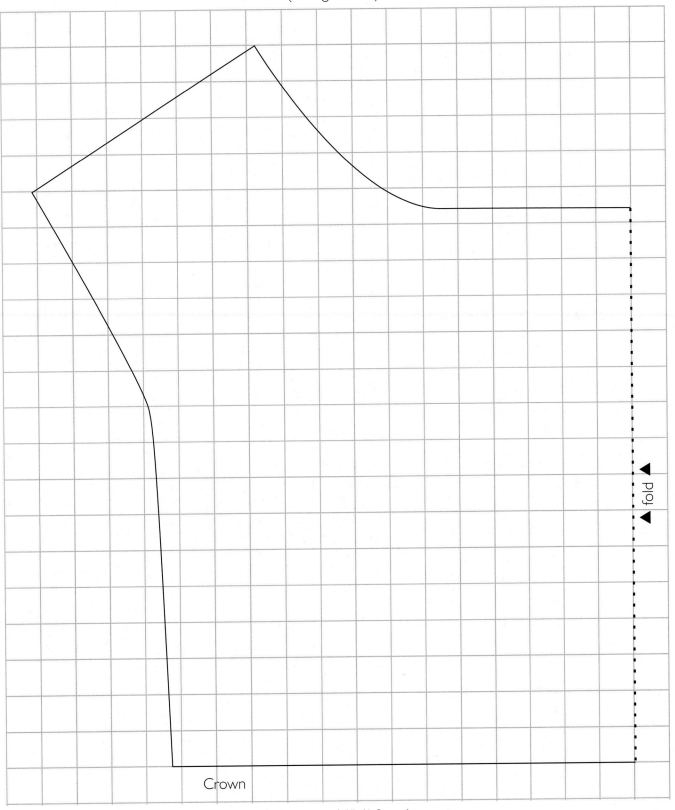

Crown

1 square = ½" (1.3 cm)

fold

My Own Lunch Bag
(enlarge 200%)

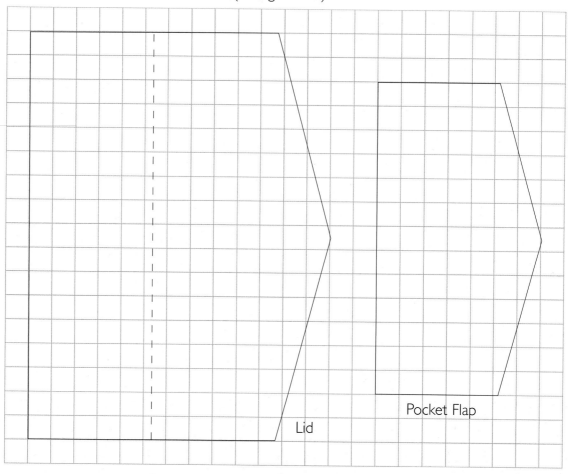

Lid

Pocket Flap

Retro Kitchen Placemat
(enlarge 200%)

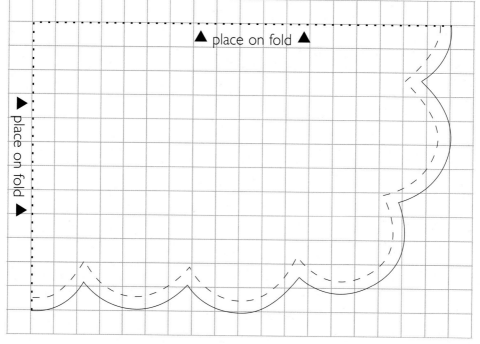

▲ place on fold ▲

► place on fold ►

1 square = 1/2" (1.3 cm)

Autumn Leaves Table Runner
(full size)

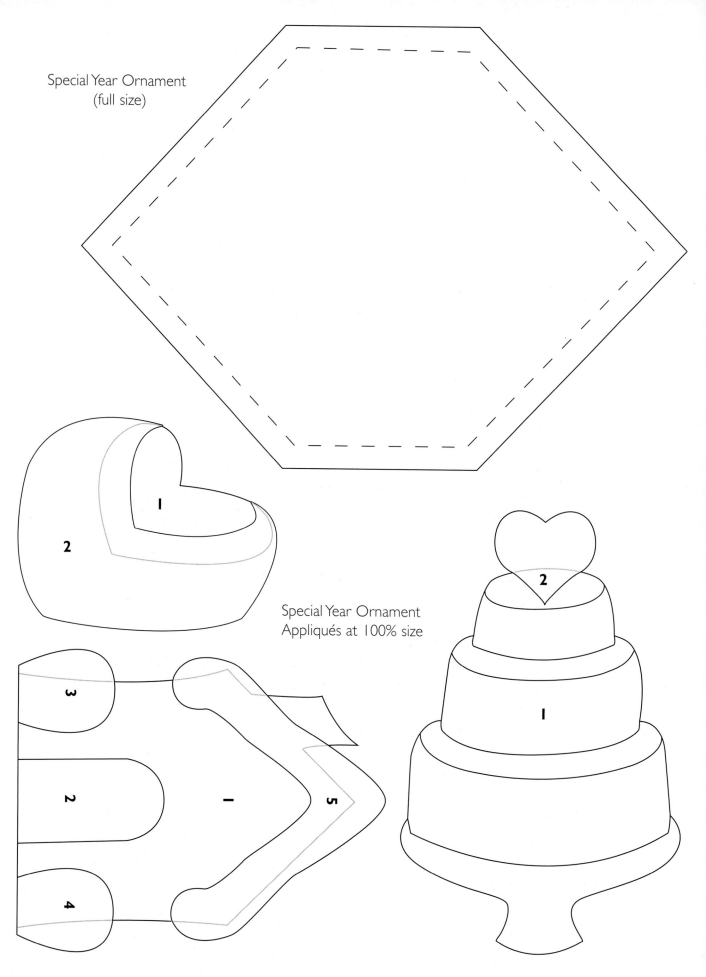

Special Year Ornament
(full size)

Special Year Ornament
Appliqués at 100% size

GLOSSARY

APPLIQUÉ. This French word refers to a decoration or cutout that is applied to the surface of a larger piece of fabric. Many methods of appliqué are used, including simply machine stitching around the outline of the decoration.

BASTE. Any diagonal line intersecting the lengthwise and crosswise grains of fabric is referred to as bias. While woven fabric does not stretch on the lengthwise and crosswise grains, it has considerable stretch on the bias.

BORDER PRINT. This fabric is printed with a bold pattern, usually larger in scale than the rest of the design, running along one selvage. The border pattern is often used along the hemline in a garment, which means the lengthwise grain of the fabric runs horizontally on the garment.

CASING. A fabric tunnel is sewn into the garment, often at the waistline, to carry elastic or cording.

CLIP. Small, closely spaced cuts are made into the seam allowances of a garment or other project, usually along a curve or into a corner. When the item is turned right side out, the seam allowances can spread apart and lie flat where they have been clipped. Small clips are also used for marking the location of notches or dots from the pattern.

COURSES. Corresponding to the crosswise grain of a woven fabric, the courses of a knit fabric run perpendicular to the selvages and ribs. Knit fabrics are most stretchy in the direction of the courses.

CROSSWISE GRAIN. On woven fabric, the crosswise grain runs perpendicular to the selvages. Fabric has slight "give" in the crosswise grain.

CUT LENGTH refers to the total length at which fabric should be cut for a project. It includes allowances for hems, seams, matching any prints, and, for Roman shades, additional length for mounting.

CUT WIDTH refers to the total width at which fabric should be cut for a project. If more than one width of fabric (selvage to selvage) is needed, the cut width refers to the entire panel after seams are sewn, including allowances for any side hems or seams.

DARTS. Fabric is folded and stitched to remove excess fullness and give shape to an item. For instance, darts are sewn at the front corners of a chair seat cover to make the fabric conform to the front corners of the seat.

DIRECTIONAL PRINT. The design printed on the fabric may have definite "up" and "down" directions, such as flowers growing upward. All pieces for a project should be cut so that the print will run in the correct direction when the project is finished.

DROP LENGTH is the length of a tablecloth from the edge of the table to the edge of the cloth. It can be anywhere from 6" (15 cm) to floor-length.

DROP-SHOULDER. This garment design feature means that the seam joining the sleeve to the front and back is intended to fall down off the edge of the shoulder, rather than align to the shoulder crest. Drop-shoulder styles are rather relaxed, less fitted, and generally have more room in the armhole.

EASE. Some fabric length, beyond what you have calculated, will be "eaten up" by turning under and stitching any double-fold hems, heading, or rod pocket. Also, when a treatment is gathered into a rod, the length may "shrink up" a bit. By adding 1/2" (1.3 cm) to the length before cutting, your finished length will be more accurate.

EDGESTITCH. With the machine set for straight stitching at a length of 2 to 2.5 mm or 10 stitches per inch, stitch within 1/8" (3 mm) of a finished edge. With many machines, this can be achieved by guiding the inner edge of the right presser foot toe along the outer finished edge.

FABRIC IDENTIFICATION LABEL. Found on every bolt or tube of fabric, this label informs you of the fiber content, width, and care method for the fabric. The labels on patterned decorator fabrics also indicate the length of the pattern repeat.

FACING. A fabric extension or addition that is sewn as a backing to another piece protects raw edges or seam allowances from raveling and gives the item a neat, finished appearance. For instance, a jacket front and neckline have an outer layer and an underlayer, or facing.

FINISHED LENGTH refers to the total length of a project after it is sewn. For a tablecloth, this includes the table length and twice the drop length; for a Roman shade, finished length is measured from the top of the mounting board to the windowsill or apron.

FINISHED WIDTH refers to the total width of a project after it is sewn. For a tablecloth, this includes the table width plus twice the drop length. For an inside-mounted Roman shade, the finished width is the inside width of the window frame; for an outside-mounted shade, the finished width includes the window frame width plus 1" (2.5 cm) beyond the frame on both sides.

FLANGE is a border of flat fabric that extends beyond the stitching line around the outer edge of a pillow, pillow sham, or duvet cover.

FRENCH SEAM. Two pieces of fabric are joined together in a two-step seam that encases the raw edges. First a narrow seam is sewn with the wrong sides together. Then the fabric is refolded on the seamline and stitched again with the right sides together. This is especially useful when an item will be sewn from both sides, such as a shower curtain.

FULLNESS describes the finished width of the curtain or valance in proportion to the length of the rod or mounting board. For example, two times fullness means that the width of the curtain measures two times the length of the rod.

GATHER. Two rows of long machine stitches are sewn along a seamline. When the bobbin threads are pulled, the fabric slides along the stitches into tiny tucks. Gathers are sued to fit a wide garment section to a narrower section while at the same time adding shaping.

GRADING. Seam allowances on faced edges are trimmed to graduated widths to eliminate a bulky ridge. Often the garment seam allowance is trimmed to 1/4" (6 mm) and the facing seam allowance is trimmed to 1/8" (3 mm).

HEADING is the portion at the top of a rod-pocket window treatment that forms a ruffle when the curtain is on the rod. The depth of the heading is the distance from the finished upper edge to the top stitching line for the rod pocket.

HEMMING. The outer edge of a project is given a neat finished appearance by turning under and securing the raw edge in one of several methods. It may be turned under twice and stitched, encasing the raw edge, as for the side and bottom hems of a curtain panel. It may be turned under once and fused in place, as for the Roman shade. The round tablecloth is hemmed by stitching welting or bias tape to the outer edge.

INSIDE MOUNT refers to a window treatment that is installed inside the window frame.

INTERLINING is a layer of fabric encased between the top fabric and the lining for the purpose of preventing light from shining through or to add body for items like window toppers or valances.

LENGTHWISE GRAIN. On woven fabric, the lengthwise grain runs parallel to the selvages. Fabrics are generally stronger and more stable along the lengthwise grain.

LINED TO THE EDGE means that a fabric panel is backed with lining that is cut to the exact same size. The two pieces are joined together by a seam around the outer edge; the seam allowances are encased between the layers.

LINING is a fabric backing sewn to the top fabric to provide extra body, protection from sunlight, and support for the outer hems or seams.

MARK. It is often necessary to give yourself temporary guidelines or guide points on the fabric for cutting, stitching, or matching seams. There are many tools and methods for doing this, such as marking pencils and pens, chalk dispensers, tape, or pins.

MITER. Excess fabric is folded out at an angle to eliminate bulk. You probably miter the corners when you wrap gifts.

MUSLIN. This mediumweight, plainly woven, cotton fabric is relatively inexpensive, so it is often used for drafting patterns when paper isn't feasible. Unbleached muslin is off-white with tiny brown flecks; bleached muslin is white.

NAP. Some fabrics have definite "up" and "down" directions, either because of a surface pile, like corduroy or velveteen, or because of a one-way print. When laying out a pattern on napped fabric, cut all the pieces with the top edges facing the same direction.

NOMINAL LUMBER. The actual measurement of nominal or "stock" lumber differs from the nominal measurement. A 1 X 2 board actually measures 3/4" X 1 1/2" (2 X 3.8 cm); a 1 X 4 board measures 3/4" X 3 1/2" (2 X 9 cm). Be sure to measure the board for accuracy.

NONDIRECTIONAL PRINT. The design printed on this fabric has no definite "up" or "down" directions, and pattern pieces can be laid out with the top edges facing in either direction.

OUTSIDE MOUNT refers to any window treatment that is installed on the wall above and to the side of the window frame.

PATCH POCKETS. One of the easiest pocket styles to sew, these are sewn to the outer surface of the garment like a "patch."

PATTERN REPEAT, a characteristic of decorator fabrics, is the lengthwise distance from on distinctive point in the pattern, such as the tip of a petal in a floral pattern, to the exact same point in the next pattern design.

PIVOT. Perfect corners are stitched by stopping with the needle down in the fabric at the exact corner before turning. To be sure the corner stitch locks, turn the handwheel until the needle goes all the way down and just begins to rise. Then raise the presser foot, turn the fabric, lower the presser foot, and continue stitching.

PRESHRINK. Fabric that shrinks, especially natural fibers, shrinks most in the first laundering. If you intend to launder your finished piece occasionally, you should wash the fabric before cutting out the pieces, so the item will not shrink after you make it. "Dry clean only" fabrics can be preshrunk by steaming them with your iron.

PRESS. This step is extremely important to the success of your sewing projects. Select the heat setting appropriate for your fabric, and use steam. Lift and lower the iron in an overlapping pattern. Do not slide the iron down the seam, as this can cause the fabric to stretch out of shape, especially on the crosswise grain or bias.

PROJECTION is the distance a rod or mounting board stands out from the wall.

RAILROADING. The lengthwise grain of the fabric is run horizontally in the window treatment, eliminating the need for any vertical seams. Some decorator fabrics are intentionally made this way, in widths that can accommodate floor-length treatments.

RETURN is the portion of the curtain or top treatment extending from the end of the rod or mounting board to the wall, blocking the side light and view.

RIBBING is a very stretchy knit fabric, usually with pronounced ribs. It is especially suitable for necks and cuffs on knit garments, since it can easily stretch to go over heads and hands, yet spring back in shaped once in place. Most ribbing comes in much narrower widths than other fabrics and, because you use less of it, it is often sold by the inch (centimeter) rather than the yard (meter).

RIBS. Corresponding to the lengthwise grain in woven fabric, the ribs of a knit fabric run parallel to the selvages (if there are any). Knits are usually more stable in the rib direction.

ROD POCKET is a stitched fabric tunnel in a certain where the curtain rod or pole is inserted. Stitching lines at the top and bottom of the pocket keep the rod or pole in place.

ROTARY CUTTER AND MAT. These time-saving tools for cutting fabric may also take a little practice and serious precautions. The blade on a rotary cutter is extremely sharp. Cut slowly, watch your fingers, and always retract or cover the blade between cuts. The rotary cutter cannot be used without the special protective mat.

SEAM. Two pieces of fabric are placed right sides together and joined along the edge with stitches. After stitching, the raw edges are hidden on the wrong side, leaving a clean, smooth line on the right side.

SEAM ALLOWANCE. Narrow excess fabric lies between the stitching line and the raw edges. The standard seam allowance width for garment sewing is 5/8" (1.5 cm); the standard width for home décor sewing is 1/2" (1.3 cm). The seam allowance gives the seam strength and ensures that the stitches cannot be pulled off the raw edges.

SEAM RIPPER. It doesn't really rip. Use the sharp point to slide under and cut stitches one at a time. Avoid the temptation to simply slide the cutting hook down the seam. You will inevitable cut into your fabric. Even the most experienced sewers rely on their seam rippers.

SELVAGES. Characteristic of woven fabrics, this narrow, tightly woven outer edge should be cut away. Avoid the temptation to use it as one side of a cut piece, as it may shrink excessively when laundered. One exception to this rule is sewing long vertical seams on sheer or loosely woven curtains, where trimming the selvages off could cause excessive raveling. In this case, leave the selvages intact and clip into them every 1" (2.5 cm) to allow them to relax.

SEPARATING ZIPPER. Zippers that come completely apart at the bottom are intended for use in items like jackets or the tote on page 293. Check the label carefully in the store, to be sure you are buying the correct zipper style.

TACKING. Short stationary stitches, sewn by hand or by machine, hold two or more pieces of fabric together a little less conspicuously then a row of stitches.

THREAD JAM. No matter how conscientious you are in trying to prevent them, thread jams just seem to be lurking out there waiting to mess up your day. The threads become tangled up in a was on the underside of the fabric and the machine gets "stuck." DON'T USE FORCE! Remove the presser foot, if you can. Snip all the threads you can get at from the top of the throat plate. Open the bobbin case door or throat plate, and snip any threads you can get at. Remove the bobbin, if you can. Gently remove the fabric. Thoroughly clean out the feed dog and bobbin area before reinserting the bobbin and starting over. Then just chalk it up to experience and get over it!

TOPSTITCHING is a decorative and functional stitching line placed 1/4" to 1" (6 mm to 2.5 cm) from the finished edge of an item. The stitching is done with the right side of the item facing up. Sometimes topstitching is done with a heavier thread or two threads through the machine needle, to make it more visible.

UNDERSTITCHING is straight stitching very close to the seamline that connects a facing to the garment. After the seam allowances are trimmed, clipped, and pressed toward the facing, stitch from the right side of the facing to keep it from rolling to the outside of the garment.

ZIGZAG STITCH. In this setting, the needle alternatively moves from left to right with each stitch. You can alter the width of the needle swing as well as the length between stitches. A zigzag stitch that is twice as wide as it is long gives you a balanced stitch, appropriate for finishing seam allowances.

INDEX

A

B

H

I

J

K

L